ERSIN PAMUKS

SELDA TERE

UNTIL THE LAST TOXIN

Take Care Of Yourself

DESTEK
yayınları

DESTEK MEDYA GRUBU

DESTEK YAYINLARI: 1001
GÜNCEL: 81

ERSIN PAMUKSUZER - SELDA TEREK / UNTIL THE LAST TOXIN

Concession Holder: Yelda Cumalıoğlu
Executive Editor: Ertürk Akşun
Publishing Coordinator: Özlem Esmergül
Translator: Sibel Hill
Book Cover Design: İlknur Muştu
Page Layout: Cansu Poroy
Pictures and Drawings in the Book: Tuğçe Budak
Social Media - Graphics: Tuğçe Budak - Mesud Topal

Destek Yayınları: September 2017 (2.000 Edition)
3rd Edition: September 2017
4rd Edition: November 2018
Publisher's Certificate No. 13226

ISBN 978-605-311-481-9

Abdi İpekçi Caddesi No. 31/5 Nişantaşı/İstanbul
Tel. (+90) 212 252 22 42
Fax: (+90) 212 252 22 43
www.destekyayinlari.com
info@destekyayinlari.com
facebook.com/DestekYayinevi
twitter.com/destekyayinlari
instagram.com/destekyayinlari

Deniz Ofset – Nazlı Koçak
Sertifika No. 40200
Maltepe Mahallesi
Hastane Yolu Sokak No. 1/7-B
Zeytinburnu / İstanbul

DESTEK yayınları KARAKARGA BEYAZ BAYKUŞ genç DESTEK

Emotional, Mental and Physical Purification…

ERSIN PAMUKSUZER
SELDA TEREK

UNTIL THE LAST TOXIN

Take Care Of Yourself

Translator: Sibel Hill

DESTEK
yayınları

CONTENTS

CHAPTER TWO

CHAPTER FIVE

FOREWORD BY ERSİN PAMUKSÜZER

Why This Book?

I read the book *The Seasons of a Man's Life* at a very young age. This book tells us that the lives of human beings are composed of phases and that we go into particular activities and give life a meaning according to those phases. I also have passed through my own phases, and for the last five, ten years, for my own benefit, I have stepped into the journey of spreading useful things to society and the world I live in, which I call "The Giving Period."

The book you are holding needs to be evaluated in this way. I wanted the book to transfer the lessons from my process of actively restructuring my life for the last fifteen years, as well as the things I cared a lot about and thought to be useful during the journey.

I believe that if it is possible everything must be done with an expert or left to an expert. However, if I do not have the choice, without hesitation, I roll up my sleeves and get to work. I never get self-conscious or worried or think of something as wrong if it is not liked by others.

In this manner, when I proposed my idea to people in Destek Publishing House, to whom I was introduced by a friend, they suggested that I do this job with Selda Terek. Thus my journey with Selda started. In our first meeting, I told her my idea and she happily agreed to write this book. Actually, she could have said, "I'm a novelist, what has a health book got to do with me?", but on the contrary, she said that she had worked in the health sector before, and she had a natural affinity for the subject matter, and it excites her, too. The title of her first book Amygdala, which she had came out with during a chat with a brain surgeon, also supported this.

Three days after deciding to make the book, we met in The LifeCo's Bodrum Türkbükü Center. My team and I started to explain to Selda what we know and would like to share in this book, so that she could start writing. We also included her in a detox program. At the reception of the center, they asked her, "Shall we write you an 800-calorie or a 1200-calorie diet?" Selda answered, "3200-calories if possible" and tried to escape. However, in the end she agreed to a 1200-calorie detox because of massages, yoga, Turkish bath, meditation and colema. Yet, we all understood from the start how important it was for Selda to eat! ☺

Anyway, we started to talk and she took notes.... Our intention was that we (my team and I) would give the ingredients and she would cook the food, but after a while I looked around and saw that the woman had disappeared, literally as if the ground had split open and she had gone into it! On one hand, I was wondering and worrying; on the other, I said to myself, "She will know; give her time, Ersin." Yet Selda turned out to be more interested than I thought. In fact she thought that I was not enough of a source and she referred to a lot of other books and sources. She had disappeared to read, research and gather information.

In time I understood that, in the direction of what I want to say, she was going to write her own book. "Why not?" I said, because maybe, being disconnected from the audience, I might have been losing clarity. However, Selda, as a writer, could manage to touch more people and move towards the goal better than I could. So, I immediately went on to a new route. I have decided to give an overview of the subjects by writing a preface and a summary, leaving the actual writing to her, but contributing my own sentences and different ideas to the book from time to time. I thought that because the health field is full of different approaches in this book, which is such a synthesis that Selda and I having different approaches should not be an odd thing at all. In fact, seeing different sides of the picture might attract people's attention even more, I thought to myself. Thus, we started a very pleasant journey. It was a stimulating journey for me.

Now I leave you face to face with Selda. Of course, I am here, and from time to time I will make small touches because Selda allowed me to do so.

This is how I look at the world: It's an open buffet; whoever wants be able to take whatever they want in their plate and eat it or leave it. Therefore, it must be noted that everything that is written here are the reflection of one's choices (either Selda's and/or mine). The things on the table are ideas which have been covered thousands of times before, either in books or nowadays in videos; you may have seen and be familiar with them. Do not expect a brand-new concept: it's just that everyone has a different way of eating the yoghurt, as the Turkish saying goes.. That's all! The authentic aspect of what we are saying is that we are talking out of our own experiences.

Ersin Pamuksüzer

FOREWORD BY SELDA TEREK

Mr. Pamuksüzer and I met at Destek Publishing House. When we sat at the famous lucky white table, he asked for water, and me, for coffee. By the time we left the table, shaking hands, in total he'd had two glasses of water and a cup of herbal tea containing hibiscus, and me, four cups of coffee and two small teas, and a cigarette on top. It was the end of November...

While this project was in progress, the point I reached was this: my water consumption went up to the level it should have been, tea and coffee went down to a reasonable amount, my eating rhythm has changed. I started to eat greener and raw vegetables, my breathing got more comfortable and more over, as my perspective of the world has changed, I started to like myself more. I started to talk about health, detox, free radicals and antioxidants with my friends. My habit of interfering with my spouse and kids about what they need to eat has never changed. I haven't become ill once and have started to ask those who get ill about their means of nutrition. At the moment, I feel like stopping everybody passing by, sitting them down , explaining things to them, and generally interfering with their lives. The worst thing is, I think I actually do this from time to time!

In this book, we talk from the health customer's point of view, not from the seller's.. All we explain is the knowledge we have gained over time, as people who have tried, believed and got results from this knowledge as well; in order to use it, not to sell it. That is what is different about this book. We have made selective health consciousness to map our journey. Also, without maligning or offending anyone...

Selda Terek

INTRODUCTION

- ❖ WHAT IS THIS BOOK ABOUT?
- ❖ THE REPRESENTATIVES OF HEALTH

"Be silent or let thy words be worth more than silence..."
Pythagoras

WHAT IS THIS BOOK ABOUT?

We have some things to say to remind you and ourselves about happiness... Most of these words occur when we look at the inconstancy of happiness and health. This is why we started this journey. As we pointed out before, on this journey we are the consumers of health, not its sellers. We have tried to share what we chose for our own bodies, spirits, feelings and health, as well as the logic and the knowledge behind these choices. Our approach was not to believe everything said about health, jumping from this doctor's approach to what another one said. We wanted you to design a lifestyle for nourishment, self-discovery, loving and valuing your body, and writing the prescription for yourselves.

This book is a compilation of what we have chosen for ourselves. Firstly, not to repeat the mistakes we have done to our bodies, minds and feelings, and to reach a healthier, happier life, this book is compiled with the guidance of a lot of medical doctors and alternative treatment methods, implemented in personal, real-life, in-the-flesh examples. We can say that it is a sort of synthesis of different experiences. This is our map of the journey. We would like you to evaluate this map simply as a set of suggestions that we present. Our aim is merely to create (one more) awareness and gain friends among our readers who love their bodies and existence, and who can be happy with every breath they take...

It is good to remember this often:

When we manage to take control of our lives from the hands of our weaknesses, we are definitely going to be happier and more joyous individuals.

Just like an orchestra conductor who succeeds in making wonderful sounds from the harmonization of many musical instruments, instead of drifting with life, being able to manage it and catch happy tones is the essence of the art of living.

On Living

Living is no laughing matter,
You must live with great seriousness,
like a squirrel, for instance -
I mean not expecting anything above and beyond living.
I mean living is all you must do.
You must take living to heart.

Nazım Hikmet

The poet has put it nicely. The metaphor "like a squirrel" opens the subject that we want to enter into. In fact, it is true: animals, that are an inseparable part of nature, do not pretend like many human beings do. They do not eat until they burst; they eat until they are full. In the animal world, you cannot find habitually drunk mice, druggy otters or platypuses that lose themselves in the world of junk food. They sleep when they get sleepy, drink water when they are thirsty, and do whatever needs to be done when they breed. How about humankind? We spend the day forgetting the fact that this world we have created is artificial. We're so clever! Making things difficult and complicated is our job… We dress for fashion, eat for the taste, and drink for joy. Many of our acts are done to be sociable. We randomly have our body cut for beauty, wear shoes that are against foot anatomy because they bring sexual attraction, and spray chemicals on ourselves not to smell bad. Building roads, getting stuck in civilization, missing nature. We are human beings: we are weird in nature.

Now, hang on to your hats! There is a range of sentences coming in which the word "nature" is used exactly twelve times: We, human beings, cannot be ***natural*** like animals, because this is our own special ***nature***. In other words, ***naturally***, we organize the balance of ***nature*** according to ourselves. Because we cannot change this fact, we need to live in peace with it, but also remember that we are a part of

nature. And the more we are in harmony with ***nature***, the better it is for our body and soul. We need to remember this often. Why? A day might come when the ***nature*** that we have become distant from, and which we try to manage according to ourselves, unexpectedly reminds us of something, and we might not know what to do. For example, when we are alone in ***nature*** without any tools, if we don't know how to find food, shelter and security, we are finished. It is a fact that while humanity is knowingly and willfully trying to rule ***nature***, it is not aware that it is growing away from it day by day. But still, what we expect from life is always the same… Could saying "***nature***" this many times bring us back to ***natural*** life? If only… Well then, why is it necessary to go back to ***natural*** life? Because the source of the thing we are looking for and pursuing is there.

To cut a long story short:

In fact, all of us are pursuing the same particular thing all our lives:
Hormones!

Maybe we can word it better:

In fact, all of us are running after the same particular thing all our lives:
Whatever our hormone levels make us feel
in our happy moments, that is it! ☺

Or shall we say it like this?

In fact, all of us are running after the same particular thing all our lives:
The feeling of happiness…

Yes, that is the fact: Whether the name is serotonin, endorphin, oxytocin or dopamine, we are all after the conditions that are going to form this chemistry of "happiness."

We want to be in love, successful, healthy, beautiful, lucky, able to have fun, complimented, looked up to… Why? The answer is hidden in those few hormones. We are after the energizers of those hormones, which make us feel the happiness. Let's take falling in love as an example. Affection and love are energized psychologically at first, and the combination of these feelings, together with many hormones being ready in the body and rising fast, can cause a total reaction. The feeling is pleasure… And pleasure is definitely irresistible…

In this century, everything is in such an interwoven state that while we are talking about health, it is possible to find ourselves discussing communication, and while talking about communication, discussing the economy. The strange thing is, all these things play a role in health. So, we wouldn't dare to ignore life conditions and prescribe the same recipe to everyone, being smarty pants and making utopian sentences about health or recommending health experiences, which are wrong to others by showing a one-sided approach. However, we can do this: We can say, "Keep away from un-healthiness and live a quality life in any situation."

If only there were one health approach, which could be packaged like those colourful pills that the pharmaceutical industry makes us buy (or tries to make us buy.) Then it would be easy. We are trying to walk on slippery ground where two times two does not make four. What makes it difficult is that the parametric value, which plays a role in everybody's health, is different for everybody. Therefore, there is no "illness" but only a "patient" in the end. When every person should be looked at individually, using the common ground is suggested; it's as simple as that.

Therefore, we believe that:

The best prescription is the one we write for ourselves.

Every living being is unique. Although we have many common characteristics, none of us are the same. Yes, we have similarities and we even expect the same things from life: satisfaction, happiness, pleasure, peace, trust, success etc. So, is there a common description to reach the high quality and happy life that we dream of? We can at least try to find that description.

The first thing to be done is to know how to choose the appropriate thing, to be able to separate right from wrong. Eat right, move right, breathe right, think right and feel right… Once you know what is right, practising it is just down to being strong-willed.

"Well, what is right?"

When we say "Right," we roll up our sleeves presuming that each of us wants to live a healthy and high-quality life. But we have to make an exception and be sceptical at some point. For example, if you feel happy among the blessings of the world (food, drink…), which give short-term pleasure and then make you suffer, we cannot produce common ground for that.

THE PRACTITIONERS OF HEALTH

There are four types of people in the world who work in health.

1. Medical Doctors: We mean the representatives of medicine nowadays, as it is taught in the universities and accepted scientifically in the world. They spend many years in education to attain the title of medical doctor. On top of that, they have their specialization, academic career etc. They make the proven truth their map for a journey, and their education never ever ends: they constantly follow the literature.[1] We need to pay attention to them. In emergency treatments, it is necessary to stay on modern medicine's course. Medical doctors are the ones who should be consulted during the acute stage of the illness; if you have a wounded limb, are bleeding or have a broken bone, they are the people you should go to immediately.

2. Alternative Medicine Specialists: It is a name given to those who carry out some traditional or current practices, the effects of which cannot be proven with scientific methods, but which can allegedly cure. These specialists have developed diagnoses and treatments using methods, which are outside of modern medicine. They offer their services not in hospitals, but in their own private clinics. It can be said that, together with modern medicine specialists, there are benefits in taking them into consideration. Although some of the methods they apply may cause a placebo effect, we observe that they work. (e.g. homoeopathy, neural therapy, reflexology, acupuncture, family constellation, mesotherapy, magnetic field treatment, prolotherapy, hypnosis, manual therapy, osteopathy, chiro therapy, kinesiology, O-Ring tests, phytotherapy, oxygen, respiration, ozone etc.)

3. Traditional Healers: These are experienced people who treat the patient by using plants, pastes, waters, dressings or burning and other methods which they

---

1. The approach named 'evidence-based medicine' in English. Also, in medicine itself the value of these pieces of evidence has started to be questioned. For example, tablets containing sugar do good to 40% of depression patients, but actually the patient does not know that he/she is only taking small sugar pills. There are many studies showing that, although it is known that the treatment is not going to help at all in last-stage cancer patients, unnecessary chemotherapy is being applied. Sounfortunately, it is difficult to say that modern medicine acts only according to the evidence.

see as effective, according to the medical perception and the background of their times, e.g. the representatives' of 2000 years of Chinese Medicine.

They are experienced specialists who offer preventative and healing treatments, just like Alternative Medicine Specialists. If you are ill, it is not a mistake to knock on the doors of both healers and modern medical doctors. Since their methods are always natural, they won't hurt you. However, since they do not have modern medicine's imaging devices with their analytical abilities and tests, if you do not have tolerance towards the natural food that they suggest, and you are faced with an allergic reaction, you should plan what you are going to do.

4. Wounded Healers:[2] The term Wounded Healers comes from Chiron in Greek mythology.

The mythological story goes like this:

Chiron, who got his name from the half-horse, half-human mythological being called Centaur, was the son of Saturn and the water nymph Philyra. Because his body was half horse and half human he was seen as a monster in his mother's eyes and was abandoned. The god Apollo protected him and brought him up. Apollo gave Chiron his education and led him to gain many abilities: Chiron became a soothsayer, doctor, teacher, musician, archer, hunter, and expert in the arts of war. He even became the teacher of the children of the kings and the gods. He was Achilles', Hercules' and, the god of medical science, Asclepius' teacher. It is said that the first culture of scientific experiment came from Chiron.

And the story which has caused him to have the name 'Wounded Healer' and has had a part in forming the symbolism belonging to Chiron is this: while Hercules was taking lessons in the arts of war, he accidentally wounded Chiron on his leg with the tip of an arrow which had been dipped in snake venom. Since Chiron was immortal and could not die, he would carry it as a wound and be crippled all his life.

→

2. **Wounded Healers:** This is a term, which was created by the psychiatrist Carl Gustav Jung. The idea indicates that an analyst becomes obliged to treat patients, because the analyst himself/herself is "wounded." The idea might have its roots in Greek mythology. Research shows that 73.9 % of consultants and psychotherapists underwent one or more wounding experience, which led them to choose their career.

Because Chiron was expert in medicine and alternative treatments, he developed methods and made medication all the time to heal his own wound. At the end of this, he did a huge service to the medical field: he figured out the formula, which would heal the wounds of all warriors. However, he could never heal himself in any way. In the end, because he got fed up with living like that, he made a fatal exchange with another half god, Prometheus, who had stolen the light from Zeus and was convicted to live in the underworld of Hades, chained to a rock for his whole life. According to the agreement he had with Zeus, he would be free only if an immortal wanted to take his place. And Chiron did so. Prometheus was freed and Chiron went to death in the underworld.

Sources:

Melanie Reinhart, Chiron & the Healing Journey

Ariel Guttmann and Kenneth Johnson, Mythic Astrology

Liz Greene, Mythic Astrology

www.stariq.com archive articles

Chiron's story always touched me. The wound, which a son got from being abandoned by his mother must be bigger than the unhealed wound of that arrow. It is not surprising that one day people's repressed instincts occur in front of us, manifesting themselves in new, unbalanced forms. These can be physical or mental illness. Chiron in his mythological story could not ease his pain and finally could not stand it and chose death. What it is, is a pain that cannot be eased, which means an incapacity that goes on forever, a horrible suffering. There is an important lesson to learn from this situation: if there is a feeling of longing or pain about any matter which is very difficult to resolve, what needs to die is not the person who feels the pain, but the cause of the pain. This means that to treat a wound we need to destroy the source of the wound, not the wounded one.

According to belief, there cannot be a healer/curer who does not have a wound, because the real power of the curer comes from the wound itself.

"The doctor can influence only if he too is affected.
Only wounded doctors can make the patient well.
But if a doctor wears his own character like a steel vest, then there is no effect."

Carl G. Jung, *Wounded Healer of the Soul*

The real fight for "recovery" starts after the process of "operations and treatments with medication" which modern medicine carries out against our symptoms. For example: One's problem of high blood pressure can only be reduced, not cured. When medication is stopped, the problem arises again. Recovery would be possible with a change of lifestyle and of the environment and conditions causing the illness. And the most important part of the recovery process is "embracement." If "belief/embracement" is not ensured, the recovery process would either go backwards or stop before starting, with evasions and revisions. These fluctuations could drag the patient to the point of system failure. The other important factor to ensure embracement is that the person who is leading you in the recovery process is someone who has experienced the recovery process before. A doctor who had fallen from a roof would have more empathy with a patient who fell from a roof, so to speak. It makes one a better disciple on the way to recovery. I came across the term "wounded healer" when I was discussing the behaviour of an alcoholic friend who I hadn't understood for a long time, and a doctor friend who had been through the same experience himself clarified the subject easily. When I asked wonderingly "How did you make that connection?" he said, "I lived through those days too."

Ersin Pamuksüzer

Well, in this case, the idea of the saying "Do not ask the doctor; ask the patient" has become clear ☺ and, between you and me, I do not mean to create a rift, but these four human types that I mentioned above, who deal with health, have curled their lips at each other's disciplines from time to time. However, this book tells you that all these approaches are beneficial individually; we only draw your attention to when you might apply which one. The approaches, which prevent illnesses before they occur are those which can protect us from acute illnesses. That's why we give an ear to what healers and alternative medicine say. It is necessary to keep the system up, straight and healthy, and behave in line with health consciousness. It is the idea of staying healthy, instead of trying to have it back after it is lost. Despite all this, if we couldn't prevent the illness or if we have a broken bone or a wound that needs stitches, of course we resort to modern medicine.

I heard this conversation with my own ears:

"Medicine improved, improved a lot. The technology being used in recent years is unbelievable!"

"Yes, it's clear that medicine showed incredible progress in the area of 'diagnosis,' but what would you say about the fact that it's still using the same methods of treatment? Information technology has overflowed in the last fifty years, and science is improving at a speed that is impossible to follow in the world, but medicine isn't managing to implement the same modern methods in terms of treatment."

"That's totally wrong! Even the operations are done by robots!"

"Yes, but at the end, what they do is an operation. Let's talk about progress when they provide the recovery without cutting someone."

While people keep waiting for medicine to improve, we have some very valuable information in our hands:

With the taxonomical name Homo Sapiens Sapiens,[3] so-called human beings, the only living species in the homo type of the primate group, despite not being able to figure out what this miracle is which they are a part of and why it happened, have already discovered that natural renewal and mending apply to their own

3. **Homo Sapiens Sapiens**, means "one who can think about what he has thought." This idea was propounded first by Rene Descartes. Today's modern people belong to this sub-species; however, they are mostly referred to as Homo Sapiens.

bodies too. Good news: Human beings already know that as long as they create the conditions which make them better, nature will get the job done... ☺

The Journey of Medicine: From the Yellow King to Hippocrates, and from There to Today's Modern Medicine

TCM (Traditional Chinese Medicine) starts with the Yellow King in China having kept a record of his experiences, and continues with Hippocrates's approach, "Let food be thy medicine and medicine be thy food", whereas the approach of today's modern medicine is (except integrated medicine) formed in accordance with the management of emergency situations. In short, the main occupation of modern medicine today is to take the diagnosable symptoms under control. We can see it as "The art of symptom management focused on operation and medication." However, in the old terminology the concept of "healing" aims at full recovery, and recovery is a process for which one is responsible oneself.

Ersin Pamuksüzer

With this book the only thing we are offering you is:

A key!

You are going to decide which door it will open in your life. We wanted to provide you with a guide for a higher-quality, healthy and happy life. The only thing you have to do is reach out and take the key, and take care of yourself UNTIL that LAST TOXIN.

CHAPTER ONE

QUALITY OF LIFE

- ❖ IS IT POSSIBLE TO BE AGELESS?
- ❖ INTEGRATED HEALTH
- ❖ OH, THOSE FREE RADICALS!

"Cheap health leads to expensive treatment."

Selda Terek

IS IT POSSIBLE TO BE AGELESS?

We Need That Child....

We were all children at one time. Well done to those who have been able to keep that spirit inside!

Those who had loads of love when they were kids are lucky, because the most valuable nutrition a child can get when growing up is LOVE. In fact, it is the most valuable nutrition that any living thing can have. Love teaches people tolerance. Giving without expecting anything in return, attention, patience, too... It's not a coincidence that a lack of love underlies the individuals who create conflicted societies today.

When children reach adolescence, with some exceptions, they emulate those older than themselves, not the younger ones. This is the normal process of growing up. The virtue of having a child's spirit is understood at a much later age. When we remember that we too were adolescents at some time, we can see this: there is a childhood that we have forgotten about because of the rush to grow up. So, what is it that makes us forget that we were kids?

When we analyse the activities of kids, we see that claims based on feelings trump those decided by logic. For example, if a child is playing a game that she enjoys very much, she might not pay attention to or even forget about her hunger. Or if she is hungry, she might prefer a hamburger with a lot of mayonnaise and ketchup together with crunchy fries and a cold coke to a plate of fillet steak, broccoli and salad. These decisions come from the orientation of the feelings (and of course the eating habits formed by the family.) The desire towards repeating the conditions, which were known from before that give pleasure. So, in fact, loving hamburgers for children comes from the positive feelings that they've had when they ate their first hamburger. The opposite is applicable too. A child who was forced to eat by his/her mom might become more selective and even, as a reaction, might develop completely opposite habits as a grown up.

Human beings, as they grow older, start living according to what they are supposed to desire, not what they want. Of course, I am talking about the grownups, who are educated, read a lot, and are enquiring. In modern society, a rational grownup should know the importance of a balanced diet and behave accordingly. This is not only about eating; they prefer particular actions about every issue (or do they really?) Even in developed societies, from time to time living conditions push us to behave inconsistently and even rebelliously about either feeding, about our ethical approach or on the subject of social order. Although we know the necessity of staying away, when we are very hungry we can be hooked on one of the chains of a fast food company; if we are very bored in traffic, even though we know we shouldn't, we end up driving on the hard shoulder or even playing a game on our mobile phone. I don't even count fighting with our body hanging out of the car window when we are angry!

How many of us still enjoy playing games? (I don't mean computer games.) And how many of us still watch animated movies? Maybe if we look for it we will find our inner child in the sameplace our busy adult life took away from us; but how many of us spare time to do that?

It feels like I hear some of you saying, "I still play games and watch animations." How beautiful that you managed to keep that child inside you like that. Childhood is a good thing, but you are who you are now because of that child too. And if you have a bad habit that you need to change, you have to persuade that child inside you as well.

If you have a bad habit that you need to change, you have to persuade that child inside you as well.

The importance of this subject being included in this book is that we can only understand the cause of our preferences today by looking at ourselves in our childhood. Whatever we push too far or avoid in our reactions today is caused by our childhood experiences. We carried lots of things with us from our past to today, like what we eat or do not eat, how much we move, what our reactions are, what we enjoy, our obsessions, hobbies, talents and inabilities, ethical approach and more. Hence, whatever it is that makes us forget about our childhood, we need to cut it off, go back to the state when we were children and look at ourselves from there as well. Because:

To be happy, we need that child ...

A Few Notes on Being Ageless

Being ageless? Is that really possible? How many people do you know who are ageless, in good physical condition, witty, enjoying life, laughing in a carefree way, tolerant, not worrying about their age, at peace with themselves and their surroundings, who can run up the stairs, can look at the world and its troubles with an open mind, not panic immediately, not look for answers in rage, turn a blind eye to some things they actually see, are happy with their situation, who are at peace? Well, I'm kind of joking, but when I say "ageless person" I am actually thinking of the handsome, wise person in my dreams. ☺

By the way, talking about agelessness, I want to indicate that the experiences which the years recorded in the archive in our mind, the lessons and knowledge learned from them, should stay where they are: the child living inside, her/his excitements, and the happiness she/he gets from simple things should also stay. But can the body be ageless too? Aren't we asking for a bit much? ☺

The Formula for Happiness

So, what about happiness? Nobody knows that they have the magical formula for feeling happy, and actually everybody carries the potential inside them to create their own formula. Believe me: what needs to be developed is only a piece of awareness, a little sense of humor, and a bit of faith. To have the awareness of being happy, the past or the future are not what need to be looked at; it is now. In other words, we should focus on our own life conditions and ourselves, not on anybody else's or anybody else, and on what we can do with what we have. Maybe we should try to love ourselves before anybody else. Do not take this as selfishness or arrogance: we can look at this as a sense of responsibility. It is the same logic as "Put the oxygen mask on yourself first and then on your child"? To be beneficial to other people, first we should be upright and well, shouldn't we?

The only promise that I can give you for a formula of happiness might be the one in the box below. If you count it as a formula… I wouldn't want to disappoint you by saying something vague, but I can guarantee that with some sense of awareness and gratefulness on the journey towards integral balance, which we will be talking about throughout the book, you will be equipped to write your own formula.

You cannot find inner happiness by looking outside.
Look for it inside yourselves…

Being happy is an awareness issue. Of course, it is partly in proportion to quality of life, but it is a fact that everybody designates the parameters of happiness themselves. Before everything, let us have a look at the subject of the quality of life.

Happiness/Fulfilment

While happiness is a feeling, which belongs to the moment, "fulfilment," in other words "contentment," is the constant and lasting foundation of happiness. In my way of looking at the world, being fulfilled comes before being happy, because being happy, most of the time or all the time is not possible. Also, being happy all the time tires people out. When we live a full, fulfilled life, having sad moments is as normal as having happy ones. When we lose somebody close, no one would expect us to be happy. However, being a fulfilled person, we could spend this moment thinking of good memories of times we spent with the person we lost and how they affected our lives, and thus manage a natural separation. The journey to fulfilment keeps us serene during negative moments as well as positive ones. Underlying our fulfilment is our peace with life and with ourselves. It is beneficial to turn our antenna that way.

Ersin Pamuksüzer

Quality of Life

Although when the game finishes, both the king and the pawns go back into the same box, it is important to be able to spend the life we have with pleasure and happiness, because life is the time when we are able to breathe. Don't pay attention to those who behave as if they know what will happen next.

For a person who spends most of his/her life ill, sad, in depression or worry, what is the difference if he/she is a king or a queen? Well, this is the point where the criteria of quality we make for ourselves become important. Living, but living how?

Look what participants said about the criteria of life-quality during a brainstorm:

Financial power
Family
Health
Peace
Welfare
Democracy
Freedom
Natural Nutrition
Security
...

Luxury consumption
Education level
Work satisfaction
Quality of sex
Quality of sleep
Gender equality
Rate of literacy
Justice
...

And a dozen of more words like these... The list was dragging on, so I eliminated many of them. For example, have you ever said a prayer like, "God, please don't let me fall off the elephant"? Or got upset, saying, "I'm too weak. I can't pass the ball as far as number four"? To be able to say these prayers, first you are supposed to be on an elephant or play in a volleyball team. These are both nice experiences though. You are going to say, "A happy person can get worried too!" Of course! But if worries force us to the level that ruins our quality of life, then we need to be careful and increase awareness. For you, which criteria from the list can measure your quality of life?

In fact, each item in this list can be a minor or a major parameter indicating a modern person's quality of life. Alone, none of them are enough. However, there is one among them without which the others mean nothing and that is Health!

There are three important subjects that need to be emphasised which we always face, and which carry us to old age and later to death. If those did not exist, we might see death as a phenomenon that happens only by accident. However, it is not. We always run towards that obvious end under the influence of these three items.

Here are the common problems of every person:

Attention!
Three main factors that bring us, to death:

- Being Poisoned (Toxaemia)
- Poor Nutrition (Deficiency)
- Constant Stress (Continuity of sympathetic mode)

Every passing day, because of these three factors, we can say that life is getting shorter. Unfortunately, we need to point out that we are living in the most toxic time in history. As has been said before, there are hundreds of toxic items even in new-born children's blood. Being constantly under the effect of those, provides the ideal environment for chronic illnesses, feelings of exhaustion, and getting old. So, what is the response? The illnesses caused by getting poisoned and collecting toxins, muscle loss and lack of power caused by lack of nutrition, and the immune system destroyed by a life under constant stress would bring us the end fast. The items that were listed in that brainstorm: How ordinary and meaningless they look beside this, don't they?

Yet we can slow down ageing and death, which are inevitable, and even postpone them considerably by applying the following:

How can we resist the three main factors, which bring us to death?

- Being poisoned	→ Cleansing/Detox
- Poor nutrition	→ Conscious nutrition
- Constant Stress (Sympathetic)	→ Resting (Parasympathetic)

However, no healing will be long-term if these three factors do not come together healthily:

Physical condition + Emotional Condition + Mental Condition

Before we go into the details of these, we can say that the quality of life is a condition, which is about how good and balanced the three approaches we mentioned above are in our lives. The rest is meaningless: property, schmoperty! Money, schmoney! These don't matter. . I have seen many people in clover, living in luxury, but they aren't really happy because they do not have awareness....

The Logic of Anti-Ageing...

What a nice story Benjamin Button's is![4] It is about a man born old, but getting younger over the years. I wish! Of course, beside people getting older day by day, this bizarre state does not fit and causes other problems. Still... As fantasy would have it...

If we come back to real life, yes, we call earth circling around the sun in a a year "time," and measure human age by that, but who could insist that we age by the same amount every year? Getting old is not just a concept about time. It is also the

4. **Benjamin Button:** The Curious Case of Benjamin Button, a 2008 film, adapted from the short story by F. Scott Fitzgerald, published in 1922. The director is David Fincher and the screenwriter is Oscar winner Eric Roth.

bodily rate of decay that we allow and cannot avoid at certain times. We even say that if we don't allow this to happen, **"it is even possible to get younger!"**

You already see, hear and read what we say as anti-ageing. Yet do you believe it? Do many of you see it as a commercial to sell products? Believe it: many of these statements are true.

Getting old is the steady reduction of a human's physical and spiritual functions. And everybody knows that difficult life conditions, too much sun, situations that wear you out, bad nutrition and harmful habits accelerate this process.

On your birthday, if you answered the question "What is your age?" not according to the years, but according to how much damage those years have done to you, how old would you say you were? I would say something like thirty-one, just because saying twenty-eight would be pushing it a bit too far. ☺ To be able to say "I am ageless," would be the best answer, wouldn't it? There are people who have managed to seem ageless. So, why don't we start working to keep young and beautiful always, right now?

Since we mentioned youth and beauty:

Youth and beauty are well-being from inside.
Aesthetic intervention done from outside divides the energy flow.
Unless it is necessary, we should keep away.
Beauty cannot be a template.

When I say "agelessness," I would like to emphasise again that I mean fitness, health, happiness and being attached to life. Physical transformation and looking young are only the side effects of this effort…

Although preventing the ageing process, which is affected by many different factors, completely is not possible, it is surely possible to postpone it to a serious degree. In fact, you know exactly how that happens. As I indicated in the table above, toxins are gathering in our body constantly; as long as we flush our bodies clean of toxins regularly by detox and antioxidants, it means that we are taking the first step to keep the system seriously young. And we should know that, however much we eat, we lack some of the necessary materials for the body. In this case, food supplements and a rich and varied diet become important. I will cover the subject of stress in detail in the coming chapters. But 1 would like to indicate that, for agelessness, youth and beauty, these are a must.

Anti-ageing literarily means "against age." Yes, as people who know more or less the destruction years cause, if we could take some precautions before we wear our body and spirit out, we could seriously slow down ageing.

So, what should we focus on?

1. Renewing the skin texture and binding cells.
2. Getting rid of hormonal imbalances.
3. Natural techniques that increase the sexual power and health.
4. Illnesses.
5. Metabolic rate.
6. Nutrition.
7. Activity.
8. The mind, sense and feelings.
9. Hygiene and naturalness.
10. Life conditions.

We could add more to these items. Here is a question: What is the main target that makes us rebel against getting old? Would any one of us want to be Cher? Would it be bad if we could? Is the target to prevent power-loss and illnesses caused by ageing, and to stay young for a longer time? What is your reason? My reason is: Not to be dependent on anybody by getting weak and incapable. (My grandmother's prayer ☺: "May your hands and feet be healthy, so you need not depend on others!") Having a high quality life till the end.

The reason to stay young is to keep our life energy and sources of happiness alive and get pleasure from life. This is the best favor we can do for ourselves.

Nowadays the stages of ageing can be measured and changed. It might not be the right thing to apply the same prescription to everybody, since the illnesses that people might get in their old age and the hormones and substances in the body can in fact depend on hereditary factors. I am one of those people, who believes that every person's diagnosis should be individual.

To be more precise, you should know your enemy well in order not to become aged. There are many reasons for getting old of course, but if the fight starts against these aspects, it won't be bad:

1.Free radicals.
2.Decreasing hormones.
3.Unhealthy life conditions.

Somehow achieving all this, if we can manage the mental tiredness and emotional burnouts, we can protect our youth for many years by starting a war on ageing.

Yes, but how? Good question…

And Maladjustment to the States of the World…

When we look at our world, in every area we see many changes that make us say, "Where did we start, and where have we come to?" The transition from a system where a 100-people-society lives together, to the cities where 20 million people live is not a joke. Also, it is unfortunately a fact that mountains of concrete have taken over our green, natural living environment. Immobility, since we can sort out everything from wherever we want, has taken over from our naturally mobile state, which should be a part of our daily life. When two thousand people are playing Angry Birds and eating by ordering fast food through their mobiles, they need a reason to move. We never thought that we would be tired from being inactive, but that has happened too.

→

We have turned the food we ate directly from the tree into commercial products on shelves. That's why we have no place to rest nowadays. Today, in our world, 93% of death is due to the illnesses of lifestyle.

In short, what we eat and drink, mental state, lack of movement especially in the environment we live in, the reflection of our lack of adaptation towards nature, cause these lifestyle illnesses. When the Creator and nature equipped us, they created us in peace with themselves, whereas finding it not sufficient, we changed nature and created 21st Century life. Now we have houses protecting us from nature, cars so that we don't need to walk, greenhouses that prevent us from eating our vegetables in the season when they are just right, shoes made out of plastic that cuts our attachment with the earth, sunglasses and sun lotions that prevent us from being directed by the sunbeams and also stop the activation of vitamin D, poisonous air that surprises our lungs. In short, we have turned into confused people who create every type of fault about life, and when it comes to paying the bill (depression, illnesses, pains etc.) we ask, "Where did that come from?" We live a full life, yes, but full of all the wrong materials. Instead of happiness, unhappiness; instead of health, illness; instead of a body for which everything is possible, legs that avoid walking have become our reality. It is nonsense to rise-up against this reality because it is not possible to change it in the short term, so we have to sort it out for ourselves. How? By managing the damage, which we get from what we eat and drink, our mind being inactive, and the environment we live in. The world is what it is today and living well in this world is our responsibility and our talent.

From Birth to Today: The Frame of Reference

We are born with our parents' genetic structures; our immediate family and the close environment format us. After this, religion and the existing dominant culture affect, who we become, and school adds the final main brushstrokes. On top of that, work, social life and experiences come as a polish. This is our conceptual environment.

→

Our conceptual environment plays the main role in our sense of the world and what is happening around us. All our character and identity are formed as a result of these. When we notice the wrong formations, it is not at all easy to reform them. Changing habits might take years. The "us," which is programmed from before forms the root of our journey. For example, I have been actively trying to rewrite myself from the beginning for the last fifteen years. I am trying to change my habits and put more beneficial, joyous ones there instead. I know this as my process of change and improvement, and as my responsibility. For the life of me, I would have never believed that the formations given to me in my early years are this difficult to change if I hadn't tried. I've learned that to change a habit, first of all we need to be at peace with it, and accept it as it is, without making bargains with frailty; filling their space with new and better activities. And to have the new and good ones stable, we must have determination and awareness that we cannot abandon. I have learned these things through living. And here is what I am trying to say: May God help us all.

There is no point in blaming those who gave us the formations that we don't like. They are also living according to the formations they were given by others, so what can they do? The problem comes from the links in the chain like me, who question this. Change starts in these links.

Ersin Pamuksüzer

INTEGRATED HEALTH
(Holistic Approach to Health)

If they asked me what the most popular two words of the last five years have been, I would say:

1. No problem.
2. Holistic. ☺

BODY
HEART
MIND

Really, don't we hear these very often, or is that just my selective perception?

When you ask someone "How are you?" if the person who is about to answer is actually thinking who she is instead of automatically saying "I'm fine, how about you?" be sure that she is asking herself these three questions:

1. "My body, are you okay? Is there anything you want or need? Or does anywhere hurt?"
2. "My feelings, how are you doing? How do you feel right now? How shall we respond to this question?"
3. Oh my mind, what is going on inside you? Is there a million things in there? What are you busy with?" ☺

Well, today's condition of "being well" is possible when these three are in balance. So, you should know that the person who can respond to your question with, "I am well…" is taking the average of all three and responding. When doing this, nobody needs to think for a long time; because the stimulants are already constantly scratching the doors of the brain, the answer spills out very quickly:

"Oh, don't even ask! I haven't been able to pull my head off the pillow for days. Migraine again…"

"Well, at least we're getting on with life."

"Thank God, no problems."

"What kind of state is the country is going to be in?"

"…"

Are you aware that the answers are going on inside the triangle of heart-mind-body? The answer, which moved around the curves of the brain and reached all the way to our mouth is quite a filtered inference that was blended by the effects of these three factors.

"Holistic" literally means, "integrated." In other words, it is an approach, which says that only if all the pieces, which are connected and affected by each other, are evaluated together can the quality of the being affected by them be defined. And a "Holistic Approach to Health" says that the body cannot be thought of apart from the spirit and the mind.

When we say "spiritual health," we can start by accepting that it is a projection of body and thoughts. In many holistic statements, this term SPIRIT is used. But I should confess that I am scared of this word. Yikes! Maybe it is because of the religious doctrines that we were exposed to or taking the necromancy sessions that we did by writing down letters on paper that we took too seriously as children, that this word gives me the feeling of another energy dimension that lives outside of the body. Not to get stuck on this unknown all the time, and instead of trying to remember or remind you of, the definition I made (projection of body and thoughts), I prefer to analyse the holistic approach through the **Body-Heart-Mind** triad. Together with this, although my intention is to examine these three concepts separately, I am also aware that I am talking about an inseparable triad, the elements of which affect and trigger each other, and which can be both each other's cause and effect.

Being both the cause and the effect of each other...

For instance, there is research showing that the intestinal flora of people in depression is different from that of those who are not. The fact that the microbes living in our guts can affect our mood demonstrates the significance of holistic approaches, as well as being interesting. Similarly, it has been found that mice carrying healthier bacteria in their guts have more possibility of staying alive after a heart attack than those carrying unhealthy bacteria. The cardiologists who know that heart health can be related to the flora of the intestines: hands up! ☺

Look at the Stones Thrown at Modern Medicine!

As you know, modern medicine is under serious critical attack. Why? Critics say that it gives symptomatic treatment and most of the time does not look for the real reason of the illness. It is a great injustice to slander today's medicine like this. Yet, although I find this generalization mistaken, it does make you wonder if there might be some small validity to this idea. According to some approaches, it is said, that *"Modern medical education is predicated on the 'cell' as a structural unit. In this case, the scientific research always stays at that level (cell level) and this explains modern medicine's limited structure, which is confined to just the physical body."* Well then, what about the approach which has been known of and discussed for years, in which atomic and subatomic particles (Higgs Boson[5] or the God Particle) activate the power of thinking, meaning, *"Whichever program we download to our mind we live according to that?"* Doesn't this underlie many philosophies explaining the power of thinking? As well as believing it, we want to believe it.

Yes, emotion, mind and body are a whole. A problem in one of them can seriously damage the other. The thoughts filling our minds appear as the reflection of each of our feelings. And vice-versa.

Since modern medicine focuses more on the physical body, this leads to the accusation that most doctors (excepting those with a holistic approach) cannot terminate the source of the illness, but make do with sorting out the symptoms. We are telling you: If your doctor's approach is this, instead of slinging mud at the whole world of modern medicine, you'd better change that doctor.

If we discuss chronic illnesses, because the symptomatic treatments applied to psychosomatic illnesses, in other words, physical illnesses caused by psychology, do not actually heal the illness but only remove the symptom, most patients can be addicted to medicine for a long time, sometimes a lifetime. And if the treatment stays at the level of medicine, it is very difficult for this to change. Full recovery cannot be experienced. When people ask for an example of this, the first things that come to mind are fever or high blood pressure. Ok, it is fine to regulate the blood pressure of a patient with medication (if high blood pressure is not regulated, either with medicine or lifestyle and diet, it is like a ticking bomb: it can cause strokes, heart attacks, and problems in

5. Just a millionth of a second after the Big Bang, which is accepted as being the beginning of the universe, the first particles spread out. These particles were pure energy and did not have any mass. It was suggested in 1964 that the mechanism, which gained them mass was Higgs Boson.

the eyes and kidneys) but isn't it better to find the reason for the high blood pressure and try to eliminate that? What does the pressure, which becomes high in order to pump blood to every part of the body, actually try to tell us? That is what we need to understand. No doubt solving the problem, which causes the high blood pressure will be the real recovery and repressing the pressure will merely be a palliative solution.

Sometimes palliating the problem with medicine is no different from switching off the power of an alarm system. Of course, they should be palliated when they are at a level at which they are threatening health, but if this feels like the problem is past and the patient is sent home with the verdict, "Okay, you are cured," it should be known that the situation here is not one of being cured. If the doctor who says that, doesn't research the real problem, which caused the symptom, then there is a problem. High fever is the same kind of a problem. It is important to find the reason for this rather than suffocating the patient with medicines, because the body is fighting something by producing fever. Instead of helping it with its fight, we take its weapon away. (In fact, I'm being smarty pants, affected and paralysed by the things I've read. I know how much we need the medicines that we call "bad" and which remove the symptoms, even if we have a cold, to be able to sleep well. I don't want to put you in a dilemma, but I'm trying to bring this awareness in this book: If the symptom is at a really disturbing level, of course - preferably in natural ways - try to solve the cause of the illness by getting rid of that disturbance. But don't think that you are cured when you have just eliminated the symptom for that moment.)

What do the wounds in our body, allergies, dandruff, headache, etc. try to tell us? Triglyceride is high, cellulite is increased, or there is decay in the teeth... Oh! What's happening! I hardly eat, but I'm on the edge of being obese. Come on! I now have osteoporosis, but I am still hoping to get better by continuing not doing the things that I didn't do, is that right? Well, at this point we should look not at the thing on the surface, but deeper. The things we mentioned are not the real problem itself, but signals.

So, why are they giving modern medicine such a hard time? What can be the doctors' problem, that although they know the illnesses better than all of us, they deal with symptoms and cannot go into the real source? Again according to some approaches, *"In fact, it is not that they cannot; but they do not most of the time. It cannot really be possible nowadays for a standard medical approach to locate the source of the problem"* they say, because there is such a perception: *"Medicine, which is getting more and more commercial every day, approaches everybody similarly, so it cannot have personal results. It cannot spare time for that when there is a queue of patients waiting at the door. E.g. The person who approaches a doctor saying, 'I have an inexplicable headache' is immediately sent to an imaging device like x-ray, MR (Magnetic Resonance) or tomography, if not EEG etc. Between us, the doctors, who send a lot of patients to the imaging devices are adored by the hospital management. Ah, bloody capitalism! They ask the patients if they have insurance and before diagnosis the invoice starts getting longer and longer. The patient necessarily/unnecessarily gets radiation. Investigations continue; headaches too… The patients are happy and hopeful, just because they are not alone with that horrible pain at home, but thinking that somebody is sharing their pain, and because of the hope, 'Maybe I can find a solution to my problem.' If there is no tumour or any other trouble seen, it is most likely the doctors will lay emphasis on the migraine pains; although they think about the psychological and spiritual dimensions, they don't have time to deal with them or they don't even attempt to ask about it because it is not their area. In this case, they direct the patient to another specialist, a psychiatrist. What happens there? One of the three to five - well-known antidepressant medicines in the sector is written in that prescription and the patient starts watching life from behind a curtain of mist, half smiling and half not understanding it."*

What I want to say is that the more you get away from an integral approach more difficult it gets to find the source. In other words, getting lost in detail, missing the whole, not seeing the wood for the trees is what I am trying to say. At this point, the approaches, which find doctors' specialities guilty step in and say: *"Having specialities inside specialities blunts the ability of the doctors to look at the patients integrally. The source of chronic illnesses is mostly psychological conflicts. When an illness occurs, the* ***organ***, ***brain*** *and* ***psychology*** *tend to give a mutual symptom or separate but concurrent signals, by triggering each other. And the way to make this discomfort better is not just making one of them better. Getting rid of a psychological stomach ache by medication wouldn't radically fix the psychology. It would be a more correct approach to ensure that the stomach pain goes away naturally by fixing the psychology."* So, what? Shouldn't they look at the patient closely?

These are the pretty pessimistic generalizations made about modern medicine. Shameful! Okay, we are not very fond of this either, but because of a few bad apples, the image is damaged for the good ones as well as the bad ones. And there is no reason to add fuel to the flames by saying where there is smoke there is fire.

While we can say a lot of things about health because of modern medicine's explanations, isn't it very cruel to make a generalization because of a few doctors who don't do their jobs properly?

OH, THOSE FREE RADICALS!

Just in the middle of our conversation, when we were bubbling so delightfully, please don't find it odd that I've brought this subject up so abruptly! There is such a reality in our lives and if you dig into it a little bit you'll be shocked. That reality is Free Radicals.

If you ask, "What on earth are free radicals?" the definition in chemistry is this: Molecules, which generally include one oxygen atom, which has lost one of its electrons. Chemically they have lost an electron from their outmost electron orbit and they have an attacking character, trying to share other atoms' electrons to be able to fill the electron gaps.

"You don't say! Really?" ☺

Okay, you're right: This does not say anything to me either. So, what if I say that these shameless molecules bother their neighbours; they long to possess their electrons and when they get the chance (here, the word "chance" is very important: I will tell you about it soon) they attack greedily here and there and damage the structures of the cells. It's a disaster. No way! Nobody wants these types around him or her. No, they don't, but these circulate inside us. What do you say to that? You didn't hear it from me, but all of us are feeding enemies within!

And Now We Have These to Deal With

Unfortunately, the oxygen that we need to live is at the same time the source of the free radicals. These molecules have extra energy. By pouring this energy into the cells, they hinder and change their normal functions. You might be familiar with the names "hydrogen peroxide" or "lipid peroxide." They can occur as a result of metabolic procedures. E.g. they might occur as a result of the metabolic reaction that oily nutrition processed at a high temperature creates in the body. These are the most dangerous ones among the free radicals. They can cause a vast variety of illnesses, e.g. cancer! Heart disease! Fast ageing! Aching joints! Weakened bones! Getting white hair, shedding hair, skin dryness, wrinkled skin, etc...

I don't know: Did I manage to draw your attention to free radicals?

In fact, the thing is: During energy production in the cells, as a result of the fats or glucose reacting with oxygen (turning fat to energy or burning fat) oxy-radicals occur. These are toxic waste; we do not need them at all. As soon as our much-loved oxygen molecule, which needs to form a compound, gets into a reaction with fat and glucose, the oxy-radicals start to be produced. There is no way out of it, because there is no way oxygen can move through the body without this by-product occurring… It's like a bad joke! Moreover, even one of our cells has the ability to produce vast amounts of free radicals. Really, it's a very complicated process. Well, it makes you want to give up burning your fats with oxygen, so as not to produce any free radicals…

A healthy cell getting on with life happily.

Free radicals pick on the healthy cells to replace their missing electrons.

Antioxidants give them an electron from themselves and stop them bothering the healthy cells.

However, I have good news too: From time to time, free radicals are good for metabolism. The body can use the power of the most harmful free radicals in the immune system and inflammatory reactions. How? The macrophage cells[6] in the immune system take bacteria and viruses inside them. This process is called macrophagy. And after that, together with oxy-radicals, which occur by separating electrons from oxygen molecules so that they can take via blood circulation, they wipe out the microbes. Take the doctors' word for it! Aggressive usage of the types of toxic oxygen becomes impressively successful in protecting the body against infection-producing organisms. But there is a possibility that this process is out of control and, in the case when too many free radicals are produced, many harmful

6. **Macrophage Cells (macrophages):** They swallow and digest bacteria, some substances and infarcts, which are foreign to the organism, by phagocytosis. Macrophages are cells, which have the characteristic of migrating inside the body. On the other hand, these cells undertake a duty in the immune system of the body.

chain reactions can be triggered, too. Even here, the logic of "too much of a good thing is bad" applies.

If you say, "Write that down in language that we can understand!" I would only say: If we do not want the free radicals taking the electrons they want by damaging the structure of our healthy cells, we will have to regularly consume food containing **antioxidants**. There is no other way; we will do it, because if free radicals get what they need from antioxidants, there is no reason left for them to damage any other structure in the body. To cut a long story short, this is the reason for the increased demand for foods containing antioxidants…

Note: Somewhere above I said, "When they get the chance they attack here and there greedily…" and I said that I would explain the use of the word "chance" later; so, this is the reason. It is possible because of antioxidants not to give a chance to free radicals.

At the end of my research, I saw that we are being exposed to external substances that largely cause the occurrence of free radicals in our body, e.g. the ingredients that are used to produce some of the convenience food and drinks that we buy contain quite a lot of agricultural chemical substances. And by using these substances directly we open the way to the production of free radicals. I sat and read quite a lot; I came across a compound called "Lipid Peroxide." Processed foods generally contain a high dose of lipid peroxide. It causes the formation of free radicals, which harm the cardiovascular system very seriously. It is very worrying what happens in our body because of weird compounds that we wouldn't even recognize if we saw. Of course, I panicked! Since then my cupboard never lacks cranberries, which have a very high antioxidant value. Don't ask! They are pretty expensive too!

Also, let's not miss out the fact that all types of electromagnetic radiation and exposure to too many sunbeams can also cause free radicals to occur. And this causes the skin to become aged, wrinkled and roughened. When exposed to sunbeams too much, free radical formation in the skin can cause skin cancer by seriously harming the tissue of the skin. Again, we have a case of "too much of a good thing is bad."

And stress… That is the major factor in everything. In an environment of too much stress, our body starts to produce free radicals more than needed, and this causes a series of troubles in the body, like running out of energy too quickly, feelings of exhaustion, hardening of the arteries, etc. Besides that, during stressful moments, our body apparently starts producing the hormones cortisol and catecholamine (I love writing these Latin names, which I don't understand and will forget in a minute) in our metabolism. And later, these hormones turn into harmful free radicals in the body. We know that the environment we live in and modern world conditions cause our stress level to get too high. So, it means there is yet another reason to decrease our stress level.

Free Radical > Antioxidant = Degenerative damage in the body

Yes, this is what happens if free radicals are more than the antioxidants in the metabolism: Degenerative damage.

It is said that as we age the body is exposed to the formation of more free radicals. For goodness' sake! Just one more year until I'm fifty, and you are saying this! ☺ Here is exactly what they say: "If the effective power of free radicals is more than the antioxidant level in the body, the cells in the body lose their functionality, get defeated, and ageing accelerates. Besides, the production of antioxidants in the body gets lower gradually with ageing, and physical and mental collapse occur. We need to supply antioxidants from outside, from more or less age twenty-five. What if there is no antioxidant? If there is no antioxidant in the body, it can even cause death. It's no joke...."

"What do you say, doctor?"

So, what shall we do to be protected from free radicals?

1. Take antioxidant supplements: nutrition, pills, minerals, vitamins, etc.
2. Be, walk, run, dance, etc. in environments where the oxygen level is high.
3. Stop harmful habits like cigarettes and other stuff right now.
4. Persuade yourself not to start smoking again.

Let's not forget, as each of us gets older, the speed of wearing out is increasing because of the free radical reservoir in our tissues and cells. The natural antioxidant system of the body cannot fulfil its job properly in this period. That's why the organs and tissues start to lose their function in time and die. We need supplements from outside. Let's take our precautions before it is too late. However, the more important thing is to have this awareness.

Here Are the Most Powerful Antioxidants Known In Nature

The antioxidants contained in vegetables and fruit vary in quantity and type. Antioxidant compounds are not in the same proportion in every food.

Ascorbic Acid (Vitamin C): It is contained in vegetables and fruit like oranges, lemons, kiwis, tomatoes, green-leaved vegetables (broccoli, spinach, Brussels sprouts, etc.) and potatoes. The extra vitamin C is got rid of in the urine. It increases resistance to illnesses. Should preferably be eaten raw.

Alfa tocopherol (Vitamin E): It is contained in grains like wheat, millet and rice. Also contained in oils like sunflower oil, corn oil and cottonseed oil, in dry fruits like walnuts, almonds and peanuts, and in green vegetables.

Anthocyanin (purple): Blackberries, cranberries, black mulberries, cornelian cherries, black grapes, savoy cabbage, aubergines, black prunes or black raisins... These are the warriors against cancer. Their antioxidant values are very high.

Beta-carotene (Vitamin A): It is contained in yellow coloured fruits like peaches, apricots, butternut squash and nectarines, and in dark-green-leaved vegetables like spinach, rocket and parsley. The best source is carrots. Strengthens the immune system, increases resistance, lowers the risk of cancer, protects from cardiovascular illnesses.

Flavonoid (yellow-white): They are the pigments contained in many fruit and vegetables in a high ratio. Fruits like apples, strawberries, grapes; chocolate and especially tea also include flavonoid.

Lycopene (red): It is the substance, which gives tomatoes, cherries, raspberries, pomegranates, beetroots and turnips the red colour. It has been found out that it affects cardiovascular illnesses and cancer and has positive effects on the immune system.

Lutein (green, dark green): Spinach, rocket, parsley, dill, courgettes, green cabbages, asparagus, leeks, green peppers, broccoli, Brussels sprouts, green apples, green grapes and kiwis are lutein and indoline sources. Lutein is a very powerful antioxidant. It gives skin beauty and freshness.

Coenzyme q: It is on the agenda due to its positive effects, especially on cancer and particularly neurological illnesses. It is at a high ratio in meat products like liver, heart and kidney, and in fish too. It can also be taken as a pill..

P.S.: Vitamin E is damaged in food, which is deep-fried and during the milling process of grains. That is why it is healthier to consume the products, which contain vitamin E without deep frying, but raw or boiled, especially with unprocessed grains.

I would like to introduce you one more term: ORAC (Oxygen Radical Absorbance Capacity.) It is the value, which shows how rich fruit and vegetables are in antioxidants. It has been found that if we consume the value of 3000 to5000 ORAC daily, we gain serious protection against free radicals.

Clove, sumac, oregano, cinnamon, sorghum, turmeric, acai berry, cocoa, cinnamon and parsley are the ten ingredients that have the highest ORAC level.

Health and Illness

Health and illness should not be seen as opposites. Quite a lot of contemporary illnesses attract our attention when they become acute. In fact, in the process of chronic development, illness and health live as though each is within the other. If I could draw a scale from 0 to 100, putting health at one end and illness at the other, each of us would be at one point of this scale. When we wake up one morning we think we are well. At that moment, we would be at health level 40 on the scale; the next day when this number drops to 38 we become ill. In short, dropping from 100% healthy to health level 38 does not happen overnight. In chronic illnesses, the total of the mistakes we have made over time is the illness. The healing process is not only the getting rid of the symptoms: it is the journey towards health at level 100.

Illness Management

When the journey from illness to health is described step by step, the first step is faultless nutrition. In other words, not tiring the body by malnutrition and supporting the healing process by taking beneficial food into the body. If on one side the illness results from toxic pollution, purification/detox is an important step too. Purification is the most important medicine of wilful healing. It is not possible to heal under stress. Certainly, every healing process should be augmented with a serenity process. A range of high-dose vitamin C, omega-3 supplement, etc. accompanying proper nutrition and purification will accelerate the healing process.

This part of healing is the real healing journey to be made when there is no need for emergency action. Emergency management is modern medicine's attempt to get rid of the symptoms by using medicine, operations and similar systems. In every healing, after the emergency management, we should not forget the need for a healing process for which the patient is responsible and which may take months.

Ersin Pamuksüzer

CHAPTER TWO

FOR PHYSICAL HEALTH…

- ❖ THE BODY
- ❖ A SPECIAL NOTE TO MY MOM
- ❖ GETTING DIRTY (RETOX)
- ❖ GETTING CLEAN (DETOX)
- ❖ DETOX AND BREATHING
- ❖ DETOX AND CANCER
- ❖ BE CALM

"There is not a type of treatment that is more effective,
less harmful and cheaper than hunger".

Aidin Salih, M.D.

THE BODY

Examining humans I talked about howwe need to look integrally because we are talking about a living thing which doesn't only have a physical area but mental and emotional areas too. All through the book the importance of these three areas being in balance is going to be restated, talking about a healthy life. Although these three elements cannot be held separate from each other, in this chapter, taking a step back from emotion and mind, we are going to focus on "Body."

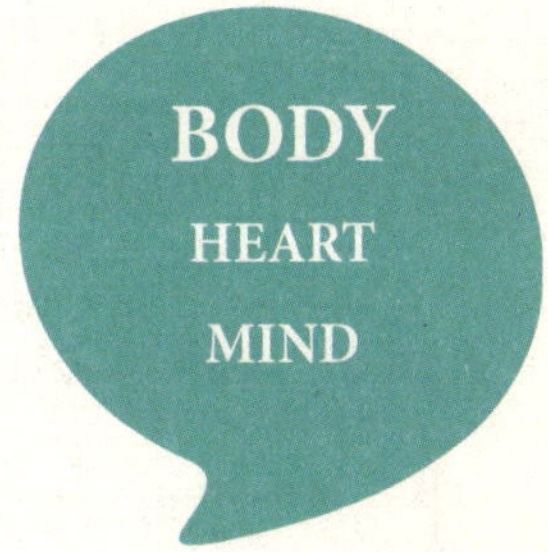

Why Do We Get Ill?

"😐 Why not?"

"What kind of an answer is that?"

You're quite right, so I'll put it this way: As long as we don't take "overdoing" out of our lives, we'll get ill. In other words, when we overdo and exaggerate things, the natural protection mechanisms rebel; springs burst; the system overheats.

Stress, continual worrying, sympathetic nerves working constantly, not being able to get rest, emotional conflicts, acid-producing food, malnutrition, preservatives in food, pleasure-giving substances, harmful habits, addictions, modern city life, base stations, mobile phones, radio waves, geopathics… In short, environmental, nutritional, emotional, and magnetic pollution and overexposure to them make us ill. Also, after getting ill we don't know how to overcome this illness by using emotional, mental and physical detox; moreover, we don't believe that we can. However, we can overcome illnesses in such ways. This is the thesis of this book…

The Characteristics of a Healthy Person

Well, let's go in reverse. Let's not talk about un-healthiness, but about being healthy. What does it mean to be healthy? What do we miss and want? What are the properties of a healthy person? Would you like to make your own description in the space below? Dream about the thing you want to be:

....

....

....

....

I believe that a healthy person is:

1. Energetic, full of desire, eager, motivated.

2. One with hobbies, life-pleasures, priorities, curiosity.

3. Creative and active.

4. One with hopes and life-projects.

5. Who enjoys family and friends.

6. Filled with peace and serenity.

7. One who feels beautiful.

8. One who is at peace with sexuality and can enjoy it.

9. One who has good judgement.

10. One who can harmonise logic, emotion and the senses.

11. One who can manage to stay in the moment, in peace with his/her past, is not worried about the future, or who can manage all these emotional states well.

12. Active.

13. One who is self-sufficient physically.

14. One who likes his/her body, himself/herself and nature.

15. One who respects the modern, the good and the beautiful, and stands against the bad.

16. One who can express oneself.

17. One who has values.

18. Happy.

...

Of course, it's possible to add quite a few more items. I know there will be many items that match the description of a healthy person that you've made too. The description on the list you made has particular importance: The things you've written there are your priorities. You should focus on them. You should find out how many of the things you wrote you have or do not have,and try to add the missing ones.

First, we should know very well that each of us is a miracle. If we, who start by dropping into our mother's womb and witness countless miracles all through our lives, can manage to learn how to use many natural facts that we take for granted, everything will be so much more beautiful.

Nature and the living things contained within, have a property of mending, healing and renewing themselves. We, who get wounded and recover, who get ill and get well again, should be grateful to nature for even knowing this. Lucky are those who are aware and can be grateful for this.

We can start the day by learning to be thankful and smiling for the things we have... Being grateful for what you have is a very important act of awareness.

What are Toxins and Detox?

'Toxin' literally means poison. Substances that damage the natural harmony of our body diminish our health and quality of life and can bring us to death unless they are eliminated. Life is already toxic in nature. According to the research called Body Burden, carried out by the organisation called the Environmental Working Group in America, in the blood of nearly every child born in America nowadays, there are more than 200 environmental toxins. Insecticides, heavy metals, Teflon, and even rocket fuel are among these. Although nature is ready to tolerate these toxins to an extent, it reacts against them when they are too many and decreases the lifespan.

We generally take toxins from outside, but some of them we produce in our own body too. We get them by breathing, eating, drinking and physical contact. The metabolism has to work for us to be alive. As long as the metabolism works, the body produces toxins. In other words, every time we breathe and take in oxygen, our cells use this oxygen and burn glucose fat to turn it into energy. However, during this process, as I mentioned in the first chapter, free radicals occur. They attack the healthy cells and damage their structure. Unless they are hindered, they can cause ageing, cancer, cardiovascular diseases and many more illnesses.

City life means toxins anyway. We are exposed to toxins too much, and of every kind. Exhaust fumes, cigarette smoke, factory gases, ventilation systems, and chemical substances used in industry and farming that we breath in from outside destroy our body. Of course, a high dose takes us to the finish line more quickly, but don't think that the body tolerates the lower doses. Unfortunately, even when the dose of toxin is low it continues to gather and cause damage. In this sense, there can be a destiny, starting with asthma and concluding with anaemia and cancer for those who live in highly polluted areas, that in some sense is drawn by people themselves. A weakened immune system, unfortunately, becomes insufficient to respond to the ubiquitous damage.

Moreover, as well as breathing them, we eat toxins. In agriculture, for earth and seeds, there are pesticides and sprays for fertility and resistance against what may harm them. Although we know most of them are toxic, using them to deal with other harmful organisms is similar to war for peace or sex for virginity! "Destroying the harmful with even the more harm] is capitalist society's commercial concern..." No, no! I won't finish this sentence.

Yes, what was I saying? I think I was saying that we also eat the poisonous residue onskins and leaves together with fruit and vegetables themselves. If we could see the preservatives and sprays put on the shining and colourful fruit and vegetables, which smile at us as seductively as they can, would we be able to eat them this comfortably? And also, do we know that however much we wash them, we cannot get rid of the toxic substances completely?

How about the antibiotics and growth hormones that are given to animals? God knows how long it has been since we ate a chicken without hormones. Even the water we drink contains toxins.

Homes are the same. Everywhere looking clean does not mean it is cleaned of toxins. On the contrary, the cleaning products themselves are toxic anyway. How about dust, smoke and paints? And don't think of toxins only as substances: harmful emotions, thoughts and environmental factors are also toxins for our body. News and series are toxins. Never-ending construction rumbles on our roads and streets, the roads being dug and re-dug, traffic and traffic bullies… These are all toxins. We are finished, we are! We're already dead and there is nobody crying for us. (But let's not get that sad: There are countries in the world without any of these problems, but people who live there die of lack of sun and not having a purpose!)

So, all through this book let's call every type of poisonous substance, which damages our compound of Emotion-Mind-Body a **toxin**, and the process of getting these substances out of our lives **detox**. If we look at detox as a purification process, we come across another concept that we should keep in mind: The situation that whenever the detox process ends, the action of metabolism in life's cycle pollutes the body again. And let's call this **retox**.

To detox periodically is a must for a healthy life. Unfortunately, while we who live under the effects of all these elements - some of which are controllable and some not - are trying to live a healthy life, we are constantly under attack from factors that affect us both from inside and outside. However, let's not forget that the body is a constant self-repairing structure. We can trust it. Only helping the body by making the process a bit easier is doing a favor to ourselves. Just as the sentence, "I want a healthy life" seems inappropriate coming from our mouths aswe continue doing harmful things, it is not very smart not to do the things that we know that are good for us.

The Factors that Cause Illness

External Factors	Internal Factors
magnetic pollution:	chemicals
electronic devices	medicines
computers	paints
mobile phones	synthetics
etc.	industrial additives
geopathic pollution:	heavy metal poisons
underground waters	nicotine
base stations	intolerance (opposite frequencies)
high tension lines	situations that cut the energy flow
etc.	e.g.: scars, wounds
environmental pollution:	etc.
air pollution	
poisons	
gasses	
etc.	

How Does Illness Show Itself?

Be sure that a recipe is not needed for this. It shows itself in such a way that you recognise it immediately saying "That's it!" It never needed to advertise itself! However, the interesting thing is that we only recognise illnesses when the natural resistance mechanism of the body is activated. In other words, when we come across weakness, fever, cough, etc. we say "Oh! I got ill". These signals are not the illnesses themselves; they are just the symptoms. And also, they are a part of the healing process. E.g. having a high fever… The aim of the biological system at this stage is to regulate the body, to balance the settings, to fight with the microbes and viruses. The human body has tolerance to fever up to a certain degree; we all know that. In situations, which push our tolerance levels, we might need to resort to symptomatic medicines. However, every removed symptom, hidden emotion and swallowed word is like a toxin gathered inside. Unless the trouble is figured out and the illness is sorted, healing is not going to happen.

If we talk about the body becoming polluted by toxic substances: while the liver, kidneys, lungs, and other organs are working normally, this heavy weight does not cause a lot of trouble; we don't even understand that we are ill until our immune system gets weak and the tolerance towards illnesses gets weak too. Then, because the body's digestion and organs of elimination are not in a state to bear the burden, it means troublesome days are ahead of us. As this situation continues, I mean toxic substances gathering and the organs of elimination having even more difficulties, hard times for the metabolism show themselves. I think the inability to lose weight is the easiest of all these problems…

The body is a self-mending structure. Let's help it by providing it with the necessary conditions to manage this more comfortably.

They call the body gathering toxins or getting polluted "acidification." It is something like when we didn't put the trash out of our home and it smells. If there are people living in that house, of course the trash goes out. If they don't throw itaway, of course then it is going to smell. We live in a world in which we get ill because we don't do the things we have to do. So, instead of reacting to the illness, we need to get the habit of being pro-active against getting ill. The cells that produce our daily energy leave the waste, which occurs during this energy production to the fluids outside the cell. In a healthy system, these fluids are discarded in urine and sweat anyway, and the body brings itself again to an alkali (the base dissolving in water) state. If we understand becoming alkaline as getting away from acids, it will make our work easier. You are going to hear this word "alkali" often in the rest of the book. Medical people figured that it was ideal that the pH value for healthy blood should be between 7.35 and 7.45. They say that a healthy body protects these values automatically. So, it would not be bad to help it, so that there is alkali left for the body.

In our body, a few organs are obliged to stay alkaline: Kidneys, lungs and our skin. Acids are thrown outside of the kidney by urine and from the skin by sweat. Dark yellow urine and bad-smelling sweat indicate acid excess. Again, doctors say: "People who want to lose weight should have their pH values checked frequently and encourage alkali. The most healthy diet program is a green-vegetable heavy nutrition program, which makes urine alkaline."

Apart from the kidneys, the lungs, which are the other most important acid-balancing organs that we have, are given the job of oxygen uptake and carbon dioxide release. We should help our body in this matter by making our lungs do the right kind of breathing. (See Chapter 5: Breathing). We should apply the sort of breathing with which we get the maximum benefit from oxygen, and we should obtain higher awareness about this subject.

And skin… This organ, which covers all our body is constantly functioning to release toxins by sweating. My grandma who asked, "Could you rub my back?" once a week in the bath obviously knew something about the rubbing since she periodically brought up the issue. She would do many more things, my late grandma, which I thought were just folk medicine. She would do cupping, which is an unbelievable massage technique and stimulates the acupuncture points. Also, she would do blood-letting[7]. She would stick leeches to her legs. Brilliant techniques for dirty-blood-suckers, but do I have the guts? Now, these have a very serious place in the health sector. Well, when did you have your skin aired the last time? Outfits which prevent the skin from breathing, deodorants which make it suffocate , hair dyes, cosmetics, poor quality creams and perfumes with many additives all hinder the skin in doing its job. On the contrary: It is possible that our skin, which has an ability to absorb all the chemicals used on it, instead of releasing toxins can become an organ that gathers them. We should immediately take this subject in hand and take a look at the chemicals we apply to the skin, e.g. deodorant… Using it is a problem; not using it is another problem. My friend Dilek said to me, "The solution is easy: mix carbonate with a bit of aloe vera and

7. **Blood-letting:** It is a process of draining the heavy metals, toxins, free radicals, pills being used and food with hormones which the body cannot get rid of, by creating bleeding by small cuts and by cupping.

jasmine oil and put it on your armpit; it will keep the odour of sweat away all day; this is a deodorant which does not include any toxic substance..." Since my friend told me this, my armpit does not get itchy as it did when I used deodorant. In fact, it never does. It means I was doing something seriously wrong before.

And there is another danger waiting us as well. I've learned that our muscles gather derivatives of an amino acid called glutamine. This substance is a protein. It heals muscle and connective tissue, accelerates the intestinal absorption of food, and sources the necessary energy to muscles when we do sport. If our body has too much acid, it is consumed so much that it causes muscle atrophy. Besides, in the case of lack of calcium and magnesium, an alkali mineral in our body, problems like hair loss, tooth disorders and muscle atrophy occur. Magnesium is one of the substances that is intensive in the muscles. However, when it decreases and is not supplied from outside, it causes cramps and brittle bones (osteoporosis) in the body. So now, as people who know all this, can we see the importance of stopping acidification, in other words putting the rubbish out, and supplementing the body with calcium and magnesium?

I will discuss acidification and the illnesses it causes in detail; it is an important subject.

Is There Anyone Left Who Hasn't Heard About the Gut Situation?

It must be because of the substances it contains: The intestines have always been organs, which were put aside until later, which did not get the attention they deserved, and even did not want to be remembered. Until they reminded us of themselves... Luckily, nowadays a lot of medical doctors tell us their importance and mention the importance of intestines in their books. Among the books that I've read about this subject, the best book is Intestine, the Emotional Brain by Prof Dr. Hüseyin Nazlıkul. I suggest you read it.

Even I realised the importance of intestines because of a friend who got colorectal cancer this year. This friend of mine, who always had a constipation problem, is face to face with a case of cancer for which doctors say she is pretty late because she did not deal with the situation at the right time. She decided to go with the techniques of modern medicine, and her effort is continuing. I wish her recovery. I understood that the intestines are among the most vital organs in the body and deserve maximum attention. They may even be the most important link in our digestive system.

Besides this, I used to wonder, "What does the pancreas do in the body?" To my surprise, one of the functions is this: After the food gets digested in the intense, acidic environment of the stomach and goes to the duodenum, the pancreas excretes bicarbonate to create an alkaline environment and, apparently, waste is thus prepared for the last stage of digestion without harming the body. Otherwise, when the system does not work well - in other words when the acid ratio cannot be lowered - because the walls of the intestines get damaged the holes of the intestines which absorb nutrition get wider and leak the pieces of food which haven't been sufficiently absorbed, and the digestion of which is not yet complete. Because the system senses these pieces as alien substances, it reacts. Here's food sensitivity for you: Intolerance, digestion problems, allergies, constipationetc.

Oh, and be careful if you are taking supplement pills to help your guts work! It is known that many of these cause damage to the flora of the intestines. We wouldn't want to have chronic constipation, would we? Since I've learned that the pH value in intestines that do not work steadily gets damaged and the bacteria that tries to rot the acidic food becomes active, and that the reason our excreta smells so bad underlies this, I believe that we need to take care that our intestines are working with their natural flora.

You may know that many discomforts show themselves in excreta's colour, smell and consistency. You've probably also heard that there are medical people who can diagnose a lot of illnesses by looking at the colour of the urine. Just like the tongue and urine,feces are also important information sources, which let us know what is happening in the body. Keep watching. ☺

If You Intend to Lose Weight, Please be Careful!

Despite all these systems, which try to regulate the body, if the acid ratio remains high due to malnutrition, harmful habits, bad conditions and other factors, it is known that the other systems, which are the body's safety net, step in. This is my favourite subject! ☺

I will tell you a secret: I think in nature, biologically, women are luckier than men. Why? Women have a lot of cellulite; that's why! ☺ Women's bodies are prone to cellulite formation because of their tissue structure and hormones. If you ask,

"How does that vile cellulite, which deforms our bodies, fit in the term lucky?" I will explain immediately: The extra acid which wanders around the body is captured and trapped by fat in women so that it doesn't go and stick to an interior organ and harm it. This or that part of our body is getting fat; our pants won't fit; our world becomes dark… The name of the thing that is formed is: Cellulite! Most of us don't like it much, but the work it does should be respected. Thanks to it, we're being protected from some illnesses, which could be serious, but we did not know it. Yes, you are right, as a side effect we put on weight, we look worse. That saying, "Even by drinking water, I put on weight" is right: we get swollen because the acid gathered in fats causes water to be kept in the body. (That's why excessively fat bodies lose weight fast right after starting a diet. The first thing gone from the body is the water…)

We need to know that it doesn't matter how intense of a diet we are on: fats are going to stay in the body until we get rid of those acids. The kilos lost with diets without balancing acid are unfortunately lost from inside the muscles and bones, not from these fats. You are right to panic. With senseless diets, we lose materials, which are not easy to replace. Among those we lose are our muscles, youth, and beauty too. So, be careful!

If we want to lose weight let's not do it without getting rid of the acids gathered in the fats in our body!

Yes, ladies! I am saying that because cellulite traps acids and prevents the body from harm, women's vital organs are damaged less in comparison to men's. In men's metabolism, tissue structure is different. And because it doesn't have a chance of having cellulite,acids cannot be kept away from the organs enough. They bring a burden to vital organs and count as one of the main causes of men dying earlier than women.

Love Your Lymphatic System; Take Care of It…

In other words, the immune system… In descriptions, "lymph" is a name given to the circulation fluid made up of blood plasma and lymph proteins, and which circulates inside lymph capillary vessels. And the lymph system is a name given to the organ system consisting of lymph fluid, lymph vessels and lymph nodes, and carries lymph fluid, which circulates everywhere in the body (except the brain.) It is a second circulation system in the body besides blood circulation. However, it is known to be pretty different to the circulation system in terms of structure. The function of the lymph system in the body is to move away the alien substances, dead tissues, damaged cells, bacteria, and microbes inside the cells; making sure that the tissue fluids and blood fluids are kept in balance; adding fatty acids, glycerol, vitamins A, D, E, and K, which have been absorbed in the intestines, to the circulation, and supporting the protective system of the body.

I have learned that the most frequently seen lymph system illnesses are in the lymph nodes. Well, from our childhood we hear our mothers saying, "Your tonsils are swollen!" There: The thing we call "tonsil" is a lymph node. The mothers who read this can say, "Kid, your lymph tonsils are swollen" from this time on. ☺

The Main Life Savers

Do you have a life prescription? What do you do when you get up in the morning, and what would be better if you did it? All day, how do you snack? How do you choose food for your lunch and dinner? How is your consumption of coffee, tea, alcohol, coke and fruit juice?

What are your activities? Do you take the easy way in tasks, which need natural movement? In other words, do you take the elevator, or go to the grocery store by car? Besides, which kind of activities are there that work for your body? Do you walk? Do you do sports? Is there a space at home spared for exercise? Have you made it a routine to open your body by stretching nicely every 45 minutes during the day?

What kind of beauties do you see around you? How often do you talk to them, caress them? Is your water/air clean or ionised? Which chemicals surround you? Are they in your shampoo? Are they in the air freshener in your car? Are they in your fabric softener? How many or how few are the moments when you are completely involved with nature? How can you make them more? Above all, do you have awareness?

Do you always have something on your mind? Do you get angry and demoralised? Are you stuck and can't get out of the difficulty? Are people making you tired? Are you bothered at work and at home? Do you need recipes to make your mind good? If so, what about creating them? Can you categorise your relationships? Toxic, tiring, lacking, too much, can be fixed, cannot… Here, how about switching off the ones, which cannot be fixed? If you cannot (it might be difficult to switch off mother, father, brother/sister…) how about accepting them as they are and living in peace with them? And taking responsibility and opening a new blank page for the ones that can be fixed? ... The best fixing can be done by making the opposite side feel good. You'll terminate the world's tiresomeness the day you accept that it is what it is. Can you make the differentiation between my job, his/her job, your job, the government's job, etc? And can you approach the ones other than your job as an open buffet and in a way, which is not always accepted? Be playful, take responsibility, don't be a victim, don't live a lost life leaning on excuses, but be realistic; the borders of playfulness end where your effect ends. After that, there is the cosmic world outside of you; you should accept what you have and create excellence with that.

A person writing a prescription for himself/herself is writing his/her life. I review and revise my prescription at least once every three months and recommend this to everyone else too.

Gratitude

Taking the beauties in our lives for granted as if they'll always be there and not being grateful for these beauties, we lose the value of quite a lot of things. However, when we start being grateful, our life fills with contentment and meaning. Usually, the coldness of the water we drink from the fridge or the warmth of the water we feel while having a shower are unimportant details. It means we have forgotten to be grateful. In my childhood, I would be joyful and grateful and appreciate the value if there was hot water once or maybe twice a week.

A lot of things we can get easily and suppose that they will always be there are in fact there for us as miracles. When we start knowing the value of each one of them, our life begins to be full. They are so many that you'd never finish counting. From breathing to seeing, from feeling to hearing, from kith and kin, to love… Breathing in these miracles every moment and being grateful is one of the most important factors to make our life energy higher. And not knowing the value of the miracles is the source of dissatisfaction and unhappiness.

We Ate, We Drank, What Will We Do Now?

When I asked that question to myself as a 46-year-old person who had encountered every way of life, who came from a world where fish is healthy and smoking cigars is accepted as a diet , my answer was, "This needs to be corrected." My first attempt was 7 days' detox, then eating vegetables for seven weeks, and after that another week of detox. After two months, I had gone down from 86 kilos to my 18-year-old weight of 68 kilos. Immediately, I developed a follow-up system and defined 68-72 as a range for myself. I have spent the last fifteen years in this range; when I passed 72 I did detox and came down to 68. I didn't allow margins that would upset my brain and body by putting on and losing tens of kilos. I don't even need the following system anymore: I am already in the state of staying within this range.

On this journey I've made many pit stops, from doing liquid detox once a week, every Monday, to what I nowadays term "nutritarian intermittent fasting." My most important discovery during this journey has been realising that the food sector is not nutrition-focused, but commercially focused. There is nothing left to trust about the products it offers to consumers. Taking nourishment has become an action that consumers have more or less all the responsibility for. I saw that, we need to have consciousness of maximizing the ratio of nutrition value to calories. In other words, we can say that we should prefer the nutrition according to how high the ratio in one calorie is of enzymes, amino acids, vitamins, minerals, etc., which are the building blocks of the body.

E.g.: While this ratio is 1000 in black cabbage, it drops down to 9 in one calorie for olive oil . I've also learned that dark green-leaved vegetables are the champions in this subject. Didn't they always tell us to eat meat and fish? I carried on as much as they could be, eaten either for pleasure or, if we have to, to maintain life. Yes, this is true, not a joke. Also, I started to read the labels of the products. I realised that those labels are full of fictional substances, which are not recognised in nature. We have chemicals foisted upon us, which lengthen the shelf life of food… additives to enhance flavour and at the same time ruin the balance of the constitution… and a lot of lies! It was as if all these things were telling me, "Wake up!" And I woke up! My nutrition system wasn't going to be as it was imposed on me, but how I decided it would be.

To start with, I put a green drink into my routine instead of a breakfast, a nutritious snack instead of a lunch, and a vegetable-based dinner eaten early in the evening. When it was beyond my control, in other words when I was someone's guest or travelling, I aimed for minimised damage. I allowed myself a margin, so I didn't get stressed out. I added lots of water and green tea (Oolong tea) into my life. I coded in my brain that thirst creates the same feeling as hunger. I made it a principle to eat for pleasure, and only to eat when I get pleasure. On the contrary to what we've been taught, I aimed to leave food on the plate, beer in the bottle, and wine in the glass. When full, one should be able to say "Okay." We don't have to consume everything in the same proportions as other people's standards. We can decide for ourselves. All these became the main building blocks of my new lifestyle.

From that time on, eating was divided for me into feeding and stuffing myself for pleasure. When getting stuffed I would swallow with the help of a drink and without chewing. And while feeding I was chewing to savor every taste and consistency. To those who wish to try, my suggestion is to chew something they like 40 times with the eyes shut and then evaluate it again. Most of the time, at the end of this process, the foods we like lose their tastes. In other words, I think if we could get 80% nutrition and avoid 20%, we would catch an ideal nutrition/pleasure ratio.

When we manage this ratio, the body works nearly perfectly and wears out less. In short, I am not saying not to eat; I am saying to lower the number of times you eat without awareness.

Making Peace with the Physical Keystones of Your Body

Those muscles surrounding our skeleton and the vital organs in front of or behind them, our cells, which are the keystones of our being, all our body fluids, live all together in the same moment as us. And all these organs could be under torture: The sufferers of the feelings which occur due to a greedy brain and the input via its senses. Think about stuffing two portions of meatballs, tapas, desserts, a lot of drinks and bread into a stomach, which is as big as a fist… If this isn't torture, then what is it? Redoing this torture every two or three hours makes it impossible for the structures to come to themselves. As well as that, sitting all the time while waiting for the other course to arrive instead of making our muscles and bones more powerful, we choose to be inactive. Look at the state of us! We need to flow… And to be able to do that: Yoga, trampolining, walking, exercise, running…

Have you heard about the workouts, interval weight-training, 30 seconds fast – 90 seconds slow, eight-lap runs, working out with your own bodyweight? These are the best ways to exercise physically. On the one hand, by being in a contact with the body and asking it how its different points feel, in a way you do a sort of meditation; on the other, when you work out by forcing the limits a little bit, you push those limits higher step by step, and build an excellent body.

I, too, after being promoted from being a sitting bull to exercising every morning for between 40 and 60 minutes have brought a physical work out into my life which consists of sonic vibration, trampoline, inversion and stretching, and following that a sauna and serious sweating. Walking when I have a chance, long walks in the summertime, and also opening my stomach muscles and spine on cylinders called Rolling Foam became a job I did every hour of the day. As in everything, the best we can do is our own perfection.

It is a big mistake to fall into a comparison and not to start, thinking "I could never come to this point." When I first started, I learned that my hand came to my knee; after a month I started to touch the floor. And today I can put my palm completely on the floor. In short, with determination and without dreading, we need to gain our good state and flexibility. One-pill miracles are not even in the films or tales anymore. Actually, being well happens at the end of long work and sacrifice.

Toxic Hunger, Getting Thirsty and the Feeling of Hunger

A day comes when you eat bad food, don't feel good, and search for the solution in other food, and the toxicity gets higher and higher. This happened to me a lot in the past. Or when you consume food, which doesn't have nutritional value, food full of calories and lack of consistency, you fall into a never-ending hunger. That is what toxic hunger is: the most dangerous kind of hunger. You can't get rid of it; you go into a toxic vicious circle. Although it happens to me very rarely, to get rid of it I use water, sodium bicarbonate and techniques like consuming Swedish Syrup and going for a walk. The important thing is ending the toxic hunger, getting out of the pit. One of the other points to be careful of is the similarity in the feelings of hunger and thirst. When we feel hungry, drinking water can be a simple solution. I solve this by constantly consuming water and types of green tea during the day.

The 80/20 Ratio

We are not going to deny the environment we live in. Doubtless, in today's world, everywhere around us is full of fake nutrition and processed food. So, to live in peace and not to feel under pressure, a rate of failure (which means eating for gratification and stuffing oneself) ranging between 20% and 30% is a lifesaver for us, and our body can deal with it easily. In short, while getting nutrition of 70% to %80, it is beneficial to carry a tolerable failure rate in our pocket. This balance can be on the same plate as well as provided between meals.

Intermittent Fasting

In the natural world of human beings, because there is no Asda, Waitrose, etc., there is hunger and eating when you can. In short, our natural being is set for "intermittent natural fasting". The easiest way of doing this nowadays is by keeping our eating and drinking time between 12 midday and 6 in the evening and the rest of the time consuming herbal tea and water. For us, intermittent fasting is a system which altogether solves subjects like anti-ageing, weight management, etc., and connects us to a healthy life.

Colon Health

I come from a family, which is afflicted with constipation. When I was young, sometimes I broke my own record. It's easy to say: Two weeks. Also, in my new life, this problem messed up my world, and I was open to every kind of solution. A dear doctor friend of mineLodi said to me not to have a transit time of more than 24 hours. And Dutch colon specialist Dr. Bernardson said that people who have clean intestines do not get ill: it is a must to keep your intestines clean.. On the other hand, the fact that on average each and every European carries 4.5 kilos of transit and that this reaches 5.5 in United States is scary data. A high-fibre diet, a portable enema kit and colon cleaning in clinics were my lifesavers. In that period, my 24-hour rule came to life. Also, probiotics (beneficial bacteria additives) light up my every night before bed! Like everybody, I also had worries about colon cleaning. But my doctor friends told me that, apart from Colon-Hydro other interventions are harmless, that they have been used through history in every century, and that I should not worry.

About Colon-Hydro, they said that it would be enough if I had it twice a year, five times for each of these, carried out by a doctor and specialist nurse. Now I have a clean inner world!

Ersin Pamuksüzer

A SPECIAL NOTE TO MY MOM:

Dear Mom,

There's something that I've tried to tell you for years, but you don't listen to me. You know the pains in your knees and ankles, the ones you went to countless doctors for but couldn't make any better? Well, I'm talking about them. My dear mother, there is acidification in your body! The acids you gathered so meticulously react with calcium and neutralise. When that happens, the pH balance of your body fluids goes bad and you can't become alkaline. Because of the reactions in your body, salt crystals appear and they go and sit between the joints. Then let the pain come, and the complaints… This is what you call osteoarthritis! This is also in joint inflammation or arthritis, arthrosis, cholesterol plaques occurring in veins, and even the cause of kidney stones. Even gout happens because of the same reaction. From too much uric acid gathered in the body… You don't care what I say and you don't do a serious detox to get rid of these acids, but you see yourself that it's not working with those painkillers the doctors give!

Save Your Toxins, Then Hope for Help from Doctors…

Was it easy for you to gather all those toxins? Who knows what expenses and troubles you have gone through for years to prepare those tables of wonderful dishes. Then you weighed yourself carefully, and here's the result…

Look mom, which illnesses acidification leaves us face to face with:

1. Vein diseases.

2. Osteoporosis (Bone thinning).

3. Functional decrease in the thyroid.

4. Wrinkles and dryness of skin.

5. Fungus occurring.

6. Problems in brain functions.
7. Insulin resistance.
8. Cellulite.
9. Tooth decay and gum illnesses.
10. Kidney stones.
11. Hypertension.
12. Increasing triglyceride.
13. Obesity.

etc.

All of these illnesses are the projection of poor nutritional habits, unhealthy thoughts and unhealthy feelings in the body. They occur because of the pollution in the body as a result of not enough toxins being eliminated. Since I still couldn't manage to make you believe me, here is the cause and effect relation:

1- Vascular Illnesses:

It's not the food containing cholesterol, but the food containing acid that makes the veins hard. So, we can say, "The reason for fat deposits in your body is not the fat you eat, but the acid you gathered." Yes, precisely. If the acid load gets higher in the blood, it harms the vein walls. I'm talking about those free radicals, which I wrote about in the first chapter, and about their shameless structure that attacks the neighboring molecule's electrons; yes, I am talking about the vein problems that they cause.

In fact, cholesterol is a protection mechanism. It's a process starting with the liver producing more cholesterol so that acids do not damage the veins, and this cholesterol circulates in the veins. In other words, in fact, cholesterol has a very innocent aim of protecting veins. And if we consider that a lot of hormones like oestrogen, progesterone and testosterone are made of cholesterol, it is irrational to be scared of it. Cholesterol becomes a threat only if it increases significantly in the blood, and that increase is because of acidification in the body. As I said, too much of anything is harmful. When you assume that 80% is made by the liver and 20% is taken from outside, cholesterol-lowering medicine is only bringing an intensive load to the liver.

The body, which produces cholesterol, is in fact saying:
There is oxidisation here!
I am producing cholesterol to protect the veins!
Now you know!

2- Osteoporosis

Mom, you know osteoporosis, which is known to people as "brittle bone disease"? Well, here is its cause: The human metabolism needs an alkaline substance to destroy the acid deposits that are gathered in one's body. And the alkali mineral, which is found the most in the body is calcium. It is in bones, teeth and hair roots; mostly in the long bones like the pelvis, femur and spine. The body which has lost the alkali balance, is in need and uses calcium from the bones, weakens them. And this process is called osteoporosis. That's why, when getting old, because of the oxides gathered more in the body, bones can break like crackers; hair and teeth can get weak.

Wait, mom! Right at this point, I need to send a note to our dear readers: Dear readers, unlike many might assume, milk and milk products are not the main sources of calcium for our body. Our system attacks the calcium we have stored to get rid of the acidification in our body, which occurred because of the intolerance many of us have to some substances milk contains (like casein amino acid, which is needed to form horns and hooves). And this causes osteoporosis to increase as we consume milk and milk products... So, when drinking milk, in no way assume that you are strengthening your bones. On the contrary... E.g. The "Swedish Milk Study." It was understood later what kind of a mistake had been made at the beginning of the 1970s, in the period when doctors suggested formula food instead of breastfeeding. This and research like this shows that cows' milk, which we were told is beneficial, is not that beneficial at all.

On the other hand, it is beneficial to indicate the importance of magnesium, which is one of the minerals in the bones, in making the body alkaline. The reason for the cramps in your arms and legs as you get aged is lack of this. So, it's better not to take a chance, but to load up on food, which has calcium and magnesium, or to take supplements.

The body with cramps is in fact telling you:
There is oxidisation here!
I am using the depots of calcium and magnesium.
How about some supplements?

3- Thyroid

Yes, mom, I'm continuing to explain to you the cause and effect relation. This thyroid subject is important as well. You know this iodine mineral; it functions in an alkaline environment. Iodine cannot be used as necessary if there is a lot of acidification in the body, and it causes thyroid functions to get slower. This is called hypothyroidism. Because hypothyroidism causes the metabolism to slow down, it also causes weight gain. You know you say, "I've put on weight, but I was so slim until menopause…" Couldn't the actual reason be thyroid-function failure? Besides, this isn't just caused by lack of iodine. States of emotional conflict also have a pretty strong effect on the thyroid. Lately, you depressed yourself so much, my dear. Needlessly or not, you imagine the worst. Do you know that not being able to tell our actual feelings, gulping back and having to endure in silence are just like the oxidisation from food: They create emotional pollution? Even emotional detox must be done. I'll tell you about it in the third chapter. If we evaluate from a physical perspective, when the acidification in the body is balanced, in other words, as a result of good detox, the usage of iodine is relieved and thyroid problems disappear.

A body with slowed metabolism and putting on weight is in fact saying:
There is oxidisation here! I am giving a thyroid signal.
If you do not take care of me, I will cause a lot of problems for you!

4- Wrinkled and Dried Skin

Mom, collagen, which gives the skin its elasticity, is the biggest protein in our body. As a result of acidification, it gets stiff as well. This leads to dry skin, skin cracking and wrinkles: Stiffness in collagen… Not just that, but the smell of sweat that we produce as a result of acidification is really annoying. You know the other day you told me that Mrs. Jones who comes to do the cleaning smelled terrible? You were asking, "How can I tell her to use deodorant?" I say talk to her. It's not the solution to cover a smell with another smell. Sweating is a necessary thing for the body. Sweating is detoxing. If you hinder the woman from getting sweaty, be sure that the next time she is going to smell even worse. Instead, solving the fault in her diet and relieving the skin is necessary.

At this point I would like to give a message to our readers again:

Natural ingredients for homemade skin care masks; aloe vera, lemon, cucumber, Himalaya salt, mint, almond, ginger, pollen, honey and rosemary are suggested.

Alkali practices on the skin lighten the pressure on it, like thermal springs, salt baths and scrubbing, are beneficial. In that process, the subject to be careful of is that the water, which touches the skin needs to be alkaline. Because getting sweaty by doing exercise or getting into a sauna is detox too, it has a positive effect on the skin.

Roughened, cracked and wrinkled skin is in fact saying:
There is oxidisation here!
I am giving you the signal of itchy and flaky skin.
What are you waiting for?

5- Fungus Formation

Acidification has a major role in the formation of fungus in the body. In fact, fungus is a protective signal, which breeds to stop toxins spreading in the body. It gives trouble and it shows itself by reddening and itching until the cause of the fungus has disappeared.

Fungus that occurs in your body in fact says:
There is oxidisation here!
I am giving you the signal of itching, burning and swelling. Take action!

6- Slowing in Brain Functions

Not at all mom! I'm not implying anything! On the contrary, I'm saying openly that even the reason for your statements like, "I forget all the time, do I have a brain left?" is this: Acidification! Missing salt and minerals in the body, an acidic environment and not consuming enough water cause slowness in contact between the neurons in the brain. For neural conductivity, it is important that the body's mineral balance is in place and cleaned of acids. Sodium chloride (salt) is important for the body, but this salt must not be refined and needs only to include sodium and chlorine. Because of this, use the salts, which are sold with the name Himalaya or sea salt, instead of easy-pour table salt (and the easy pouring might be caused by aluminium added to it.) I gave you such beautiful salt grinders as presents! Buy salt in granules, not as dust. Look, I'm serious…

Forgetfulness is in fact saying:
There is oxidisation here!
I am giving you a signal slowing down your brain functions.
Think about this!

7- Insulin Resistance

Glucose is an important source, which lets us produce energy in the cells, and the hormone which lets glucose be absorbed by the cell is insulin. When cellular debris, in other words, toxins, which occur during the production of energy in our cells, gets too much, it damages the cell membrane. In this situation, which in time causes degeneration and lowers the sensitivity of receptors, the commands coming from insulin cannot receive proper answers and glucose cannot produce energy as it is not being absorbed into the cell as necessary.

What is colloquially called "low blood-sugar" is this. But in fact, it is wrong. When glucose cannot go into the cell as necessary, the blood-sugar does not go lower; on the contrary, it gets higher. So, calling it low blood-sugar is incorrect. The main reason for type 2 diabetes is not altogether the sugar itself; it is the collective effect of many of the factors, which cause the sugar level in the blood to remain high all the time. Nowadays, a sedentary lifestyle and too much calorie intake are the main reasons for this. Especially the combination of processed carbohydrate (flour) and animal protein tire out the pancreas. Type 2 diabetes, which is known as an adult illness, can even be seen in children now. Hamburgers are also a combination of processed carbohydrate (flour) and animal protein. Glucose not being absorbed into the cell as needed… Dizziness and a feeling of faintness… All are caused by this. This is why diabetic people keep away from sugary foods. It wouldn't be bad at all if people who are not diabetic and keep eating sugary foods are also careful about this: If excess sugar cannot be absorbed into the cell because of acidification, the blood sugar will rise and the pancreas will work to deal with this situation, tiring itself more than necessary to supplement the insulin. For this reason, diabetic people should constantly take care and adopt a sugar-free diet for the rest of their lives.

Your blood sugar getting too high
and the feeling of dizziness is in fact saying:
There is oxidisation here!
I am giving the signal of insulin.
Well, suit yourself!

8- Cellulite

Mom, not that I don't appreciate your effort to get rid of cellulite with your neighbor, Jeanie. By the way, I need to give you an important reminder of what I pointed out in previous pages by saying, "If you intend to lose weight, watch out!" because the fat tissues in the body (the cellulite that you don't like), by absorbing acids and trapping them, are trying to stop these acids from harming the body. If we don't get rid of the acids first while we are trying to lose weight, there are inconveniences. As I said, cellulite - the scary nightmare of women - in a way works as a protective shield, and to an extent hinders the acids from harming the internal organs. These tissues, which look like orange peel, are in fact lifesavers. Now, don't get into a chain of reasoning like, "Oh, that is fine then, I'll make more cellulite so that it protects me," because there is cellulite if there are toxins. Cellulite increase means more toxins. Let's use our minds mom, please.

And look, I'm reminding you again: It's very dangerous to start cellulite treatment before you get rid of acids and toxins. When the body is full of toxins already, the other toxins, which will occur as a result of broken cellulite can cause illnesses of the liver, kidneys, intestines, lymph and skin. Nowadays, in the treatment technique called mesotherapy, the medicines, which are injected directly into cellulite tissue cause these toxins to come to light. The released toxins make their way to internal organs. If you are thinking about getting rid of your cellulite with this system, I would say that beforehand you should apply a serious detox program.

In fact, cellulite is saying:
There is oxidisation here!
I am giving you a signal in the vision of an orange peel.
Get it already!

9- Tooth Decay and Gum Disease:

Saliva also gets its share from the acidification of the body. Acidification reveals itself in unpleasant smells. The function of the amylase enzyme, which is needed for carbohydrate digestion, decreases and so the digestion of glucose and carbohydrate becomes difficult. Of course, this too is a condition, which is going to increase the acidification of the body. The situation of acidification causes new acidifications to occur much more quickly, because after each acidification one more body-enzyme action is being lost, and the body comes to the point where it is not able to resist acidification. In this situation, as receding gums and bacterial plaque start to occur, decay can be seen. The body, which is trying to balance this formation of acid, will use the calcium in the teeth unless extra calcium comes from outside, and so decay and tooth loss become unavoidable.

The problems in the teeth are in fact saying:
There is oxidisation here!
I give you signals like smelly breath and receding gums.
What more should I say?

10- Kidney Stones

What a thing acidification is… It harms everywhere in the body, and does not spare the kidneys either. But you look like you don't believe what I'm saying, mom. Never mind, I'll tell you anyway; don't listen if you don't want to.

If your urine is dark colored, know that you are not drinking enough water and you are not turning your body to an alkali state. Don't forget, urine with high acid content is preparing the way for infection and stone formation. If kidneys have difficulty fulfilling their functions and can't match this increased load, kidney sand and stones form. Acidification, to which emotional factors like stress, anxiety, worry and fear also contribute, causes this painful process. Although it is possible to break and pass these stones in bodies, which are so afflicted, there's no need to go through that painful process. Isn't the important thing getting rid of the factors which cause the formation of the stones? Please, drink water! Oh, I'm doing everything in my power to talk you around, just so that you drink water…

Kidney sand and stones are in fact saying:
There is oxidisation here!
I am giving you the signal of dark and smelly urine.
Don't say I haven't told you!

11- Hypertension

I'm sad to hear the same things every time I call you. "My blood pressure is high, this happened and that happened…" Do you know that high blood pressure is again one of the precautions body takes to protect itself? High pressure is just cells trying to pump blood to the body so that it can get nutrition; but just as too much of anything is harmful, too much of this attempt at protection is harmful too. This can even be fatal, I'm telling you. You know I talked about the sensitivity of the cell membrane getting lower because of the acidification of the body? Well, high blood pressure is about breaking this cell resistance. Besides, you should take psychological factors into account and not forget the role of emotional conflicts, sudden increase of stress, and getting angry when you think about your blood pressure getting high.

Hypertension is in fact saying:
There is oxidisation here!
I am giving you a signal by making the blood pressure high.
Pay attention to me!

12- High Triglycerides

You think I'm being smarty pants! You look at my face like you don't believe me, but I listened to you when I was a child, didn't I mom? I haven't forgotten you running around after me with a spoon in your hand at home, saying "Plane coming! If you don't eat, it's going to cry!" What about feeding me anchovies when I was a baby? My grandma told me. You gave anchovies to a baby whose enzymes hadn't yet developed; what more can I say? Then, you gave my kids sugared water when they were babies. I ignored it, but I was very angry. These are totally harmful things, my dear. Now, we will be even! It doesn't matter how bored you are, sit down and listen!

Maybe you've heard and maybe you haven't at all, but there's another very important threat, which occurs as a result of acidification: Triglycerides… While the body is storing fat, both the fatty acid, which is the excess of fat, and glycerol, which is excess of sugar, combine and form triglycerides. This formed substance is stored in fat cells. Well? So? What happens if it is stored? Let me tell you immediately: You know I talked about insulin resistance getting higher in the case of acid excess? So, an increase in the insulin hormone causes metabolic syndrome and creates the desire to eat even more sugar. This is the reason for the sugar crisis. When blood sugar drops, emergency energy is taken from the fat. For this, the glucagon hormone is used. Insulin and glucagon work in opposite ways. Glycerol from triglyceride turns into glucose again in the liver. Don't look like you don't understand. Just reduce sugar, flour and oil!

Triglyceride excess, especially at levels higher than 500, can cause hardening of the blood vessels. For those who have a very high triglyceride level, it is a fact that the risk of having a stroke based on the vascular occlusion of the brain increases. If triglyceride in the body is high and HDL cholesterol (good cholesterol) is low, the risk of stroke and heart attack increases. Be careful!

The fact that I'm telling you all these medical terms is a little bit because of my need for revenge (the anchovy incident in my babyhood) and also a little bit because I'm showing off… In plain language, it is this: The other names for triglyceride are shortbread, pancakes with extra syrup and whipped cream cream, flaky pastry and doughnuts… ☺

Increased triglyceride value is in fact saying:
There is oxidisation here!
I might have a stroke, I might have a heart attack, I am signalling.
Solve the problem!

13- Obesity

Here, I am talking both to you and to the readers mom. Let's come to the illness of our time: Obesity… Yes, the kilosthat we cannot get rid of are a headache; they threaten both our health and our happiness. Although our physical appearance being liked by others is important for the relationships we form, our emotional life and our sex life, if you prefer let's make an evaluation first according to health.

Obesity is, in fact, telling you:
There is terrible oxidisation here!
I invite every type of illnesses and I am signalling.
I say, get rid of your unnecessary load.
What are you waiting for?

Solve the problem!
The job needs to be done and it's not that difficult.

1. Get rid of acidification (apply detox).
2. Apply a diet, which will get rid of the fat.
3. Make healthy eating habits your lifestyle.

***

Is it that difficult? No, it is not. We must remember that unless our style of feeding becomes our style of life, the temporary diets which mess up the system and the kilos lost are not going to be sustainable. After heavy diets, it's not right to go back to harmful food again. All your efforts would be wasted.

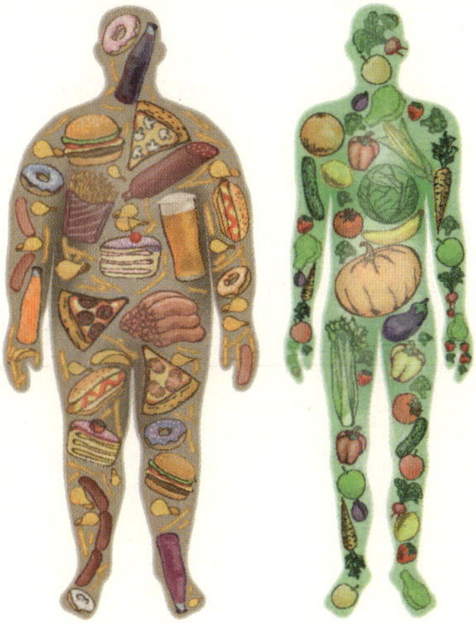

While this problem is being solved physically, emotional and intellectual conflicts should be considered too while acting. As we pointed out before, an important amount of the physical body's troubles are caused by emotions and thoughts. The opposite is valid too, but especially for people who have an obesity problem, their eating habits and the meaning they attach to food should be solved at the first stages of this treatment.

I Have the Problem: I Have the Solution

Humankind loves the term "refer to." As one can say "I refer you to God", one also can refer one's illnesses to one's doctor. However, although the word "doctor" comes from Latin and means "adviser, teacher," illness is still the work of the patient, and the process of getting well is totally a personal fight. Our raw materials are washed, we eat the right things, have a mental state that is at peace and ease with itself and supports healing, a mind that wants to get healed, and also natural support therapies which will accelerate the healing. Everyone who wants a recovery/healing beyond symptomatic treatment should fight as a "player" (with a sense of maximum responsibility) not a "victim." In recovery processes, in situations when emergency response is needed, the help that you will get from modern medicine is undeniable. But modern medicine's hands are tied regarding "complete recovery" in the stage following emergency response. During the complete recovery process, one should turn to oneself and face the responsibilities.

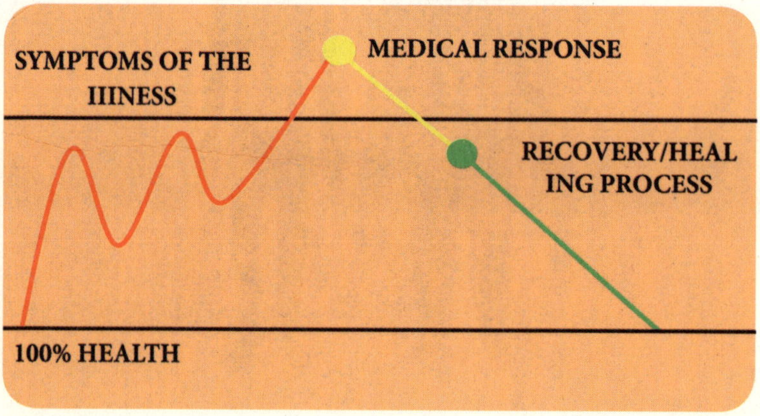

Ersin Pamuksüzer

GETTING DIRTY (RETOX)

"Getting dirty is beautiful" is the slogan of an advert... And let it stay like that. We need cleanness. Before talking about this cleanness (the body getting clean of toxins) we need to touch a little more on the subject of getting dirty.

In short, detox is getting rid of toxins and alien substances from the body, which the body does not need and which cause deformation in the body. Our metabolic system can throw away these toxins itself to a certain extent, but after that it needs help. Moreover, nowadays before there is timet to get rid of the toxins, we are exposed to a bombardment by more of them. For this reason, we should act fast and help our remaining system by doing detox. Don't look so surprised! To accelerate this state and make it effective, it will be enough to consume particular nutrition regularly and apply the things you're going to read soon.

Let's focus on the getting poisoned part of this table:

Three main factors which bring death before time:

- **Poisoning (Toxaemia)**
- Lack of Nutrition (Deficiency)
- Constant Stress (we can say the continuation of the sympathetic mode or continuous fight or flight mode)

First, it is beneficial to know that any type of poison, which is left in nature will most definitely reach the microcosmic bio-system of living things sooner or later. In other words, even if you turn your back on the waste you left in nature and get away from it fast, it manages to come your way one day.

I'm not saying that each poisonous particle of poison is fatal, but one way or another, cumulatively, it definitely harms living creatures. It is being too well-intentioned to imagine living happily in a peaceful environment with the toxins we unavoidably take into our system. Toxins don't go away just because we don't care about them; on the contrary, when we don't care about them, like cheeky visitors they each settle completely with their bag and baggage and attempt to set up their colonies in our territory. And if we keep not caring about them, they capture the system. They look for the least expected time to remind us of themselves. Usually bad times… You know, the times when we revolt against life, saying, "Throw the stones one at a time, will you!" Well, they wait for those times. Their intention is chemical reaction…

Toxins, which pollute the environment and nature, are in fact one of the outcomes of people's senseless search for a modern life. Exhaust fumes are because of the increase in the number of cars, factory waste or smoke are because of production; all of the chemical substances that we use are either for the trend of looking pretty or to live more comfortably… It is also wrong to make toxins themselves our enemy because they pollute the environment. This vicious circle is going to continue unless those human beings who release those toxins get smart. It is a very well-known example, but is it logical to spray chemical disinfectant to get rid of thousands of flies flying around the smelly rubbish that decomposes more quickly by getting into a state of reaction, and by the effect of heat every summer? Can it be logical to spread poisóns that threaten the ecosystem? Of course, not. Moreover, it is the worst mistake. Instead, what needs to be done is separating the trash and trying to get rid of the organic waste as much as possible. However, when all the trash of the huge housing complexes is piled up in front of the door, who is going to do it? Each chemical disinfectant/poison spray isn't just going to harm the flies, but all living creatures living in nature. It's our mistake not to search for a solution despite knowing this. No offence, but right is right! The species, which poison themselves to get rid of the flies is called humanity.

Today, it is not for nothing that the trash is separated into glass-paper-organic in sensible societies. In nearly every modern house there's a food waste disposal unit inside the kitchen sink. Nobody who is environmentally aware sends fruit and vegetable peel and food waste to the trash anymore, because they know that this matter is vital for a clean environment. Sooner or later we must also learn that everything that pollutes the environment one day is going to threaten our bio-system as well… So, is it too difficult to carry out waste separation in our homes? If we look at it from the "After me, the flood!" point of view it's even impossible… Shouldn't we just change those minds first, eh, before detox? ...

So, do the bodies of those people who even separate their trash and live in a modern society, not need detox? On the contrary… Even if environmental pollution is not an issue, the human body already produces toxins as a natural waste product as a result of digestion. When glucose and oxygen are burnt in the cells to produce energy, other poisonous waste products occur as acidic waste and carbon dioxide. E.g. lactic acid is toxic waste, which appears as a result of muscle work. (Lactic acid also appears with heavy sporting activities where too much load is put on muscles. Because of this, it is not recommended to do heavy sports during the detox process.) When the new cells form to replace the damaged cells, the old cells get destroyed and melted by body enzymes, and this cellular wreck becomes poisonous waste, which needs to be thrown out of the body. In a healthy body, this waste belonging to the metabolism is eliminated from the body automatically by the excretory organs.

In normal conditions, this waste, which is produced and released by the body is not harmful. However, in some cases, situations occur which lead to blood poisoning, which is called Toxaemia. As I said before, illnesses occur because there is blood poisoning, and it is poisoning itself that destroys the body's natural immune system and offers a suitable environment for illnesses.

Dr. Theodore Baroody, who carried out deep research on these subjects and wrote a variety of books, says in his book Alkalize or Die:

> *"The countless names of illnesses do not really matter.*
> *What does matter is that they all come from the same root cause...*
> *too much tissue acid waste in the body!"*
>
> *Alkalize or Die, Theodore Baroody, M.D.*

There are two main reasons that toxins gather in the body:

1. Exposure to unnatural environmental toxins in food, air and water.

2. Inability to excrete as much as necessary because of unhealthy personal habits, too much tiredness and a weakened nervous system.

So, detox is a must!

Big Spring Cleaning

If there is an operation which is not an emergency, but which is waiting for you, if you are bothered by different symptoms of illness, or if you are feeling that you need a change in your lifestyle and spiritual and physical renewal, do what I do: Three weeks of "shop cleaning," in other words "Purification/Detox."

Sometimes, after these three weeks of clean life and purification, the symptoms and complaints disappear, and sometimes the curtain of mystery opens, and the real problem appears. If the subject is change and renewal, a favorable atmosphere and spiritual state occur. A lot of my friends stopped smoking and became freed from habits that they do not want. And some of them, while they were getting ready for important operations, decided together with their doctors that the operation was not necessary. There was even someone who escaped from having a stent inserted. Especially the cleanings, which are done in spring and autumn are a perfect way to stay young and fit, together with a general purification.

Ersin Pamuksüzer

So, how are we going to get rid of the toxins we've gathered? How are we going to change our habits? What are we going to do? How are we going to get clean? Before we talk about this subject, it will be beneficial to start this next section:

The Difference between Being Nourished, Eating and Stuffing Ourselves

These three; feeding, eating and stuffing, although processes starting from the mouth and ending in discharge from the obvious place, are not the same things.

There are three main differences between them:

1. The consumed substance/ingredient is different.
2. The time of consumption is different.
3. What they leave in the body is different.

Stuffing is eliminating the feeling of starvation senselessly, in a rush; eating is an activity done for pleasure and being sociable; feeding is a technical accomplishment for which sometimes even eating something is not necessary. Let's ponder this subject too.

Are you aware how popular the subject of gastronomy has become in recent years? Local and foreign food programmes on television, the desire of high school graduates to do their postgraduate study on the subject of gastronomy, the restaurants which are highlighted by gourmets, cooks and gastronomy specialists, the ratings given worldwide to foods and restaurants, and the effect of this on tourism are only some of the indicators of this phenomenon.

Eating food is not only an activity, which is done to be full, but also a feature of socialising and discovering tastes, pleasures and cultures. But eating out of habit or physiological discomfort are not the types of eating that we want to come across. While stuffing is an utterly harmful activity for health, which makes the fast food chains rich and opens the door to obesity, one's main need from feeding is one of the most important subjects for a person. While it is possible to develop habits that do not conflict with the pleasures of eating, stuffing and feeding are not two terms, which should often stand beside each other.

Foods with low nutrition level, flavor enhancers, and those additives mixed in foods to make their shelf life longer, not only spoil the nature of the food, but also give the body more harm than benefit. Do we get full? Yes. However, consuming those nutrients that leave toxins in the body with every gulp instead of giving nutrition, should not be confused with feeding.

Now, from this chart, let us look more closely at the subject of poor nutrition.

Three main factors which bring death before time:

- Poisoning (Toxaemia)
- **Lack of Nutrition (Deficiency)**
- Constant Stress (we can say the continuation of the sympathetic mode or continuous fight or flight mode)

The state of taking insufficient nutrition to meet your body's needs, not being able to have the energy we need, consuming just one type of non-beneficial nutrients, body tissues not forming as they need to, and the body becoming weak is called poor nutrition. The human body needs a wide variety of sources like minerals, salt, vitamin, protein, and energy to give other nutrition. The reason we need a richly varied diet is that there are important substances that we get from each nutrient. Because eating only one type of food will cause a lack of the other necessary substances and minerals, it will cause poor nutrition in our body and leave us weak. So, for poor nutrition, we can say both nutrition that is taken insufficiently and also eating just one type of food.

In a lot of food nutrition, deterioration occurs because of faults in storage and cooking. So, despite being consumed enough, because of the change in the content many nutritional elements are lacking. This is one of the factors deceiving us, even though we eat enough.

Warning!
The number of people who think that they eat enough,
who are even eating more than enough,
but are not getting nourished enough is a lot.
Eating food does not mean getting nutrition.

The illnesses that are seen in people who do not get enough nutrition, and feed in an unbalanced and unhealthy way:

1. Defects in the growth, development and function of the body.
2. Weakening of the immune system.
3. Decrease in physical power and productivity.
4. Mental retardation.
5. Obesity.
6. Lifeless hair.
7. Pale and problematic skin.
8. Swollen stomach.

9. Tiredness.
10. Lack of appetite.
11. Lack of motivation.
12. Unhappiness.
13. Headache.
14. Hunched shoulders and back.
Etc.

In this case, for someone overweight, because the balance mechanism of the body is broken down, it will become more difficult to lose weight as long as the person continues with an unbalanced diet.

What is intended by detox is, after getting the body to achieve the state of a balanced diet, keeping it in alkaline form and cleaning it of toxins.

A short anecdote: I've told you about Mr. Pamuksüzer joining forces with food supplements, minerals and vitamin pills when he became interested in these subjects. In addition, he doesn't hesitate to meet with people who work in this field and, of course, to be friends with them. One day he was invited to the house of a doctor, a private health consultant called Jon Cotton. They chat, and of course the subject was health. Time passed by and the doctor asked him, "Shall we eat?" Mr. Pamuksüzer answered back, "Yes sure, let's eat." After a while, Jon came back with a tray in his hands. On the tray, there was nothing else but a variety of mineral powders, pills, enzymes and two glasses of water… ☺

Should this situation make you laugh or cry? What if this is what awaits us in the future? One day, are we going to feed entirely on pills and forget about our natural nutrition sources? What about the taste we get? The pleasure we get from eating? Just like the shift from the accepted sense of beauty seen in frescoes of women with fat legs, to the sense of beauty nowadays where a more athletic form is accepted as beautiful, in the future are we going to evolve to look like Martians, chinless and skeletal?

Speaking of Getting Nourished

N/C (Nutrition/Calorie)

Food substances (vitamins, minerals, enzymes, amino acids, phytochemicals etc.) are the sub-elements that build each and every part of our bodies, or which energise them. These constitute the getting nutrition side of the "Getting Nutrition-Stuffing" duality. In contrast, stuffing can be just eating for pleasure and consuming the things of which the nutritional value is insufficient, outside of the real needs of the body. The Nutrition/Calorie index is a chart on which the nutrition quantity of every unit of food content we consume is indexed. E.g.: While black cabbage hits the ceiling with a value of 1000 nutrition, sugar hits the bottom with a 0, whereas olive oil represents a nutrition value of 9 per calorie.

Comparison of Getting Nourished – Eating/Stuffing

While "Getting Nourished," we prefer food with a high nutrition value, e.g. unprocessed vegetables, dried nuts and fruits like sun-dried apricots and raw almond, and fresh dark greens. However, food usually enters our lives as processed nutrition. Fresh ingredients are deprived of nutritional value by cooking, deep-frying, boiling, grilling etc. and come in front of us with, at best, only their mineral content, creating an empty diet style. In short, if we want to get nourishment we should consume our food by keeping it in its natural state. For example, cold extraction is a method of obtaining oil without heating. Despite the fact that it has a structure, which is heavy in calories, its nutritional values have not been changed by heating.

Food Supplements

Nowadays, there is a need for food supplements caused by the need for a "core" type of diet in order to restore the missing eat-drink balance of humankind. Food supplements are excellent supplementary nutrition.

The most popular ones are "digestion enzymes" and they have a major effect on easing the digestion of cooked food. "Probiotics," which are beneficial bacteria, support the immune and digestion systems. If you have difficulty falling asleep or suffer from insomnia, you can use "melatonin" supplement, as an anti-inflammatory "omega-3" and "turmeric" and - as a general vitamin-mineral support - "green fig", all made of a variety of plants powdered or in supplement form. Food supplements have become a necessity for a healthy life in today's world.

Wake Up, Brain!

Despite the fact that our body is one of the most important parts of our being and integrity, we ignore its needs and do not care what it is saying. On the journey of life, we load a lot of jobs onto our body and it tries to do those jobs adequately too. Supporting and helping it do not cross our minds when everything is how it should be. When it does its job well, we should be grateful and reward it; when it cannot do its job and becomes ill, we wail and say, "What is wrong with you?", "Where did this come from?"

Our body has the capacity to do trillions of activities at the same time, and the input to this system is what we eat and drink. Generally speaking, we pass on the inputs we know that our body needs and only listen to our brain or make the choices, which give attention to the commercial successes of the shop owners. Choosing to eat cheesecake makes our brain happy, and Cheesecake Factory, too. With this choice, we give our body the message "Work/get dirty, I don't care!" We don't abstain from giving this message until things go wrong. Well, right at that point a "Wake up!" call to our brain is necessary.

Dr. Fuhrman's feeding pyramid

Everything we put into our mouths goes on a journey to be a part of our body. Being nourished comes after being sure of the arrival of the right materials in the right places; the rest is stuffing. "Why do we stuff?" – For pleasure. "Whose pleasure?" – Mine. Right at this point, while we are saying "Mine," we should be honest and say "My brain's," because the answer "Mine" involves our whole body.

Apart from being nourished, we also eat to cover up our emotional state. Whatever the name, it is "emotional stuffing" or "crisis eating," trying to cover our mental troubles or the knots we cannot undo by stuffing, dragging us into a vicious circle. In this pattern, stuffing is sometimes done for pleasure and sometimes because of trouble. In this circle, the needs of the real subject are not asked about. However, when problems occur in the system of the subject, or major malfunctions are experienced and then resistance starts. During this resistance, the most frequently asked questions are these:

"My god, why me?" and "Why do all these illnesses find me?"

Please let's not stuff ourselves; instead of covering them up, let's choose to solve our problems.

Ersin Pamuksüzer

Even Physical Beauty Comes from Inside

"Well, Selda, you said a couple of pages ago, 'So, detox is a must!', and so we're waiting for you to tell us about detox. You, on the other hand, talk about getting nourished, stuffing, then beauty… Why are you not coming to the point, but beating around the bush?"

Well, whatever you say, you are right. I will say another word and then come to the subject of "getting clean."

Yes, even physical beauty comes from inside. No cosmetic surgeon can provide glittering eyes, healthy skin with natural brightness, or a big, sincere laugh. Besides, as long as beauty is searched for in form, humanity will not step up to a higher level. In this book, you are going to read again and again that being beautiful occurs with health too, and it is going to be looked at as an integrated (heart-mind-body) harmony, no other way. ☺

I would particularly underline that having a haircut is the most harmless of all the changes that we want to make to our physical appearance because of ambition or some such reason. We do not suggest surgery unless absolutely necessary, because it all makes are cuts and new joins in the body. However much it is healed and not visible, scar tissue will affect the energy flow and blood circulation. So, this will cause curvature and symmetry faults during the perpetual change (growing, ageing) to the organ that is altered, e.g. a nose with a bump removed, although it may look very beautiful after aesthetic surgery, in years to come might show such things as drop or curvature. In other words, once the external interferences start, they will go on incessantly. Nevertheless, when deviation or an obsessive desire for a change occur, I think it is fine that the decision is taken by the patient and the doctor together. Of course, it is also important not to find ourselves having to deal with the damage which occurs to the spirit, while trying not to leave any damage on the body.

If a body is first of all not exposed to toxins, and also has no problems in the emotional state, the mind will get along with it and we will end up reaching that integrated state of well-being and beauty. At this point, the thing we must be careful about is:

Beauty is the side effect of being healthy and happy.
Beauty cannot be a template!
Templates are nothing else than the sense formed by the material pattern of the world that we live in.

Look with what symptoms blood acidosis[8] and pollution of tissue show themselves in the body: Heartburn, allergy, headache, purulent wounds, sinusitis, fungus, gastritis, smelly sweat, psoriasis, arthritis[9], vaginal infections, depression, tiredness, hair loss, anxiety, cancer etc.

In an acidified, unhealthy body, what unimportant details the look of your eyes and eyebrows become! So, that's why beauty is a state of well-being, which comes from within…

Two Opposite Ends on the Same Axis: Health and Illness

Imagine an axis where absolute health is 100 and death is 0. We all travel on this axis all through our lives. In the 70-80 range we are very well, in the 20-30 range things get complicated; we might even fall ill. In short, illnesses, especially chronic ones, do not come overnight. Our journey towards them takes years. Today's extremer pleasures, the logic of "Never mind, let the horse die from barley," as we say in Turkey, are the seeds of tomorrow's illnesses. When it is looked at in this way, our destiny comes from our own selves. This is not a bad thing, as long as we are conscious of it. God rest his soul, my dad was such a person, but he was consistent. Without complaining, he paid his bill. He died at the age of 69. He could still have been with us, only his choices were different.

Ersin Pamuksüzer

8. When too much acid forms in the body, if the amount of bicarbonate ions that makes this acid ineffective is not enough, metabolic acidosis occurs. In that case, the pH level in the blood and tissues degenerates.
9. **Arthritis:** Joint inflammation

GETTING CLEAN (DETOX)

Do you know why I said all these words? So that I could make you say, "Detox is the most effective protection weapon against toxins, which pollute our body and make us vulnerable to illnesses and microbes." However, it should be accepted that getting cleaned from toxins is not as easy or as much fun as getting polluted and gathering toxins! Besides, even though the duration of applying detox is a period of a week each time, if we and our lives and diet styles are not changed afterwards, it is difficult to get an effective result.

As Mr. Pamuksüzer says, life offers us an open buffet. On that table, there is bad beside good and harmful beside beneficial. They are simply laid together in a line. It looks like the devil has his finger in the harmful ones: They look more attractive. We are beside the table with an empty plate in our hand. And, after a while, our life is going to form according to what we reach out for.

Traditional Chinese medicine, which was written over two thousand years ago, says that in nature everything is in balance. That is why all traditional Chinese medicine practises are based on the principle of dynamic polarization.

YANG	YIN
Hot	Cold
Empty	Full
Dirty	Celan
Acidic	Alkali

If we can identify the problem, we can switch to applying the solution. It is often not that easy to identify the problem. There is a treatment system that we have been used to for years. You go to a doctor, who prescribes medicine , you buy it from the pharmacy and start in the evening. You tell neighbours, relatives, and friends that you are on medicine. You gather "oh dears" and "what a pity" and start waiting for the miracle. Of course, there is something called illness psychology. Without getting ill, you can be ill all right! Although the solution is clear, let's question ourselves about how much of this we actually apply. Let's say we got polluted: the solution is getting clean.

The first and most important step of any detox programme is taking out the acidic residues from lightly alkali blood, lymph, cellulite and other body fluids. Nearly all the toxins in the body take the form of acid. So, it is necessary to bring the blood and other body fluids to an alkali state. How? You can start learning the answer to this by getting up and getting yourself a glass of water and drinking it.

During the detox process, it is highly beneficial to drink a bit more water than you usually do because it is a vitally necessary step for diluting, neutralising and getting rid of the acids and other toxins which come out of the tissues during the detox process.

Preferably drink alkaline water (your weight x about 40 ml)!

Balancing the pH level in the blood and tissues is important right after the acids are washed out and eliminated from the body. We are told that when all the vital fluids in our body are functioning at their best, the pH value is between 7.35 and 7.45. Most of our vital fluids and tissues are alkali, except stomach liquids and a few others. If the pH value of the blood drops under 7.1 or goes over 7.5, the symptoms of unbalance show themselves, and if this is not fixed immediately it can even cause sudden death.

The pH balance of blood and tissues is important!

People's hearts pump 130 lt. of blood per hour. If the blood becomes saturated with acidic waste, these acids harm the heart tissues and then the heart muscles, while circulating inside. Besides, acidic waste decreases the capacity of the blood to carry oxygen.

Oxygen level, which is related to breathing in the right way, is one of the techniques of the body to control the pH balance in the blood. As mentioned in the fifth chapter's fourth subject, breathing by increasing the gas transaction in the lungs to the highest level is important in taking the carbon dioxide out of the blood and feeding the blood with fresh oxygen.

Pay attention to breathe in to the depth at which you feel you are stretching your diaphragm muscle!

Lungs hindered by cigarettes not being able to do their job properly after a while would hardly be a surprise. Because the lungs cannot take enough oxygen and carry it, they are not going to be able to ensure that the pH level of the body is alkali, and so in all the tissues and cells a state of chronic hypoxia and acidosis is going to occur. This state sends an invitation to microbes and tumours.

Stay away from cigarettes!!! It's no joke.

One of the main jobs of the liver is to filter the toxic acids from the blood. And another function is to produce the vast amount of alkali enzymes that the vital functions and the immune system need. If the blood gets polluted by extreme acidic excesses caused by wrong feeding habits, alcohol, heavy usage of medicine, stress hormones and other factors which cause acids to occur constantly, the liver will be under too heavy a load, get blocked by toxic waste and come to a stage at which it cannot do its job. Body acids start showing themselves in the form of tissue pollution and calcification.

It is important to have a healthy diet and not to tire the liver. During detox, no alcohol! If you do not have to, don't take any medicine either!

Also, the kidneys help acids to be eliminated by filtering 1lt. of blood per minute. When a wrong diet, pharmaceutical medicine and lifestyle harm kidneys, together with the acidification of the blood it might cause the formation of kidney stones.

Again water, always water…
Get adequate and balanced nutrition: Drink water!

Oh, by the way, let's mention that coffee, tea, fruit juice etc. cannot take the place of water.

It is important to exercise and keep the metabolism functioning. Besides, enjoyable sports like trampolining can be done to regulate the blood flow. Yoga, meditation, walks in the open air and swimming ensure the body gets rid of the toxins more easily. It is suggested that you stay away from heavy sports during detox because such sports gather lactic acid in the muscles. And this causes acidification.

Yoga, walking and meditation make detox easier!

Sweating, sauna and steam baths are also important aspects of a detox programme. Toxins, which gather in the lymphatic system are eliminated from the body easily by having saunas and steam baths. These are also good for losing weight, avoiding liver fattening and pains in the body, and making the skin more beautiful. An infrared sauna may be preferred, particularly because it allows sweating at far lower heat and allows relaxation.

Sauna and steam will help sweating!

Massages also allow toxins to be eliminated from the body by stimulating the lymphatic system. Stomach massage especially is just the job for those who have constipation problems.

One massage per day during the detox period!

Nowadays, in this high-paced and stressed-out world, where resting by keeping calm and doing nothing are referred to as time-wasting, one of the preconditions for any detox being effective is… resting. In that period, the way to avoid the feeling that one is not doing anything may be to feel the awareness of doing a very important thing for one's own health.

Do not get tired; get rest, keep calm, but stretch your body!

During the detox period, a special diet should be practised. To keep the intestines working, every night probiotic pills are beneficial. Special mixtures in which fruit and vegetables are prepared by cold press, vegan nutrients, food with high antioxidant value, plenty of water and herbal tea are taken. The body is kept alkaline. The aim is to eliminate by liquids. Breathing exercises are done. It is important that the metabolism works, but does not get tired.

What does a Detox Programme Include? (The LifeCo Turkey)

Sample Detox Programme:

The programme below is a 1-week sample programme, which is already being practised in LifeCo.

- First off, on the first day, together with the programme manager, according to one's needs, health situation and expectations, six different detox and diet programmes and therapies are described, and these are turned into a weekly programme.
- After that, your measurements are done by the centre's nurse: Blood-pressure, sugar, the ratio of body fat-muscle-water.
- Meeting with the doctor is alwaysdone on the first day. Necessary adjustments are made to the programmes, according to the health situation of the person.. If the person is using medicine, it is possible that the doses of these may be adjusted or completely cut.
- Generally, yoga and meditation are suggested between 9:30 am and 11:00 am. (For those who miss the morning sessions or who want to do the second session, it is between 2 pm and 3 pm)
- 5 pm – 6 pm – live informative chats are held. After detox, there is a workshop for nutrition, juice and raw food, and the medical benefits of detox are explained.
- 7 pm - boot camp fitness is suggested.
- 8 pm – informative documentaries are watched.

During the gaps in this main programme, therapies are carried out.

The Programmes Supporting the Body and the Digestive System:

Colema - Colon cleaning is applied by self-administered machines called Angels of Water, as instructed by the nurse. While in a master detox it should be done every day, in other programmes it can be every other day, or if the person does not want it, it can be skipped.

Turkish bath – A Turkish bath is absolutely recommended, particularly on the first day, so that the scurf is got rid of by scrubbing and bubble massage.

Massage – It is beneficial to have one massage per day.

Steam, sauna – Sweating every day with an infrared sauna and sinuses opened in the mentholated steam room is vital. Infrared saunas cause sweat by increasing the internal heat of the person for 30 minutes without going higher than 50 degrees, make weight loss faster by making you burn 600 calories, and also ensure that the lymphatic system is clean. One third of toxins are eliminated by the skin (16% of the body), which is our largest organ. So, it is a very important part of the programme.

Vascular access practises (vitamin mineral mixtures given intravenously by serum) – Vascular access practises, which increase one's energy, immunity and youth in the medium and long-term, are suggested 2-3 times a week. There are 6 different mixtures as supports for anti-ageing, anti-tiredness, anti-stress, the brain, immune system, and liver.

Ozone – Ozone, also known as a restorer of cells, a rejuvenator, and in general an immune system enhancer, can be taken in 3 different formats: Rectal, in the blood or by sauna.

Lymph drainage and skincare - With lymph drainage, one of the beauty and body carers, oedema is eliminated, and speeds up metabolism.. With Venus (a machine working with the technique of frequency and heat, reforming the body by destroying fat) fats get broken down, the body is shaped, and a lifting effect is given on the face.

Oxygen – By taking pure oxygen for 20 minutes every day in the nurse's room, the cells become alkalised.

Luminette light therapy - It helps for better quality sleep.

Resting – Resting all through the day is very important as well. Sea, sun, chat, sleeping, resting, reading, digital detox…

Fitness – With the support of a fitness trainer, trampoline, inversion, Turbosonic and other instruments may be used.

Awareness – Additionally, with therapists who come to visit for a short term, programmes of meditation, breathing and mindfulness are run. People also find the chance to have mental, emotional and spiritual relaxation.

Besides all this, walking in nature and free time activities, which don't tire the body are allowed. Below there is a weekly sample programme. This programme can differ according to one's preferences.

Sample Menu for a 1200 Calorie Programme/ The LifeCo Bodrum

First of all, breakfast, lunch, snacks and dinner are eaten at 9 am, 12 pm, 3:30 pm and 6 pm respectively.

Breakfast

* **Chia pudding** – Coconut or almond milk, chia seeds and fruit pieces on top or

* **Porridge** – Oats, almond milk, walnut and small fruit pieces on top or

* Cashew cheese, tomatoes, cucumber, olive, raw crackers.

Lunch

* **Lasagne** – Cashew cream between courgette slices and tomato sauce or

* **Sushi** – Cucumber between cauliflower rice, carrot and avocado slices or

* **Spaghetti** – Courgette, cut like spaghetti with a spiralizer, marinara or pesto sauce on top.

Snack

* Guacamole and raw crackers or

* Raw cake with apple and carrot.

Dinner

* Meatballs prepared with walnut, spices and salad or

* Biryani prepared with cauliflower rice or

* Beetroot ravioli prepared with cashew cream in between beetroot slices.

P.S: By the way, as a person who has stayed in LifeCo, I can comfortably say that each of these recipes is unbelievably tasty.

Avoiding the Possible Harms of Detox

In any detox programme, the excretory organs work overtime to get rid of the toxic waste from the body. We need to give some reminders so that the tissues are not harmed because of these extra toxins, which are loaded to the excretory organs.

There are four main conduits by which the toxic wastes are eliminated from the system:

1. Skin
2. Lungs
3. Kidneys
4. Bladder and Colon

The Ways of Eliminating the Toxic Waste Before It Harms Those Organs:

1- Skin: The skin is an organ, which releases toxins by sweating. So, it is very important to sweat all through detox. However, if toxic waste reaches a high density while passing through the skin, it might harm it. Bad body odour and sticky and cold sweat are some of the indicators of body pollution. To decrease the harm to the skin, we can choose to have sea salt or Epsom salt (diluted magnesium sulphate) and essential oil baths, which ease toxic waste exiting from the pores. Swimming in the sea is highly beneficial, not just because of being active, but also for the salt water to come into contact with the skin. We shouldn't gloss over steam baths and saunas either.

Do not ignore salt baths, swimming, steam baths and essential oils to protect the skin.

2- Lungs: We talked about hypoxia as the decrease of the amount of oxygen in body tissues. When blood is too toxic, like during detox programmes, its capacity to carry oxygen decreases. That's why hypoxia might occur. This increases the possibility of illness and damage. Deep breathing becomes important here. Breathing in the right way feeds the blood and tissues with oxygen. In that way, it eases the carbon dioxide and gassy waste, which cause acidosis in being eliminated from the body. Steam baths also work in this process. Besides, to support the detox process during sleep, having a negative ion producer in your room can be another technique you can use.

Breathe deeply!

3- Kidneys and Bladder: When toxic wastes are acidic, of course they can be seriously harmful to the bladder and the kidneys. That is why at the time of detox, it is suggested to consume a good many herbal teas, which are diuretic and help in cleaning the kidneys. Besides, it is important to drink at least 2.5 – 3 lt. alkali water per day.

Water, water, water, water, water…

4- Colon: Among the organs of excretion, the colon is the organ that works most, and so it is exposed to the most toxic waste. During a detox programme, it is necessary to clean the intestines from toxic waste as much as possible. For that, psyllium[10] seeds mixed with water can be taken at least twice a day. Besides, again, it is very important to drink water.

10. **Psyllium:** It is a plant of Indian origin. Its seeds are used as a cathartic under the name of Psyllii Semen.

Water and Psyllium Seed… Remember!

Washing the colon (colema) is also a very effective method. Colema is, with a simple mechanism set on a toilet, doing a similar procedure to an enema by yourself. It is one of the most beneficial stages of detox. Blockage in the digestion system can cause the body to be unable to clean itself enough. When that stage is interrupted, weight control gets difficult too. It prepares the ground for many ailments from pain, gas, and aches, to the occurrence of cancer cells. During detox, the most effective way of getting rid of the toxins is colema. Foreign substances, which cannot be eliminated from the body over time, like antibiotics and food additives, stay in our intestines and gather, getting even more acidic. They may enter the blood by secreting from the mucosa layer in the intestines. Colema is the most effective technique to get rid of that layer.

Detox programmes without colema do not provide real purification because, like a blocked sink, the large intestines can only be cleaned with external intervention; your energy will come back.

At that stage, another alternative is probiotic (good bacteria) support.

After the application of colema, the person will clearly have increased energy levels, improved digestion, a stronger immune system and find it easier to control weight...

Cleaning the colon… Remember!

Source: Daniel Reid, Detox

Problem	Solution
Stres →	Resting
↓	↓
Strain →	Relaxation
↓	↓
Physical/emotional/mental tiredness →	Physical/emotional/mental relief
↓	↓
Atony (tiredness in sympathetic phase) →	Renewal (resting in parasympathetic phase)
↓	↓
Underexcretion (intestines, lung, skin, kidneys) →	Quick and effective excretion (intestines, lung, skin, kidneys)
↓	↓
Gathering of toxic waste →	Elimination of toxic waste
↓	↓
Blood poisoning (acidosis and hypoxia*) →	Purification/Detox (alkali body and enough oxygen)
↓	↓
Acute diseases →	Healthy long life

* **Hypoxia:** Decrease in the quantity of oxygen in body tissues.

WHAT IS A KETOGENIC DIET?

If you are definitely going to go on a diet, you might as well do a ketogenic diet. In fact, preferably do not do a diet at all, because the psyche desires whatever it should not desire, and whatever is forbidden becomes valuable. When you say, "eat that," "don't eat that," the brain eats whatever should not be eaten. That is the principle of how the brain works: It only senses the order "eat" and the "eat" part of "don't eat"... So, instead of working on a diet or regime, if we revise our nutrition content a bit I guess our job gets easier.

Despite that, I would like to explain a ketogenic diet. If the contents of the food we eat evolve to be what I am going to tell, I'd happily get rid of those extra kilos. ☺ Here is the logic of a ketogenic diet: Limiting the consumption of carbohydrates and sugar, while favoring food heavy in fat and protein... It's that easy... Instead of bread, rice, pasta, sugar, cake, we have meat, fish, butter, olive oil etc. As you know, the body first appeals to carbohydrates to turn into energy. When it cannot find any carbohydrate to burn, it goes directly to fats. Fat turns into energy and life into heaven! ☺

When carbohydrates are not taken into the body, the glucose level in the blood and, in relation to this, insulin decrease. The body in search of energy directs itself to fats. When the body starts burning fats for energy, entities called "ketone" occur in the blood. The occurrence of ketones indicates that the body is in the process of ketosis[11]. This process is the process of burning fat. The breath of the person who is in ketosis smells like acetone, which is a very strong smell.

The actual benefit of a ketogenic diet is known to be strengthening the resistance of the body against illnesses. As follows: Carbohydrates and sugar raise the risk of inflammation in the body. These are the types of food, which ruin the protective mechanisms of the cells and even cause cell death.

---

11. **Ketosis** is a metabolic illness related to hyperketonaemia or acetonemia lipid metabolism, which develops because of ketone particles (acetone, acetoacetic acid, beta-hydroxybutyric acid) being gathered in the blood.

A ketogenic diet is a type used in the treatment of many illnesses, starting with diabetes, epilepsy, Alzheimer, Parkinson, heartburn, high blood pressure and even cancer. It is known that cancer cells are fed on carbohydrates and sugar. Decreasing carbohydrate consumption and increasing fat and protein will slow down the growth of cancer cells.

You may say, "What! Where's the joy in this life, when we can't even dunk biscuits in our tea?" You're right, but we can have, less can't we? We don't have to drink tea with food, which has already got a high sugar level, do we?

A ketogenic diet has been extremely popular in recent years. It motivates us, of course, when it is said that it burns fat and you can eat as much as you want. Look at what there is in this diet: Butter, olive oil, dried fruits and nuts, milk and milk products, meat, fish, avocado and eggs. Foods that are not supposed to be part of the diet are bread, rice, pasta, flour products, all sugary products, potatoes... Even fruit is limited.

What there are and
are not in a ketogenic diet

There are	There are not
butter	bread
olive oil	pasta
meat	rice
fish	sugar
egg	honey
milk products	molasses
dried fruits and nuts	potatoes

DETOX AND BREATHING

The Breath-taking Effects of Breathing

Don't say you haven't heard how much importance this subject has gained and how popular it's been in recent years. Yes, we are talking about the subject of breathing. In an integrated wellness approach, it would be a mistake not to mention the effect of breathing the external air, which we constantly inhale and exhale.

People who do meditation will know the importance of breathing. Besides, nowadays, in sports centres we go to, breathing is used in the exercises being done by trainers, is it not? Have you ever thought how important the breath that we inhale and exhale nonstop from the moment we are born is? And in fact, many of us still do not have basic consciousness about this subject.

Breathing exercises are one of the methods of balancing the oxygen that we take from outside with blood pH. The most basic act is learning to breathe more deeply by using the diaphragm muscle instead of the upper chest. Oxygen is necessary to provide a sufficient alkaline environment in the blood and tissues. Acidosis happens because of insufficient oxygen being taken in. So, it would prevent acidosis to transmit oxygen to more points in the body and to increase the amount of oxygen taken in too.

Breathing correctly and deeply gains the body these: Oxygen raises the quality of blood. Blood with raised quality brings the cells together with the oxygen that they need, and this helps the toxins to be eliminated from the system. Foods are digested more comfortably. The digestive system's organs work better. The brain, spinal cord, nerve centres and nerves become relaxed. In the health of the nervous system, rectification is provided. Metabolism feeds better. Health spreads to the entire body from the nervous system, which reaches every part of the body.

Rejuvenation will be seen in the glands of the body. If you ask why, the brain needs three times more oxygen in comparison with the other organs. That means, when fed sufficiently, the glands that it controls work better and help the metabolism's rejuvenation. Skin rejuvenates. Wrinkles decrease, and skin becomes smooth.

Deep and slow respiration lightens the load on the heart. During deep respiration, the movement of the diaphragm stimulates blood circulation in the internal organs by having a massaging effect on them. Besides, it also means lower blood pressure and so less possibility of heart disease. Deep and slow respiration also helps weight control. If you have extra kilos, the extra oxygen that you take will help your fats be burned more effectively. In other words, breathing correctly helps control your weight. Slow, deep and rhythmic respiration slows down the muscles, allowing your heartbeat to slow down, and as a result, it also helps your mind to relax together with the body.

When we get really bored, you know how we take a deep breath and then let it go fast? Actually, the body calls out for this act as a protection mechanism. It aims to provide revival by sending more oxygen to the body.

Breathing right helps with weight loss the right way, relaxing the nervous system, eating the right nutritious foods which in turn raises your blood circulation and makes you feel and look good with improved skin and complexion.

P.S.: The subject of breathing is touched on in detail in Chapter 5.

DETOX AND CANCER

The Nastiest Illness of All Time: Cancer!

Cancer is the name of the nightmare that brings us to death as a result of cells which reproduce in an uncontrolled way, producing tumors and them leaping from here to there in the body. It is still the most terrible illness of our time.

In the environment we live in, not catching this illness is more difficult than catching it. You are thinking, "What are you saying? Perish the thought!" but that is the situation. Even though medicine has made progress on this subject, it is worrying to see, when we take the stimuli that cause cancer into account, that our chances of not catching cancer are decreasing with every passing day.

On this subject, we need to keep our awareness level always at the peak and keep away from the things that we know the harm of. This is the first "must" regarding life quality conditions. However, you may ask, "What about babies and children?" They can get this illness before they've even seen the dirty face of life. That's true. We cannot ignore hereditary factors.

We know that neither modern medicine nor traditional cancer treatments can manage 100% success in advanced cancer cases. In fact, there are people even saying that modern medicine has increased tissue pollution in a serious way, that it restrains the natural cleaning and healing reactions of the body itself and causes progress of the illness. When it is asked why, it is said: "Because modern medicine is trying to fight cancer like it fights microbes. They are trying to stop cancer cells and cell reproduction by poisoning them with toxic chemical medicines, burning with radiation therapy and cutting them off by surgery." In other words, can we say, like in our known example of trash, instead of getting rid of the trash that causes flies somewhere, they are trying to cut the reproduction by killing the flies? If that is the situation, ☹ I have no other words to say. The things being done for cancer treatments bring that to mind. They can take the cells out completely and hinder reproduction, but what about the wreck left behind? The system itself is harmed way too much.

I wouldn't want to say extreme words and get the reaction of the oncologists; it is not up to me to say things at all, but if I speak for myself, I do not like the wreck the existing cancer treatments leave behind; I'm even scared of it. If that trash stays there, there will also be even more joining it, and I think that will establish an environment for an increase in tissue pollution and cancer returning.

There are always cancer cells in the body, but a healthy body knows how to destroy and terminate them. Maybe the doctors who say, "We caught the cancer in the early stage of the illness!" and apply immediate surgical, chemotherapy or radiotherapy techniques are right; however, are immediate surgery and declaring war with a chemical weapon a must? This is what I am not comfortable with.

A hundred years ago from today, the rate of death from cancer was below one in a thousand. Today in England, one in every three people is diagnosed with cancer at one stage of their lives, and one in every four people dies for this reason. In that case, who wins the war of Modern Medicine vs. Cancer? Or, as in all other wars, is there no winner?

According to statistics, if only around 5% - 10% of cancer cases are because of the genes, then it means it is not mostly genetic as is claimed. If it were so, would the number of cases a hundred years ago be approximately 250 times less than today? Obviously, a polluted world has a serious role in this. And it is very much obvious that this rise is caused by environmental factors, eating habits and harmful choices. In this case, not to lay the groundwork for the occurrence of cancer, of course preventative factors should gain as much importance as the treatment of it. The real solution to cancer should be preventing it from forming. For this to happen, tissue pollution which increases by gathering toxins must be cleaned and toxic wastes which turn the human body into trash by entering the system through food, water, air, smoke, medicine and other sources must be hindered.

The real solution to cancer should be not letting it form.

Nowadays, unfortunately there is no way of escaping pollution completely. However, we can decrease the risk by taking some simple protective measures, making some types of basic changes in our nutrition and lifestyle habits. By not allowing the poisons, which cause illnesses to rise to critical levels in our body we can hinder cancer, heart diseases and other vital illnesses.

We should not wait until we are ill to live healthy lives. The mentality of "nothing will happen to me" is nonsense; let's not deceive ourselves. Isn't it more reasonable not to go on a journey from which there is no return, rather than to go on it and struggle?

The reason that I gave this chapter the title of "Detox and Cancer" is this: There are people who challenge their cancer by healing fast, colon cleanses, a diet of raw fruit and vegetables, therapies of detox diets, vegetable and nutritional supplements, making the blood and tissues alkaline, feeding with oxygen and all the other methods of detox. We know people who use these methods as a way of life for health protection rather than as treatment after illness to overcame their diseases. . A Doctor of Medicine offers all the possibilities of modern medicine, I do not know if the same doctor would say that it is also possible to treat cancer with the help of blood and tissue detox and suggest a treatment in that way. However, I presume that the subject of cancer treatment ison slippery ground, where a 100% success rate cannot be guaranteed in the end, the patients themselves can again make the most rational choice.

Water Fasting for Healing?

Among other approaches, the method known as "Water Fasting" or "Healing Fasting" is known as a healthy diet and aims to supply energy from body reservoirs by leaving the body hungry at regular intervals and thus getting rid of the fats, toxins and waste cells which are extra in the body. This is applied in many countries. According to research, a three-day hunger diet seriously mends the immune system.

The main cause of healing fasting is not losing weight. However, losing weight is unavoidable for those who apply this method. I mean, losing weight is one of the side-effects of this procedure. The actual cause is the cut in our appetite when we are ill and the body gives all its concentration to healing not to digesting.

Healing fasting is also a holistic process, being physical, emotional and mental.

The application of this fasting, which takes more or less ten days, is like this: (There are people who go up to twenty-five days or more; however, for people who prefer long fastings, researching in detail and doing it together with a specialist is safer).

- The first day is the preparation day for the healing fasting. Fruit and vegetables are eaten.

- The next five days are known as the full fasting days. On these five days, plenty of water, herbal teas and juiced vegetable soups are consumed. Solid food is not available. The daily target is to stay under 250 calories.

- The last four days are to adjust the body slowly to its normal functional pattern after the fasting is broken. Normal nutrition should not be started immediately. That may cause problems in the intestines and stomach.

The healing fasting is applied for these targets:

- Cellulite treatment.
- To raise the sperm quality of men.

→

- To raise the possibility of women getting pregnant.
- After the chemotherapy process (with an aim of purifying the body of the effect of the process.)
- With the aim of losing weight.
- To get rid of headaches.
- With the aim of anti-ageing.

Note 1: If the healing fasting will be used for treatment (such as after chemotherapy) it is suggested that it be done under doctors' supervision in clinics.

Note. 2: For all healthy people, this method is recommended twice a year.

Note 3: While healing fasting is not found to be healthy by some dieticians, according to some research, leaving the body hungry causes production of new red blood cells by stimulating the root cells. Besides, even in people whose immune systems are weakened because of old age, the benefits of this fasting are observed.

Those who should not partake in healing fasting:
- Children and adolescents..
- Those who are underweight.
- Patients with brain and vessel illnesses
- Those who have liver and kidney failure.
- Diabetic patients.
- Expecting women.
- Those who are breastfeeding.
- Substance addicts.
- Those with stomach and duodenal ulcers.
- Those with coronary heart disease.
- Patients who have psychosis issues.

Source: Zaza Yurtsever, Healing Fasting

Cancer and Anti-Ageing: Two Halves of the Same Apple

Cancer is the new nightmare of our world… In United States, one in every three people above 70 years old has experienced cancer. The incidence of cancer, which is in fact one of the mechanisms of the body to sustain life, started to come to us as illness because of the warps in our lifestyles. Imagine that our bodies are aquariums. Fish and cells (I mean our cells and organs etc.) would get ill in an aquarium with a polluted habitat. Instead of killing the ill fish, the best solution is to purify the liquid, which makes them ill, in other words, improving the life environment. Only in this way we can reach an ideal life environment and a healthy fish population.

Besides, the works of Dr. Longo from the University of South California, for which the link is below, focus on anti-ageing and calorie limitations and show that these are seriously supportive methods when put to use in parallel with the chemotherapy applications used in cancer treatments. We can all put Longo's methods into our lives according to our needs, such as maintaining our weight, keeping young, or as a support to chemotherapy.

8 years ago I went to a cancer treatment center for the first time. The center was based upon natural therapies with an anti-ageing aim. I comprehended there that all of the natural treatments aim for an absolute recovery process, and this can already be deemed to be the basis of anti-ageing treatments.

Ersin Pamuksüzer

https://www.theguardian.com/society/2016/jun/03/how-to-get-through-chemotherapy-decca-aitkenhead-cancer-treatment

BE CALM

They Don't Say Have a Rest and Relax for Nothing…

A pretty important aspect of how our body works during detox and retox is the autonomic nervous system… This time what we will be focusing on is the third item from the table:

Three main factors which bring death before time:

- Poisoning (Toxaemia)
- Lack of Nutrition (Deficiency)
- **Constant Stress (we can say the continuation of the sympathetic mode or continuous fight or flight mode)**

What does the autonomic nervous system (It is called Visceral or Vegetative too) do in the body? What do "sympathetic" and "parasympathetic" mean? The autonomic nervous system is identified as the part, which controls involuntary acts and organ functions. What are those involuntary acts?

- Heart speed
- Breathing
- Digesting
- Sweating
- Salivation
- Urinating
- Sexual arousal

Etc.

The autonomic nervous system divides into two as the sympathetic and parasympathetic nervous systems. When physical power needs to be spent, when we are doing tough work or in a moment of danger, the movements of our heart become fast. It is done by the autonomic nervous system. During this period, also known as the Evasion, Escape, or Fight or Flight reaction, the sympathetic nervous system works. It uses most of our body energy and if the person does not realise it, they become exhausted. We escape from many dangers that we come across in nature because of the sympathetic system's stimuli; it means we owe it for being alive; however, if it is continuous it brings us to death. In the moment of danger, all the power of the body gathers in the arms and legs to fight or fly mode. During this mode, the body's functions do not work to heal itself; the aim is merely to escape from that danger. So, the reason for not being able to stay in that state is obvious: The system cannot focus on healing.

In the parasympathetic period, on the contrary, the heartbeats slow down, vessels widen, bronchi tighten, and the movements of the intestines become faster. This period is also known as rest and relaxation, because the only method for the system to work properly is to rest the body and the mind and to relax.

As nowadays' sadly modern stressful city life causes us to be under the influence of the sympathetic nervous system too much, so our immune system is at risk of collapse. This is writing an invitation for illness. The way to escape this is to make time for relaxation.

In the mode of resting and relaxing, the body can spend all its energy on healing. This is the main reason why patients are kept in intensive care.

Brainwaves

Okay, we know the most important characteristic of humans is their mind, which distinguishes them from all the rest of the living things. We people have been saying this for years. Well then, what kind of energy does this brain which the mind shelters in, have?

The human brain is a pretty complex organ that spreads different wavelengths… It is made up of billions of cells, but its secret is still unknown. However, it is known that the brain has a power, which produces different vibrations (bioelectrical power) which is turnedinto wave energy and spreads it. Consciousness and imagination occur because of these vibrations. Humankind is the only creature that we know/ assume has the possibility of reaching the power of cosmic consciousness by means of being able to use their brain. How nice… ☺

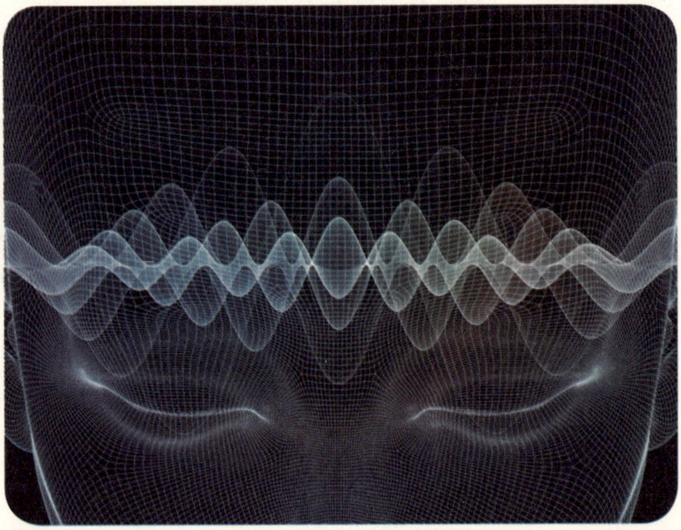

It is possible to talk about five types of waves that it spreads according to its responses: Alpha, Beta, Delta, Theta, and Gamma. (Unlike the first four wavelengths, the detection of Gamma frequency took place in recent years. Because of this, in many documents this frequency is not mentioned.)

1- Beta Brainwave

It is the brainwave of the state of stress. It is usually stimulated by fear. It is known to be between 14 and 30 Hz and is defined as waking frequency. It is the wavelength we are in when in the state of active learning, being aware, concentration, dynamism and problem-solving. It carries the person to have extreme negative feelings like stress, strain and rage. When there is danger, this wavelength steps in. It is the wavelength that occurs for example when in danger in nature such as a tiger that is ready to attack. In other words, it is the wavelength that is spread when the sympathetic nerves are stimulated. The wavelength of the states of strained muscles, high blood pressure… The state when either you run away and escape or stay and fight. Because the body is focusing all its energy on the danger, it uses all the reservoirs of energy that would otherwise be used for healing or developing the body. It is stressful and tiring to be in this kind of brainwave constantly. The immune system will collapse. Because the target of this brainwave is to keep the person alive, naturally the brain is in the mode of "I will deal with the illnesses later, once I manage to stay alive." Living in that brainwave constantly would bring the person to death.

While in beta brainwave, you cannot meditate, read, watch a film, listen or pray or focus on learning etc.…

2- Alpha Brainwave

It is between the frequencies of 8 and14 Hz It s the wavelength at which pleasure, joy and happiness are felt. It is defined as the waves of comfort, awareness, calm and peaceful understanding that we feel when we daydream or muse, and in the waves of the first stages of sleep. While reading these lines, if you are sitting with your feet up comfortably and thinking about nothing else and even better if instrumental music is playing softly in the background, this probably means you too are at this wavelength - Smile!

This wavelength is known as the "Schumann Resonance,"[12] and is also the measured magnetic frequency of our world.

When the stimulus taken from outside the world decreases, we transfer to the Alpha dimension. Our success rises in the tasks that we perform during Alpha waves. This wave is not seen at all in deep sleep or in the state of worrying or fear. It is the dimension that our brain is in while doing exercises like meditation, yoga and reiki.

12. **The Schumann Resonance:** A name given to a natural vibration, which occurs between the earth and ionosphere, explained by the scientist Winfried Otto Schumann in 1952.

Also, just before we fall into the depth of sleep, when our consciousness is open, the peacefulness that those emotions make us feel in the passing corridors is felt in the Alpha wave state. This is the wavelength of healing, mending the spirit and the body. Learning, focusing and listening occur at this wavelength and, most importantly, when the parasympathetic nervous system steps in, hormones like serotonin, dopamine, noradrenaline, oxytocin and endorphin can occur in it too. We live in this wavelength in meditation and resting moments.

3- Theta Brainwave

It is seen while transferring to sleep or in the first stages of sleep. The frequencies vary between 4 and 8 Hz and it is defined as the wavelength where there is no stress and we are in our deep interior world. Before transferring to the highest dimension of learning, we live in this wave for a while, and this wavelength also represents a situation in which our senses, which open slowly while waking from deep sleep, make us live. Also, the name "Twilight Dimension" is used for this wavelength: The darkness before light…

It is confirmed that expert meditators are in this wavelength while in deep meditation. At this frequency where, deep thought and intuitive power are alive, it is thought that artistic skills reach a peak. It is known that, especially during the artistic production of painters and musicians, the Theta dimension is at its highest and the Alpha frequency is at its lowest in their brains (meaning from 7 to 8 Hz.). So, art is hidden in between these frequencies…

According to some research, it is because of the success of healers at staying in the Theta band for a long time and in control that their healing skills improve.

4- Delta Brainwave

Delta waves occur in deep sleep stages and are the slowest vibrating waves. It is the wavelength of 0.5 to 4 Hz. frequency and it is the dimension of deep sleep and disengagement from the outside world. The consciousness steps out and gives way to peace. You know the kind of people who wouldn't wake up even if a cannon exploded beside them? Yes, it means they're surfing in Delta wavesThis is wherethe brain works least, and the secretion of growth hormone rises. In children, it brings about physical growth, and in grownups healing, beauty and keeping spry.

The very low frequencies of Delta are evaluated as the state of coma. When the brain is in the coma state it terminates consciousness. The benefit of that is this: The brain, which leaves dealing with all the unnecessary senses aside, only focuses on healing the vital organs. The immune system of a person who is in a coma is in a state of stimulation at the highest level. The consciousness is nearly at the point of stopping. All the energy flows to the vital organs. In fact, does it not tell us: "Don't bother one of your nearest and dearest who is in a coma state by taking them to intensive care?" Consciousness is what makes healing hard and keeps the brain constantly busy with what is going on… When it is in a shut-down state, the body spends all its energy on healing. Do not interrupt in this situation; do not hinder it. Leave the person alone so that they cancure fromthe deepest of sleep, by getting over the trauma, sothe chance of returning to life increases.

Don't forget!
Each mammal whose heart beats fast lives less…

5- Gamma Brainwave

Apart from those four wavelengths, the Gamma frequency, detected in recent years, is above 30 Hz. It is known to be produced due to research on connections to the higher-self and measured during the meditations of Hindu Monks. It is thought that this wave is the source of intellectual thinking. It is the brainwave beyond willpower. It is said that it is possible to travel in the astral body and to transfer to further dimensions because of Gamma waves, which occur when we meditate.

Brainwave	Frequency Range	State of Mind
Delta	0,5 Hz - 4 Hz	State of deep sleep
Theta	4 Hz - 8 Hz	Sleep, listlessness and deep hypnosis
Alpha	8 Hz - 14 Hz	A relaxed state but awake
Beta	14 Hz - 30 Hz	State of being awake and conscious
Gamma	30 Hz +	State beyond willpower

If you ask, "Why are you explaining pages and pages full of brainwaves?" My answer is: To be able to say, "As physical healing can be at Alpha and lower frequencies, if, from time to time, we can send the consciousness that keeps us so busy on vacation and be alone with our heart, we will be doing a very good thing for our physical health." ☺

Chase Life!

While living without awareness, we try to acquire many things. The things we chase turn into a very long list, sometimes like a house, car, bag or outfit, and sometimes a diploma, making a career or being in luxurious places, or even that our kids graduate from Harvard. While we are trying to acquire those things we chase, we lose years, as well as being unhappy when we cannot get close enough to our targets. Yet when we choose the factors that will bring sense to our lives, it will not be more difficult but easier to reach them, and being less connected to the outside world, happiness will come right to us. In short, after our basic needs, the factors that bring sense to life are the ones that we can reach free of charge and nearly completely through our own control. If the basis of the question, "What am I chasing today?" refers to terms like property, etiquette and being favored, maybe it is time to stop and think. If we can find this way, which will bring real sense to our lives, it will stop us from running after the artificial factors.

Seeing the Bright Side

Imagine a snow-white piece of paper. There are only 5 -10 stains on it. As long as we don't get fixated on three to five acts or characteristics of the person we are in contact with, as long as we do not have a problem with that person, we can ignore even tens of stains. However, once the black stains in the relationship start to bother our brain, the white parts get forgotten altogether. In a book that I read in my youth, called The Journey of Men, people realise the things they take for granted after losing them, exaggerate their problems and live only for the moment; this touched me very deeply. Personally, I live my relationships by paying attention to the parts, which nourish me, and making an effort to make the toxic parts better. From time to time I am successful, and sometimes this process takes a bit too long. However, if we see the bright side it can be pretty easy to maintain happiness.

Being Conscious of Your Limits

Everyone sells us his or her dreams. When we are children, our moms say, "My son's going to be a doctor!", the film we are watching suggests to us the dream of being rich easily, and in adverts we watch the promises of being the most beautiful person in the world. Of course, it is difficult to live in a world where this many dreams are being sold and this much emphasis is placed on perfection. So, knowing your limits is the first and the most important stop on the way to a happy life. In short, if you are 1.70 m tall, your expectations should be accordingly. Without help, you cannot take the book from a three meters high shelf. Our culture is outfitted with many creeds about cutting cloth according to one's means and being aware of yourself. However, despite this, there are members of society who feel the pain between what they are and what they want to be every day. I am a man who likes pushing his limits, but I also have the principle of accepting my limits and living without denying their existence.

Ersin Pamuksüzer

CHAPTER THREE

FOR EMOTIONAL HEALTH ...

- ❖ WHAT ARE STRESS AND DISTRESS?
- ❖ DEPRESSION!!!
- ❖ EMOTIONAL DETOX

"One can drink water even in depression..."

EMOTIONAL HEALTH

BODY
HEART
MIND

The second component of our health, which we analyse integrally, is emotion… When we defined it, we said it was the projection of body and mind. Our world of sensation, which occurred as a result of the stimulus of these two components, is one of the elements at the base of our behaviors, reactions, fears and decisions.

Could emotions also become toxins? Could they also cause acidification and rotting in the body? Let this be the subject that we focus on in this chapter. Let us have a look at whether we can create a term called "Emotional Detox."

Yes, there are toxic emotions in this life and they also cause us pollution just like other acidifying toxins that we take into our body. There is frustration, for example, or unfairness, abuse, being looked down on, being unwanted, being left, being insulted, being cheated, being fooled… Simply, there is the pain of love, not being able to forget, not being loved… If it was possible to live without being sucked into a whirlpool of hundreds of emotions which we don't know how to handle, there wouldn't be a title like this; however, there is…

Do you know why even newly born babies sometimes look very cute, especially those who have only just come out from the mother's tummy, despite their wrinkled and hairy skins? Not only human babies, but all living creatures look lovely when they are born. There is a simple answer to this: Because we see them that way… But why do we see them like that? (I will come back to this subject later…)

I think one of the most soothing feelings is "rebelling"… I think that burning bridges, rising up, and turning everything upside-down leave one with an incredible feeling of relief. And the reason for it is this: I see rebelling as a kind of symptomatic treatment; it takes away most of the strain. Can it solve the source of the trouble? That can be discussed… In fact, the possibility of not solving it, is high. This is like killing the headache, stopping the bleeding and decreasing the blood temperature… It paves the way for the next move you will make. I guess the final straw happening is much better than the stress caused by the worry of whether or not it is the final straw. In short, if stress is filling, rebelling is discharging… However, I do not know about whether after you burn the bridges you either get into trouble or regret, but I can say that after experiencing that discharge you'll feel very relieved for a while. Don't misunderstand me, I'm not saying go and start a rebellion somewhere. Oh, no! In fact, my suggestion is never to rise up against anything and bring yourself into such a state. Do not do it. Do not gather such toxic emotions inside you. Continue discharging emotional toxins by little exhausting movements, so that you won't have to deal with emotions for which the cake is not worth the candle. ☺ The reason that I brought up this subject is the things I am going to say now on the subject of getting rid of the emotional toxins gathered inside us. When we have emotional management that isn't going to bring us to a state of rebelling all through our lives, there won't be any need for an emotional explosion, and we will continue a balanced and peaceful life.

I am going to give the answer to why we see babies as cute, but first let us have a glance at the life we live in. What is it that makes us forget how to breathe right? Yes, we were breathing right when we were babies. The deep breath that we mention… We were circulating the oxygen through the whole body and calmly breathing out and watching our surroundings with confused but curious eyes, until coming across resistance. While breastfeeding, we stopped when full; we even got tired of sucking and fell asleep many times. What a pleasant sleep it must have been, who knows! ☺ Until a naughty wind makes us shout like a fire alarm by pressing on our intestines. We also sorted this crisis out with a heavy back massage, done with our mother's gentle healing hand, with one or two thuds and a loud burp. Whatever happened, happened after being weaned. We started to come across stubbornness and resistance there. A spoon was popping into our mouth and, before we were persuaded to swallow, a new one would come. And without a chance to say, "Stop, let me take a breath," pop: another one! I guess our beautiful moms made it a fait accompli. Those are the moments where head-turning and mouth-locking are learned. And the moments in which we learned to resist our parents, who knowus.

The rest is history. In time, we learned to live in an existing system with imposing people, to love, respect, be sad, react, be happy, be scared, talk, listen, not listen; in short, everything. Moreover, we are so highly affected by each other that we even learn to feel and fall in love with each other. The repertoire of our amygdala[13] secretes some feelings to us. We produce some part of our reactions according to the signals we get from here.

Of course, we cannot avoid our system of cultural emotion and thinking. How many more societies can dance wildly with joy, as we do in Turkey, singing "Let

13. Amygdala (In Latin, corpus amygdaloideum): Almond-shaped section of brain constructed by neurons, located in the depths of the brain's medial temporal lobe. The area, which has the premier role in the forming of emotional memory and emotional reactions. It is a part of the limbic system.

this world sink?" ☺ Here, where I write, a generation is living which grew up with heart-breaking films, which associates sadness and sorrow with innocence, and fun and joy with lack of purity. In those times when the number of channels was limited, everything we watched was embodied maybe not in our genetic codes but to somewhere in our main control room: Be sure of that.

Every moment we live, we produce our reactions from the interaction with the environment and the emotional reasoning (the mind component is switched on here) that we live inside ourselves. Our happiness and unhappiness depend on that. We are affected by television, which is the loudest voice in our surroundings, too much. Unfortunately, there are bothersome situations in many newsworthy announcements, and these subjects/news that we feel dependent on, although they are independent from us, in some way suck our joy of living out of us every day. Worry has become a constant feeling that reaches us, together with economic concerns. Not trusting our future is like a burden put upon us. Besides all this, our personal ups and downs, successes and failures look back at us as blankly as a wall. Moreover, the problems in emotional relationships crown them all. In short, we have lives full of stress and we get emotionally polluted every moment. It means the breathing that we experienced in our babyhood must have been forgotten along the complicated roads of life.

How does this component of our integrated approach to health threaten our general health? What are the illnesses and diseases caused by emotions? How can we deal with these diseases? What is emotional detox? Let us lay these subjects on the table.

No, I've not forgotten the subject of the baby! I will tell you why we see babies as very cute: Because babies have not yet met with those three troubles (toxifying, not getting enough nutrition, and the continuity of the sympathetic mode). There is no toxic substance or toxic emotion in their bodies yet. They rest their heads in trust and sleep in peace. They are carefree, without worry, innocent; the mother's milk is enough for them to feed; they awake to pleasant feelings. Well, the energy that we feel in babies is our state before getting polluted, which we miss and have lost in time. In fact, all of us push, maybe not to go back to that place, but to feel in such way and live in that serenity. We need to be as clean as a baby is. When we bring our emotions to a baby-state, there will be no problems left. So, is that possible? No, and it is never going to be. If you are saying, so why are you taking our times by saying all thesewords then, you are right, but let us not forget that even if we know that we cannot reach the target, moving in that direction is going to gain us a lot…

WHAT ARE STRESS AND DISTRESS?

With each new experience, we widen our repertoire of emotions. It can sometimes be painful to live with those increasing and at the same time ever more polluted emotions of ours. It means alarm bells are ringing. It is not possible to increase our quality of life without getting rid of this pain. Every unpleasant situation that we get stuck in emotionally will affect us physically too, and wreck our system of thought. In this case, noticing this situation and taking the necessary precautions would be the best decision to take, because the stress we are living can bring us to the point of distress.

Stress and distress are two pretty confusing terms because of how they are written, and also the similarities of their contents.

The term "stress" is a word that was transferred from physics to psychology. If any substance is not adjusting to a difficulty and keeping stable, stress occurs, and the substance is corroded. Life without stress, which is almost a natural part of life, does not look so possible.

On the other hand, "distress" is a name that is in the literature of biomedical science. The reason is the stress which living creatures come across. In other words, distress is the result, which appears when we cannot deal with stress. It is the emotional state we come to with physiological and/or psychological balance breaking down, taking hold of the organism and causing an acute or chronic problem during the processes of adjusting/enduring or dealing with the stress or similar interactions of the life we live.

In short, when stress is a situation that we come across often and must even learn to live with, distress is a risk, which involves the potential of turning into a physical and psychological illness. If not dealt with, it causes permanent physical and psychological damage. If we consider that distress is the emotional situation of not being able to deal with stress, of blocking the ways towards it, it may be beneficial to discourse a little on stress.

Getting Out of the Picture

We do not experience any emotion to the same extent as each other. Stress is a relative matter in which when one situation drives somebody crazy, the same situation may not be felt or minded by the other. It is in an amorphous structure that changes according to the point of view... Luckily, our job is not that difficult: One who has not met stress at all can only be living in seclusion, and anyway would not have anything to do with this book. ☺

When one is a part of a problem, it is difficult to be a part of the solution to it. To solve the problems which create stress, I am saying, and even insisting on, looking at the subject from a different perspective, if possible with a humorous eye, and focusing on the situation overall is beneficial. That is what I say about the subject of stress.

When one is a part of a problem, it is difficult to be a part of the solution to it. Get out of that picture; look at yourself from there...

Besides, knowing that many people experience similar problems can decrease your stress to an extent. When stressed out because of the morning rush hour, breaking out in a cold sweat, if your boss calls and says, "There is too much traffic, I'll be late," would you not be relieved? Never mind the boss: Even if two friends of yours are, like you, running late, you would be relieved. You would start seeing the problem as normal. Everyone having the same trouble would feel like it is decreasing yours. But in fact, the trouble is the same trouble still.

Not everyone is stressed about the same subject; nor do they try to deal with their stresses in the same way - there are different ways, different perspectives... Therefore, we must find our own way and develop the solution ourselves. On this subject, there is neither knowledge as easy as a pill nor a magic wand that can wipe away the stress...

I will give you myself as an example: I get stressed out; quite often, too! The method I found for myself is being proactive. I mean, instead of breaking out in a cold sweat and raising the quotient of my worry every second, I phone beforehand and let them know that I might be late. It gives relief. Another method of mine is this: "Stay in the flow, Selda" I say. "Life is bringing you to a much better place that you do not know… Every cloud has a silver lining. Life presented this stress so that it can form better conditions…" And another method, as I pointed out before, is getting out of the picture. Looking at myself from a distance, I see myself how unimportant that problem, my stress, which strangles me, actually is. Look at me and my contributions to the world of psychology on the subject of stress! Unfortunately, I do not have any place in the literature yet. ☺

The solution to many problems, which create stress becomes possible with a change in behavior and in the manner of approaching the problem.

Maybe we can start analysing by categorising the situations, which create stress. Where does stress come from?

1. **Environmentally interactive stresses:** Air pollution, noise, crowds, radiation, heat, cold, dust etc.…
2. **Stresses caused by work and shortness of time:** The worry of not being on time, heavy work, night work, too much load, tiredness, the difficulties of decision making, time pressure, uncertain roles, interpersonal conflicts, future anxiety etc.…
3. **The ones caused by psycho-social factors:**
   a. **Daily stresses:** They are the simple strains of everyday life. For example, getting stuck or having bad luck in the traffic, things going wrong at home, a crying child, a burnt dinner…
   b. **Stresses caused by change:** The stresses caused by the radical changes in life: Moving to a new house, getting divorced, changing school, changing city etc.
   c. **Stresses related to development:** The stresses about the periods of life… Starting school, starting work, puberty, menopause and andropause or, in adulthood, transferring to work life…
   d. **The crises of life:** Illnesses, birth, death, being redundant, love pain…

It would be a lie if we said there was no other source of stress. The personal sources of stresses are also too many to count. For example, the losses of the person who attributes the success of his life to a very particular situation: Suddenly an unexpected permanent physical disability to a successful sportsperson etc. Everyone who had a broken foot would be upset, but in professional sports, the anxiety would be higher.

The important thing is that these factors are got rid of before they distress the person. Although the short-term effects of stress, such as accelerating heartbeat, increase in blood pressure, anxiety, pessimism, rage, forgetfulness, not being able to focus etc. create simple and temporary situations, the long-term effects need to be discussed. The distress states, which occur as chronic illnesses (headache, heart disease), depression, phobias, personality change, hormonal changes, mental illnesses, thought and memory defects and sleep disorders, cause scores of results, like period interruption, milk coming from the breast by the increase of prolactin, brain cells dying, the brain getting smaller etc. and impair the quality of life greatly.

The Distress Tolerance

Stress is always going to exist. It is better to accept it. The real subject is to be happy despite it. In fact, it is even possible to be successful by using stress, because the right dose of stress causes one to make the moves, which will lead one to be more successful. Perception opens, concentration increases, and you focus on the target. However, the state of chronic stress is objectionable. Long-term stress, with a completely opposite effect, creates a sense of difficulty and concentration loss. Instead of making a problem out of stress, if we see it as a fact of our way of sensing or interpreting events and our resistance towards them, not mostly as outside events that we do not like, we may succeed in being more tolerant in our fight.

In psychological terms, stress is personal. It pushes, tires and might even sicken one. People want to keep their psychological, biological and social integrity against stress. They create this protection by both subliminal mechanisms and conscious efforts. The first ones that protect us are "defence mechanisms." They are some ways of protection, which work subliminally and change the reality: It does not make the problem go away, but it does provide temporary relief. It is exactly sweeping the dust under the carpet. Like repressing, developing a reaction, forgetting, reflecting, postponing etc.

Instead of solving it, if you are ignoring the problem, for instance not paying a bill or the raised rent, which is shaking your budget, not talking, not seeking a solution but ignoring the subject, then you are repressing the problem temporarily. However, even if you are not aware of the stress, you carry it inside you.

Other defence mechanisms that protect one are the attempts, which need consciousness and effort: Knowledge acquisition, widening the sense area, understanding, evaluating, new solutions, seeking alternatives etc. Each situation that has been talked over and finished with a decision is an attempt to deal with stress in a conscious way.

You Either Deal with Your Stress or Get Defeated by It!

People show different reactions to each other even under similar conditions. This is very normal because there are many parameters, which dictate these reactions, like age, gender, socio-cultural environment, education and experience. Even if these are the same, just the mood of the person that day will affect his or her reaction. When one can manage it with a relaxed sense of "Is at the end of the world?", the other can make his or her life miserable with a strain of "This is the end of the world!" It means that our personality, disciplines, life conditions and the perspective on the future are the sources which we must manage stress.

Our style of dealing with stress also reflects ourselves. Where some of us prefer to see the bottom of a bottle, some of us prefer flowering in sports centres. On the one hand, cigarettes, alcohol or too much food; on the other a healing diet, sport, regular sleep… On one side stepping back, turning in on oneself, becoming passive, avoiding facing one's own problems, ignoring, repressing or on the contrary overreacting, shouting, exploding; on the other side, analysing the problem, producing alternatives, taking the subject in hand calmly and producing a decision… Needless to say, this method is good and healthy: Do this, avoid doing that. You know best. However, I should say, one mistake cannot be covered up by another.

Two Wrongs Do Not Make a Right…

When lifestyles, current climatic conditions, social environment, political strains, everything moral and material are sources of stress, if I say, "Life without stress is possible," close this book immediately, because obviously I am lying…

In that case, if this is the illness, it is; first let us accept that. Then let us see that our duty is to lower the laser shields at the right time, is it not? ☺

We talked about the Fight-Flight mode in the second chapter and said that in that mode all the neural energy stock is used for active reactions to external situations, emotional reactions and sensual stimuli. We also indicated that it is not possible to live constantly in that mode. So, what shall we do? Here is the thing to do: Either we try to avoid the situations which put us in that state, or we develop personal methods of relaxation. If not, chronic illnesses, especially vascular heart disease, will always follow us.

Here are a Few Ways of Getting Rid of Stress:

- **Positive Suggestion:** Do you know what abracadabra means? I create what I say… ☺ Prayers, suggestions, desires should always be positive. In the face of incidents presenting negative attitudes, the negative words one tells oneself are not good for anything other than increasing the strain that is felt during that incident. It means we must focus on how something is going to happen, not on how it is not going to happen. For example, instead of suggesting, "I am too fat, I can never be thin" the suggestion "If I want, I can manage anything," or instead of "I have no chance," saying, "I create my own luck" is more effective. Also, you know the people allaround us that speak negatively all the time? It is beneficial to keep away from them as well? One does not need energy suckers in life.
- **Be Active:** Inaction brings unhappiness and boredom. Moreover, it gives tiredness. You already know that the people who regularly walk in the fresh air, travel to different places, and do different physical activities are much more at peace with stress. Walk, do your housework, choose stairs instead of the elevator, be active, don't be too lazy to do things. Believe me, when the body moves, it rests the feelings and thoughts.
- **Learn the Techniques of Relaxation:** Do you think people who give many suggestions about stretching techniques, which have become almost a branch of industry nowadays, never experience stress? Of course, they do; however, be sure that the people who know these techniques and can unwind are doing a big favor to those around them and themselves by the high awareness that they develop. It is

beneficial to learn some relaxation techniques. The most recognised ones among them are techniques like meditation, breathing exercises, autogenic relaxation[14], biofeedback[15], yoga, and tai chi.

- **Raising the Awareness:** It is giving short relaxation breaks to fight against stress. Breathing deeply, imagining being in a comfortable place, recognising the muscle movements and being able to realise the physical indications occurring in ourselves in stressful situations.

- **Time Management:** Plan your time but be flexible. Let your B Plan be that your plan might go down the plughole. Don't mind it even if your plans don't work out in the ways that you would like them to. Approaching life in a flexible way decreases stress.

- **Effective Communication:** I would like to broach the subject with an example. Telling someone who is trying not to miss the plane, "Put the computer in your bag separately and switch it on" or, "Take your shoes off and pass the device again" escalates stress. Instead, the same sentences can be said like, "We know that you are in a rush; however, there is such a procedure that we ought to apply according to the instructions we are given. Can you please take off your shoes and pass through the device? We will help you to finish the process quickly." Most stressful situations are caused by communication problems between people. Discussion of our problems with these people is a method for solution; however, most of the time there is not even time for that. Like in that example. If people can communicate with each other empathetically, they will be hindering stress to an important extent. Unfortunately, focusing on our own stress too much, we are not very careful about easing that of others... However, at least we people who have awareness can apply this in our lives and add the feeling of empathy to our communications. It is also important not to go into hypotheses while empathising.

Another method to lower stress is to make sentences by using me, not you. A sentence with "you""might be sensed as an accusation. When "you" sentences are used, usually a negative and defensive reaction occurs on the opposite side. If we care not about being reactive but about being effective, we will be much more successful in communication.

14. With the effect of autogenic exercises on the autonomous nervous system, sympathetic nerves transferring to parasympathetic state and relaxation in the muscles and mind...

15. **Biofeedback:** Watching the brainwaves, muscle cells or blood pressure with an electronic device. The purpose is allowing us to see or apply the bodily reactions according to some signals.

- Playing a Game: One of the best methods against stress is to spare time to play games. Play games with your partner, friends and children. Buy box games, make puzzles, play cards etc. Just like in your childhood. Especially when we give our concentration to highly mindful and creative games, we see that we focus on the big picture by getting away from the current stress source and staying in the moment. Looking into our problems from outside is important for the solution to the problem and lowering of stress. Those computer games which sometimes we get angry about and which take all the time of our loved ones are good excuses to get away from stress. Of course, one condition is not to over-do it.

- Eating Healthily: You cannot imagine how important it is to give the body the real nutrition it needs, eating balanced and naturally, preferring green and vitamin-rich types of food and keeping the flora of the intestines healthy to lower stress.

- Working and the Feeling of Success: Unutilised capacity and doing nothing are stress sources all by themselves. Resting is not doing nothing, as it is thought to be; it is taking the body and the mind away from the current state which creates tiredness. In addition, it should not be forgotten that we can manage to rest through physical activity too.

- Quality Sleep/Resting: Sleeping at the same time every day, waking up at the same time, sleeping enough and not resisting when sleep comes both keep the body away from stress and heal it. Sleeping time and its quality have major importance in mending the body and in the building-up of the nervous systems.

- Principles: Maintaining the principles that are created for some conditions is also one of the important factors in dealing with stress. Indecisiveness creates stress, whereas principles are the source of getting rid of indecisiveness. For example, a person who keeps to the principle of, "I won't smoke more than a cigarette per day," and who is able to apply this principle with pleasure, without getting stressed, and having great pleasure from that one cigarette, can continue that "beneficial, harmful habit" all her or his life. ☺ We say "beneficial" because it may be a principle which saves the person from addiction and prevents the increasing consumption of cigarettes. Besides that, "nevers" and "alwayses" cause a life lived under stress. Principles are what can best keep a limit on our behaviours, like "I do not drive when I drink alcohol", "I do not eat even one more bite when I get full", "I do not decide immediately when I get angry and I sleep on it for one night" etc.

- **Hobbies:** Developing hobbies, in fact setting up our occupation according to our hobbies is also an important way of dealing with stress that we can add to our lifestyle. It should be a fundamental to diversify life, give color to it and not set it up based on just one thing. Because if we lost that one thing, we would be in a state of dealing with a huge emptiness.

We suggest you watch the video below about addiction:

Power of Addiction, Addiction of Power.
https://www.youtube.com/watch?v=66cYcSak6nE

Radical Acceptance

In mental health, the first step is accepting the world as it is. Rising against the world and not accepting it, moreover going to war with it, puts us in everlasting pain. In this world, I can only carry the responsibility of the being, which is under my control. If we try to change the flow of the world for somebody else, or to do so by ourselves, an everlasting fight begins. In this fight, when the incidents do not go as we want, instead of going crazy and rebelling, it's necessary to just accept the things that happened as they are. Without this acceptance, a long and happy life can never be founded.

Mindfulness

The most basic step to go further on the subject of Mental Health is the creation of mindfulness. Mindfulness is the ability to sense our surroundings and ourselves as they are at the present time. Only then do we come to the state of feeling what we are going to accept, and which of our emotions are triggered and need to be controlled. In short, if there is no mindfulness, one does not have a chance to look at life in the right frame.

Meditation

Meditation is an exercise done to regain the property of mindfulness that we have lost. If we haven't been taken under occupation by the world of consumption that we've created, we'll be constantly "meditative" anyway. However, we practise meditation to stop our brains, which live under occupation, and to bring them back to this moment. When we come to a state of meditating as a part of the natural flow of our lives, then it means our awareness is at its peak. In that way, we come to a state where we can take the necessary steps to be able to keep our mental health in balance.

Wise Mind

Life always offers us its different faces. We have the possibility of approaching these instances emotionally or logically. It is obvious that the situations where only one of these approaches is used are going to cause problems. I, approaching emotionally under the shadows of feelings, can fall away from reality and behave unadvisedly; or, with an absolutely logical approach, I can sign my approval to major controversies and uneasiness, which I might be right about doing only on paper. We call these two thinking types being used together, not separately and one by one, the "wise mind." As well as making us approach the world in balance, the wise mind prevents us from getting worn out by living on the edges.

Validation

There are two sides to every relationship. On one side me, and on the other side the one across from me. If we do not validate the person across from us positively and reward him or her, because of the lack of acceptance in the relationship, that person will feel uncomfortable and not open her or his ear or heart to us. When this scene repeats a lot, he or she will lose hope for us, and the relationship will be wounded so much as to be unhealable.

Especially the behavior repeated while raising a child or in teamwork can become a threat to our child's or the team's future. People we approve of will be more open towards us and listen to us with all ears. In this way, they might even go as far as to change their minds. Living by approving of people also allows us to cast a positive light around us.

Aligning of the Habits

Life is a train where our habits are lined up in sequence. It is necessary to line them up and evaluate which of them affect us how, identify and write off the ones wearing us out and pressurising us, and build up the ones which positively affect us. However, acquiring new habits can be designed as a perfect life configuration. In fact, on my own behalf, I did exactly this in my new life configuration, which I started in 2002. By configuring my eating-drinking habits, sporting habits, thinking habits, my approach to life, and working habits, I became the "new me." Now it is your turn.

To be Happy, Accept Your Surrounding as They Are, But Still Say What You Think Is True…

Everybody I know is in search of happiness, but keep complaining and grumbling about being bothered by either a colleague, or a husband or wife at home, or a close friend, or the powers that be. Grumbling and complaining are the last things, which can trigger changes in our surroundings. The first thing that we need to do is to accept them as they are and emphasise how you can open a different world's doors to them. This can usually be done by sharing our views and indefatigably trying to educate. If, while providing this support, we are giving our views and sharing sincerely and with an open heart, the opposite side can be open towards us too. If we do it with an arrogant, superior mind, we will inevitably find closed doors and people whom we cannot reach, and we will start complaining again.

Ersin Pamuksüzer

DEPRESSION!!!

There is an "Unhappiness Epidemic," and they call it "Depression." (I saw the term "Unhappiness Epidemic" in Ümit Aktaş's book called Happiness Treatments - I liked it so much that I bought it immediately. I loved the book too, and would highly recommend it.) This malady has become a type of illness that is seen as often as having a cold, and which we have become accustomed to now. It is very different from stress. For that reason, it is beneficial to examine it separately.

We call depression the state of spiritual collapse when hopelessness and pessimism get stronger and the self-confidence and joy of living are lost. It should be dealt with holistically because it is closely related to hormones, the physical body, the emotions and the mental situation. A pretty serious problem that, if not treated, would drive one to suicide.

Around us, many people are in depression, unhappy and worried... In addition, antidepressants, which are thought to be the cure of this trouble, have become so common that they are virtually put in a candy dish and served to visitors with coffee. I don't want to say this and upset you, but it is useful to know that people who are undergoing depression treatment but are not suicidal become more suicidal after starting to take these pills. Here are the possible side effects of antidepressants: Forgetfulness, putting on weight, loss of concentration, dizziness, nausea, headache, lethargy and sleeplessness, high blood pressure, heart attack... What else?

I would like to repeat the thing I have been saying since the start of the book: "Symptomatic treatment will not work in the long term; the real causes need to be eliminated..." Where do I know this from? Well, what if I tell you that I lived through it? Well, that is what needs to be done in the treatment of depression too. Without changing the factors, which are causing the depression, antidepressants are only an emergency action, like sweeping the troubles under the carpet temporarily, or while tidying the room putting all the mess in the cupboards. If by any chance you open those cupboards, turmoil will crash down on you. Moreover, while trying to get over depression, taking all the risks that I named above cannot be the actions of an intelligent person.

Sometimes the source of our depression can be so deep down that we think that we are in depression for no reason. Then, what has been told to us by the doctors is this: "There is a chemical imbalance in your brain…" That is the moment when we are finished! Do we have any other choice apart from believing it? The guy learned the science of it for years; he knows better than you. So, what is it again? "There is a chemical imbalance in your brain…" Moreover, he happens to understand it after a very short session, for half of which he checked his watch. Well, ask once why there is an imbalance in that chemical! Maybe, faced with all we live, not having a chemical imbalance in our brain is the biggest disability; could having a chemical imbalance in our brain not be the right thing sometimes? In the world we live in there are all these things to cause a chemical imbalance in our brains; those who have a brain will, of course, react with their brain. If you (I am talking to the psychiatrist) are writing one of three to five known antidepressants with your pen, which was given to you on your graduation, not to send the patient away with their hands empty, and not trying to go to the root of the problem, then we cannot say that you are a good doctor as we thought you were. In short, dear reader, if you are given a prescription and if you go willy-nilly to the nearest pharmacy to get the prescription and start washing the pills down, you are washed up… I am telling you… ☺

May God protect the doctors who have become the volunteer soldiers of the industry of medicine, but with your permission, I would like to use my right to object.

"Dear doctors, is it not you who say, 'Only 5% of serotonin hormone is produced in the brain and the rest in the intestines.'? So, why are you striving with that poor 5% and trying to increase serotonin in the brain? Deal with it through the intestines. Do you not see that there is a risk of suicide? Please, have mercy on us!"At exactly this point, reader, it is necessary to share a comment that I got from friends and psychiatrists that I consulted with who deal with the science of psychology. They say: "We cannot say it that way. All these approaches are at a theoretical stage. Any of the hormones in the body can create different effects according to where they are produced. It means that there is no basis for believing that intestinal serotonin would do the same job as that produced in the brain." In that case, I am taking all my words back and I say, go to the doctor, as your heart leads you… ☺

Look on what kind of slippery ground medicine is trying to act. It is necessary to round the sharp edges of all the sentences which are formed on this subject. As I wrote before, when we talk about multi-parameter systems, every patient is special, and I guess we have no other choice than to accept that we will find the right treatment a bit gropingly (by a method of trial and error). However, with your permission I would like to be sharp on this subject: I do not like the fact, dear representatives of modern medicine, that you prescribe medicine every time, like you are trying to prove that you haven't read all the thick books just to tell us, "Increase your omega-3 sources, take vitamin D, eat pickles, consume probiotic yoghurt, be active, walk in fresh air".

Well, I am saying this, but is there no subject that they are right about and no patient that they cure? On the contrary… Although they tried so hard for themselves, there are so many patients who came around with the prescriptions that modern medicine suggested, who turned back from suicide and found peace, that one gets embarrassed about what one has said. In fact, the thing that needs to be seen here is very similar to the one I explained in the chapter on physical health. You doctors who suggest the same solution to everybody, and you patients who take the hearsay medicines randomly: In short, the waters get troubled because of lack of knowledge.

Yes, in our time, depression has grown like a snowball. Why? Because we feed terribly! Unhappiness is everybody's shared problem. Why? Because we cannot secrete the necessary hormones when the trouble of what we eat is not feeding us enough comes together with our emotional state. Because there is genetically modified food on our table. Because we still add the chemicals, which are used to protect food and lengthen their shelf life. Because, from the frequencies that we are exposed to, unhappiness is being broadcast. Because the lyrics of the songs are very depressing. Because we have a culture where who cry counted as oppressed and being oppressed is valuable. Because we do not move enough and think positively. Because making love is still a taboo and forbidden. Because instead of finding our own truths and seeing with our own eyes by questioning, we try to find our way with what the others say to us. Because we are trying to catch the conditions of artificial happiness and tiring both our body and spirit. Because we do not sleep properly. Because we live in contradiction. Because…

…Because we do not separate good from bad!

It is a known fact that lack of some vitamins and minerals causes depression, but many of our doctors who cannot take health as integrated, for example, our psychiatrist, usually avoid asking us how we eat. Whichever specialist you go to, he or she prescribes you medicine from his or her branch. You might say, "Huh... Should they write some other branch's medicine?" Well, they should not just prescribe medicine. They should try to understand. They should go deeper into the problem. Prescribing a medicine and sending the patient away has become routine. They should send the patient away with empty hands; it would not be a problem. They should tell them that they must do sports, walk this much in a day, drink this much water, eat well, not watch TV but play games, etc. Okay, okay, I'll stop preaching to the converted.

Do you know that, apparently, depression is the century's illness and that it was not known much until sixty years ago? So, what happened that it became so widespread and nearly captured all of us? Or is this the work of aliens?

What has been said is this: In 1995 some medicines were released onto the market which changed the chemistry of the brain and were prescribed to so many patients that, although they were thought to be working at the beginning, the psychological illnesses increased dramatically in our country, and this is the world in which we find ourselves. Again, I am talking from a doctor's mouth that apparently when you apply long-term medical treatments to a patient, that patient's tendency towards depression might rise... In this case, it means that the medicine given to the patient to get over the depression is itself the factor that makes the depression permanent. In fact, is there no other way rather than using medicine? 😐

Hippocrates said, "Let food be thy medicine and medicine be thy food..."

I am trying to say exactly that. It is time for us to save our brains, which we have strained with medicines from those chemicals, and to balance our brain with our body.

The strength you need is already in your noble blood ...

Atatürk

Or in your intestines... ☺

Be Free from Depression Now!

There is no magic wand or a prince on a white horse who is going to save you. Nobody will come and get you out of depression by taking your hand: You'll do it yourself. A bit of personal effort is needed. This business is nothing like handling stress. It needs serious responsibility and determination. And first, willing… Of course, there are some easing methods (and believe me there is no place among them for antidepressant medicines, tranquilisers or alcohol.)

In a holistic health approach, depression is a subject, which we need to handle physically, mentally and emotionally. You will see that many items listed below do not include only mental solutions, and that depression is related to our physical functions and what we eat and drink. Here are some of the methods, which will make your job easier:

- **Make your own probiotic yoghurt:** Make your intestines happy. Let them work from natural yoghurts and not gather toxins. Let them produce the serotonin, which is necessary for your happiness. (Although, I wish the whole job could be done with serotonin.) Be good to the friendly bacteria we live together with in our intestines. You should know that they do not like industrial products. To make them happy, do not buy your yoghurt from the supermarket, make it yourself. Making yoghurt is the easiest job in the world. The internet is full of recipes.

- **Feed naturally and heavily with greens:** I am not saying become a hundred percent vegan[16], but I suggest you become something near to that. ☺ No really, I'm not joking. If you want a proportion, considering that eating and drinking are at the same time a sociable business, I would like to suggest that you make your feeding eighty percent vegetable-based. The other twenty percent, on condition that it is healthy as well, can include animal products (meat, milk, eggs, yoghurt, etc.) However, never consume commercial food products that are modified and contain protective additives. Plants are rich enough in nature to give us every variety of vitamin, mineral and protein for life. I'm just saying…

16. **Being vegan** or **veganism** are for some reasons rejecting the use of animal-based nutrition and other animal products. Sometimes it is named as "serious vegetarianism." People who are vegan reject the nutrition, clothes and all other side products, which are obtained by using animals.

> *"Nothing will benefit human health and increase the chances for survival of life on earth as much as the evolution to a vegetarian diet."*
>
> *Albert Einstein*

- **Care about taking vitamin D:** One of the sources of unhappiness is a life without vitamin D. A life lack of vitamin D would both put one in depression and cause other illnesses… There is even cancer among these other illnesses. How lucky to live in a country with a lot of sun! However, would you believe me if I told you that many of us cannot benefit from the sun? Believe it. Our relationship with the sun should be good, but there are many wrongs that we think are right. Let me say it now that for the sun to work, we need to take vitamin D. The opposite is valid too: The sun must be such that the vitamin D we get from food becomes beneficial to the body. Well, I am trying to say this: The sun activates vitamin D in the body and right then this vitamin comes to a state in which it can play a role in our happiness. Please make sure you visit the page "Sun" in Chapter Five.

- **Try to find the real source of the problem and get rid of the cause of your depression:** Whatever the reason is: Loneliness, being out of job, economic trouble, noise, unhealthy conditions, too much workload, having no purpose, emotional ups and downs, love pain, etc., it may not be solved at all. These are not the causes of depression themselves; it is our side, which is not able to fight these problems. The depression won't go away completely by solving these problems, but by changing our approach to them. The problem might not be solved, but when our point of view on the problem changes, that subject might even be removed from the category of being a problem. It is necessary to be able to face the subjects, which put us in depression and reach the conclusion that, despite everything, life is a liveable place, by making this acceptance in principle. As long as people link their happiness to others or to conditions, without them, every time they find themselves in the arms of depression. Carrying happiness without tying it to conditions must be the basis. The thing that needs to be known is that happiness is within us.

- **Omega-3:** One of the main compounds of the cell membrane is omega-3. Omega-3 fatty acids are magical. These fatty acids let nerve cells have a healthy cell membrane. Healthy cell membrane means healthy brain functions. More importantly, the brain itself is also made up of omega-3 fatty acids, in the proportion of 40%. It is contained in salmon intensively. As well as being used in the treatment of depression, it is also a very effective substance in postpartum depression. If a woman who newly gave birth is not consuming enough fish, omega-3, which is passed to the baby by milk, gets less in the mother and if not replaced it can create serious depression. The solution is simple: Eat fish.

- Shall we forget wheat yet? Its genetics changed in the name of regenerating the wheat. Our food is full of chemical additive substances. These products', which contain chemicals but have increased shelf life and taste, lifetime has seriously increased, but whatever happened has happened to people. Obesity came; diabetes, cancer and chronic illnesses increased, and allergic reactions have virtually become natural. How about psychological problems? For a healthy and happy life are we going to take wheat out of our lives too, hmm? Today, genetically modified dwarf wheat accounts for 99% of wheat farming in the world. When the genetics of the wheat were modified with, apparently the target was to finish the hunger in the world. Hunger has stayed as always, and worse, obesity has gone wild. The reason for all this is the wheat that was modified genetically under the name of improvement. Unfortunately, the aggressive gluten in that manufactured dwarf wheat spoiled the gluten tolerance in many of us. The sad thing is that there is a serious relationship between depression and gluten. Gluten in bread, pastry, pasta and cookies can even cause inflammation in our intestines. You know we talk about the relation between the chemistry of the brain and the intestines? Here it is! One of the reasons underlying depression is the imbalanced intestine-flora caused by gluten. This is the situation. And we are a society which consumes a lot of gluten... Bad news!

- I almost skipped B 12: I almost forgot vitamin B 12, lack of which causes depression, paranoia, memory loss, hallucinations and short temper. B 12, which takes part in the creation of blood and nerve cells, is contained in nutrition like meat, liver, eggs, chicken, cheese, kidneys, milk and salmon. So, this is the reason for me saying not to become vegan completely.

- An end to putting on and losing weight fast: If you do not want to be worn out both psychologically and physically, do not gain and lose weight fast. I'm not talking about one or two kilos: Gaining and losing 15-20 kilos fast is what I'm talking about. Whatever changes one's physiology changes one's psychology too.

So, whenever you are free of your kilos, to make this permanent, you should change your eating habits and make this your lifestyle, so that you can keep the balance.

- **Consume quality oil:** Olive oil, fish oils, real butter... You should consume these oils. You can even add coconut oil to these. Especially in filter coffee, it creates an effect that lengthens the pleasure. Do not run away from oils for the sake of your brain chemistry. Not too much though, you should consume them responsibly. Don't forget, sugar makes the fat in the body, not oils.

- **Look after your thyroid glands:** Have your thyroid functions checked regularly. Sometimes depression might be directly caused by these glands too.

- **Stay away from sugar:** You are saying, "You weren't going to say this! I've lost all my taste now," are you not? "The most beautiful thing in the world is sugary food; what taste does life have without it?" That's right, but we have to tell this truth. Sugar can cause depression in two ways: The flora of the intestine and the movements in blood sugar... Sugar kills the good bacteria in the flora of the intestine and feeds the harmful ones. When the good bacteria are gone, a ground for depression occurs. Moreover, for a healthy working brain, balanced blood sugar is important. Despite the temporary feeling of happiness we experience because of a pike in our blood sugar, it must not deceive us. Imbalance in the blood sugar causes depression. To cut a long story short, we need to say goodbye to the pastries we love so much and the sweets that we cannot resist.

- **Companions, friendship, company:** Have you ever noticed?... That the depression cases come from not those who have companions, friends and subjects to share, who joke, talk and listen, but more from those who are lonely, withdrawn and isolated. The most valuable property that people can save is their companions and friends who they can laugh with. Believe this. This is more valuable than the probiotic yoghurt and omega-3 that we eat. We need other people who we can laugh together with, who do not bring us down, do not criticise us, and spend joyful time with us, rather than throwing our faults in our faces; having conversations, even if it is just speaking about sweet nothings. First, we should be companions and friends, so that we can gain companions and friends. At exactly this point, I would like to talk about an important detail that is worth mentioning: Everybody around us is in the same situation as us, don't forget. When we greet someone with a smile while passing by, that person will give us a similar reaction back. If we are like a wall, probably that person will be like a wall as well. Unfortunately, kindness of greeting is not very common in our society. For that reason, the person you greeted when passing by might be unaware and glare at you. Never mind, let's not give up. Let's keep on smiling, and the world will smile back at you. Watch what a snowball we'll be starting. If we ignore people, they'll ignore us too. In that situation, instead of being a passive mirror, let us play the role of a source of energy, and be the first one who smiles, looks, greets. If you listen to this suggestion of mine, we will get over not only our personal, but also our society's depression to an extent. ☺

- Do not give up sex if possible: Saying to somebody who is in depression already, "Do not give upsex" would not mean much. This can only be an activity, which we have to put among our precautionary efforts before we get into depression. We need those hormones. Unfortunately, not everyone has a sex partner that they want to be together with lovingly. After all, when we go to the root of many problems, doesn't something similar to this come out? Loneliness... Now, my words are to those who have a sex partner. Even if the problems of life stay in front of you like a wall, keep sex apart from them and spare time for it. In addition, let us not forget that nobody would want to take a big ball of problems near to themselves. People search for positive energies with which to share love and their bodies and life. Being alone is partly because of what we say against life.

- Think positive and let your expression be positive too: "Think positive, think positive..." You have heard this said a lot, have you not? Sometimes one wants to say, "If it's that easy, come and think positive yourself." Also, thinking is not a deliberate act either. Whatever we tell ourselves not to think, we think of even more. This suggestion should be one of the characteristics to take on in order not to get into depression. We should educate ourselves to be able to see the full part of the glass. Yes, sometimes life withholds this from people and leaves the seeds of anxiety inside us, but at least we should try. Don't forget: Because we go into the frequency with the energy we think, we summon that energy and contribute to future incidents resulting positively or negatively.

- Be active, do sports: It's not necessary to be a member of a sports club; don't find excuses for your immobility. Get away from the television, walk in fresh air, choose the stairs instead of the elevator (if you have no problems with your knees), in warm weather swim if possible, even if you cannot do all your housework do a part of it, do not be lazy, move. Most importantly, stop moaning already! There cannot be any excuse for your immobility. Use the time you waste telling someone about your neck arthritis and complaining about it to exercise that area. Immobility invites depression. The effect of exercising on brain chemistry cannot be denied because it is confirmed that the number of cells in that area of the brain, which controls memory and emotion increases during exercise. Those who work with body power are observed not to get into depression much. When you compare a student who spends his or her day doing sports with someone who spends it in front of a computer, you will see that the one who does sports is more at peace with life, stress-free, and successful. This is not a coincidence. Secretion of endorphin, one of the hormones that give happiness, occurs in active people.

- Let yourself have a hobby in this life: Only work? So boring. Don't you have any interests? That's hard to believe. If you do not have any interests at all and do not make any effort to address this, then it is better you stay in depression. Yes, really, stop reading this book too, get into bed and continue to be sad about your ill fate. However, if you have different interests, with a little effort put them into your lives as new colours. You will see that you will soon be making fun of depression.

- Do not say that you are in depression and you cannot do any of this - force yourself: Don't forget, whatever you tell your body, it believes that. When you wake up in the morning, even if the weather is terrible, just say, "What beautiful rainy and dark weather, it's just right to do my work; if it was sunny my mind would be outside." When they ask you "How are you?" instead of listing thirty-five troubles in a row, say, "I'm very well, I'm really in a good mood." Play this game, and you will see that both body and brain believe what you say. The suggestion we take has a major effect on us. When we are in a joyful, smiling, happy environment, you'll see that you pick this up and smile too. In fact, being in depression is also a choice. If you do not get out of bed, tidy yourself up, start the day, putting even a fake smile on your face, it means you are not putting in an effort. I insist that in life's mirror that fake smile is going to turn into a real one after a while. Just like your long face changes, too.... Come on, it's time to act... Fake it till you make it!

- In addition, make sure you consume these: Banana (serotonin, magnesium), green tea (antioxidant), asparagus (antidepressant), strawberry (antioxidant), avocado (omega-3), walnut (omega-3), cornelian cherry (melatonin), cashew (serotonin) and cranberry (antidepressant)...

Come on, let us just run away from this malady...

PHYSICAL ILLNESSES CAUSED BY EMOTIONAL POLLUTION (PSYCHOSOMATIC)

What is Psychosomatic Illness?

Remember the body language that appears when we are expressing our feelings. Those who cannot express their feelings are as if their organs started to talk and were trying to tell them something. They try to express themselves with the illness they have.

In medicine, "psycho" means spirit and "soma" body. They are psychologically rooted physical illnesses. It is a name given to the state of, together with the spirit having any kind of illness, the body also being affected and having a problem.

The relation between mental health and body health is obvious. Quite a lot of physical illnesses are caused by psychological factors. Psychological problems can start the illness as well as causing it to develop, and nearly every illness has different psychological sparks. What happens, happens while the body is in the effort of adapting itself to the psychology.

Psychology, which generally works in harmony with the autonomic nervous system, affects the body too. For this reason, in nearly all illnesses, which affect the autonomic nervous system, psychosomatic effects are observed. Such illnesses as bronchial asthma, skin problems that cause shedding, high tension, rheumatoid arthritis, intestine problems, ulcer and thyroid are examples of this.

In the occurrence of these illnesses, of course the effects of genetics, structural development, habits, social effects and psychosocial factors cannot be underestimated. Even the structure of character underlies the reasons for some psychosomatic illnesses. Each psychosomatic illness triggers a different area of the body. Inexpressible feelings find themselves the closest organ and start creating problems in the working mechanism of that organ.

> *What makes our body ill is the pressure of our soul.*
>
> *Sigmund Freud*

Which Ones Are They?

Have you ever had a chance to read Louise Hay's books? At first one cannot believe that the reasons for the illnesses are that psychological, but when the illnesses are examined, you observe that Hay caught the right psychological root. Interesting but true. The roots of most of our illnesses are based on our psychology. When researching in the book, for example looking up "itching," you come across something you could not deal with in the past, or when you search for "ringing in the ears," the book tells you that you are running away from something that you do not want to hear, etc. At first, you cannot believe it; you even mock, saying that she associated them well, but when you go further down to the root, you come across a staggering reality.

To cut a long story short, our psychology has a major effect on the body. Here are some psychosomatic illnesses:

- Cardiovascular System Illnesses
- Digestive System Illnesses
- Breathing System Illnesses
- Neuro/Endocrine System Illnesses
- Muscle and Skeleton System Illnesses
- Immune System Illnesses
- Skin Illnesses
- Cancer
- Psychiatric Disorders

The Sweetest Psychosomatic Illness: Love!

Of course, it is a joke… Calling love an illness is my boundless ability (!) to associate, but it is definite that it makes one ill. ☺

The psychological and physiological dimensions of love on the body submit data, which are exactly appropriate to the holistic approach at hand. Love, which freshens our hormones, is the most valuable subject of all time, which captures us with a passionate feeling… Novels, films, even life itself, walk on love and take advantage of it.

There is not only one hormone that is named the "Love Hormone." It is a composite of many. Look what has happened in the works on that subject: When the person who the subject is in love with is shown to him or her, it is observed that a few hormones of that subject suddenly change. It is confirmed that the happiness hormone, sexual desire hormone, stress hormone and adrenalin in the blood of the person who is in love increase. It is also detected that love is analgesic, which means painkilling, too. The foolhardiness of the people who are in love must come from this.

According to biology, love is a feeling, which all animals and humans must have and is important for the continuation of life. In this definition, is there a chance that love is mixed up with lust? I do not know how love is between animals, but I have witnessed some lovers becoming animals! ☺ Generally, love is observed in mammals. When the partners of elephants die, there are some who go into depression and even die, apparently. There are even those who attribute the selfless love of a mother for her child to lust. So, does it mean we should calllove related to hormones "lust"? No way! Okay, the source of selfless love, the hormones secreted after birth, I have nothing to say about this. Only women have those hormones (and female mammals); that is fine too. However, lust must be a sexual love... Be careful with the definitions.

Love is holistic. It means that emotions, mind and body are in action at the same time, and lust is the basic compound of love. Testosterone and oestrogen are the hormones of which the secretion increases as a result of lust. Neuroscience, which dedicates itself to examining the phenomena occurring in people's brains has, in the last years, observed that in the brains of people who are in love the secretion of pheromone and thyroxine increased, and identified that the secretion of norepinephrine and serotonin caused weird behavior in people who are in love. Moreover, it has been detected that these secretions increase dopamine, which triggers the brain. It is also among the observations that in people who are in love, dopamine rises up to the same level as those who use narcotics. Now I understand! That's why people in love get weird! ☺

A nice state of insanity, formed by normal abnormalities...

It is said that, when in love, too much triggering of dopamine causes an increase in the heartbeat, increase in the blood pressure, loss of appetite, sleeplessness and nervousness. Okay then, this is the reason for all this nonsense. As much as it gives pleasure, carrying these side effects constantly is both harmful and impossible. The heart rate increasing too much can cause a heart attack. For that reason, the state of being in love should not be in one's body for a very long time. If it is, it tries the body too much. I hope all our lusts turn into love and we find peace.

What if not! ☹

Then our business is tough. Why? Love disappearing suddenly is more dangerous than its sudden appearance; that's why. The end of a love can even cause suicide. As a result of the sadness that occurs with permanent separation, the norepinephrine secretion increases. Norepinephrine feeds the nerves in the body. In addition, it has an important effect on heart rate. If the increase of this secretion is more than its limits, too much anger, rage, crying crises for no reason and racing heartbeat can be observed. Moreover, it is a known fact that love pain can upset the balances of body and mind so much that it can even drag someone to suicide. Because of that, in many novels and TV series people who die or commit suicide for love are mentioned… (Besides, as the Turkish song says: "You must die for love, love then becomes love…") ☺

Psychology indicates that love is a cognitive and social phenomenon. Erich Fromm said that love is a conscious commitment and that it cannot be just out of lust. The psychological dimension of love cannot be defined as easily as the biological state of it; more precisely, it apparently shows different properties according to each individual. For some, it is a state of the senses and for some it is a need.

It is okay if I do not refer to the sociological and cultural dimension of love in this book. ☺

The reason that I spared a wide space for the subject of love in this chapter is that this integrative situation is good for humans' health in positive states, increases people's creativity by binding them to life astoundingly much, and makes them happy. The opposite is valid too of course. Love is like a very dangerous psychosomatic illness, which deceives the body with pleasure. For example, a permanent separation is equal to death… People who pass over this lightly might think that I'm exaggerating, but those who have had to separate from the person who they are in love with will understand what I'm talking about. Even so, you yourselves should not darken the world for yourselves that much just because you are separated from your loved one. Believe me, it passes over time, and you even come to a state of laughing at yourselves. When the hormones come to balance, the problem ends. Do not be sad; do not tear yourselves to pieces.

In one-sided or unrequited feelings of love, can we look at the love emotion as a toxin, which needs to be thrown out of the body? Can love's wound be cured by emotional detox?

EMOTIONAL DETOX

Like physical detox, emotional detox must be done for the purpose of being purified from toxic substances and emotions. If emotional pollution which drags us to physical illnesses is not cleaned, in the long term it can carry us to chronic illnesses and from there, to death.

While doing emotional detox, physical purification has importance too. It means people who beat themselves with cigarettes and alcohol, are in fact not doing the right thing. However, I understand them: Sometimes it is important just to pass that time as well. Anyhow, in the long term what we need is a healthy body and mind combination. Let us not ruin tomorrow's body for today's troubles.

Whatever the source of the trouble is, it must be defined properly and taken out of the category of trouble by some efforts and methods. Here, having a kind of radical acceptance of the trouble can be the first step taken for the solution to that problem.

Here are Things that Can Be Done for Emotional Detox:

- **Radical Acceptance:** When you have a problem, if you can accept it as it is, then it means you have a healthy psychology. If you do not accept it and surf in dreamland, then it means there is a problem. Yes, sometimes accepting reality according to the size and type of the trouble is accepting suffering too, and it is not that easy. First, the problem must be defined and accepted, and the act of solution must start after that. Otherwise, the name of the effort to heal would be "escape," not "solution." For example, it is not easy to accept the death of a deeply loved close person. Or, for an in-love person who is experiencing an untimely separation, accepting the sentence, "This business is finished now" will not be easy at all. These unfinished feelings leave a constant feeling of lack in the person, and for as long a time as they do not face the problem, the period of healing or being cleansed of this toxic feeling will be lengthened. Even if we do not want to, we have to accept reality; if not, we cannot take a step forward towards a solution.

- **Talking:** Talking, expressing feelings always gives relief. However, it is important who you are talking to about your feelings. To a psychologist, your mother, a close friend or a person who knows you a little bit or not at all… Although each of them would comment according to their own feelings and discipline, you would be getting rid of one more toxin each time you talked about it. However, it should not be forgotten that, according to which person that you talk to, there is a possibility that you'll give a false representation. When you cannot tell a mistake that you have made openly to your friend, so as not to be judged, the toxins will be stuck inside you. In this case, the best listeners are psychologists. They listen to you consciously and avoid commenting. Because they pay attention to you with an effective listening style, you cannot help but find yourself telling everything, many times, and even finding your own answers while telling, too. There must be people who you would not hesitate to tell about your feelings in this life. Excitements and emotions, which are hidden or suppressed cause illnesses such as gastric disorders, ulcers, herniated discs and backache. Suppression can even turn into cancer in time. Dialogue, talking, and words are all very strong medicines and perfect therapy!

- **Lifestyle:** Being a direct person, not gathering toxic emotions… We do not mean speaking without thinking and being reactive, but being an outspoken person hinders you from gathering toxic emotions. Instead of being silent against unfairness, putting up with it and trying to find a solution by quarrelling inside yourself, I suggest you express your thoughts in an appropriate style.

- **Principles:** Being decisive and principled sometimes saves us from contradictions. Too many alternatives bring indecisiveness and too few alternatives bring desperation. Let yourself have principles. Know how to say no. Believe me, you will be both trusted and respected on every subject. You will be doing the biggest good to yourselves and will be purified from contradictions.

- **Keeping emotions clean:** First of all, having clean feelings, a clean conscience and good intentions are the feelings, which give us relief. Do not let the bad feelings have a place inside you and settle there.

- **Trusting:** One who cannot trust cannot communicate; he or she is not open and cannot develop deep and strong relationships; he or she does not know how to form real friendships. However, it is relaxing to be able to trust. Unfortunately, it is not that easy to find a trustworthy person either. Despite that, you try to trust your loved ones. When you show your trust to someone, most likely that person will make an effort to be worthy of your trust. Believe me, when you cast that circle around you, both the number of your friends will increase, and you will feel better yourself.

- **Forgiveness:** Forgiveness can lift a load from us. Sometimes it feels so difficult to forgive, but in fact, the thing that people do not realise is that carrying the load of their resentments is even more difficult. You do not have to have a close relationship with the person you have forgiven; you can keep away. Still, if you are together in peace, you end up not gathering toxic feelings. You should know that you are doing this favor to yourselves, not to anybody else. Don't let yourself have any knots, which haven't been untangled.

- **Deciding:** One who is indecisive is insecure and in worry and anxiety. Indecisiveness raises problems and conflicts. Indecisive people have stomach trouble, neurological illnesses and skin problems.

- **Seeming as you are, or being as you seem:** Once you attempt to live differently than how you are or how you look, you unnecessarily put your life into stress. Take it easy; be as you are. Let whoever loves you love you this way. Remember, if you are fake you attract fake people into your life too. How can people who hide reality, pretend, always give a vision of being happy, but in fact cannot manage to be sincere to themselves or their surroundings and who possess hundreds of fake emotions, be happy for real?

- **Keeping away from lies:** Not telling a lie, but standing by that lie and being able to remember it as time goes on is difficult. For that reason, it is said that lies will be exposed eventually. Why bother nesting such a stressful archive inside yourself? Tell the truth and be free. Do not have files put together with lies; get lighter. ☺

- **Being at peace:** Be at peace, first with yourself and then with others. Do not forget that fights and arguments cannot be won. They only prolong the subject. Whatever you are going to say, say it in your own style and close the subject. The one who is right will announce their victory anyway when the time comes.

- **Curbing the ego:** You are neither superior nor inferior to anybody. We are only individuals who have different roles in this life. Do not despise anybody or humiliate them. Moreover, if you have any ego, curb it immediately and do not be disagreeable.

- **Jealously and scepticism:** Delete these feelings from your book. If there is anybody that you envy, appreciate that person, but never get into a race with anyone. Do not be jealous and do not try to be an enviable person. The most awful feelings that a person can have are jealously and scepticism. Educate yourselves about this. Whatever will be will be, in any case. Do not waste time on jealousy and scepticism.

- Paying attention to criticism: We are not perfect. We have faults, and there will be more. If people you love, respect and care for criticise you, pay attention to them.

- There is no need to be constantly defensive: Guilt gives us a need to defend. We do not have to react to every criticism with defence. Be relaxed, not everybody is judging you.

- Finding alternative solutions: Negative people cannot find solutions and they make problems bigger. They prefer getting upset, gossiping and pessimism. Believe me, those who bewail the darkness while they can light a candle to shoo it away are wasting their time. While you are a part of the problem, you cannot be part of the solution. Focus on the solution, not the problem. Spend your valuable time on what something will be like, not on what it will not be like.

- Being able to think positively: Negative thought produces negative energy, which turns into illness. Even in your worst times, if you can bring positive thought into your mind instead of worrying, and can imagine that everything will be good, you will attract those that are positive, do not forget. Of course, I am talking about a difficult thing. Thoughts will pass through your mind whether you want them to or not, but you can manage the behaviors coming from these thoughts. For example, even if a possibility of an accident or terror comes to your mind, you can lead your thoughts with consciousness and awareness and you can inspire yourselves with the possibility that everything will be okay and good.

- Getting off this boat happily: What a sweet film it was: Nadide Hayat, directed by Çağan Irmak. I suggest you watch it. In the story, the main character (Demet Akbağ), despite all the things there are making her unhappy, decides and says, "I am going to get off this boat happy!" That is, it! We need to decide to be happy and not spend life under the shadow of unhappiness. Humor, laughter, peace and happiness, or pessimism, cursing and the spread of unhappiness… In which direction would you like to use your preference? Do not forget that you live the same energy that you are spreading. You decide which kind of people you would like to attract to your side. You have control of your life.

- Knowing how to give up: Of course, fight for the things you do not want to lose. However, you might come across such things which trying would be like sinking in a swamp. Identify these situations. You can only escape from the swamp you are stuck in with your emotions, with your mind. Switch those on. To be able to let go is a virtue too.

High Acidic Emotions	High Alkali Emotions
Hate	Peace
Fear	Gratitude
Jealousy	Forgiveness
Rage	Amusement
Stress	Laughter
Sleeplessness	Positive thinking
Immobility	Resting
Using medication	Motion
Smoking	Deep breath
Radiation of TV	Meditation

Source: In some parts of this chapter, I used the book The Dialectical Behavior Therapy Skills Workbook by Matthew McKay, Jeffrey C. Wood, Jeffrey Brantley, and Cures of Happiness (Mutluluk Kürleri) by Ümit Aktaş.

Mental Health

The most important layer of being well and keeping well is leading a life away from the state of fight or flight (chronic stress) in a frame of peaceful being. Only then will the body have the chance to renew itself. In short, our state of mind is so important. If we are confused, feeling tired and distressed, then we pass on to a life, which is open to illnesses. For that reason, mental health is the keystone of living well.

The Joy of Life Where the Meaning Stops

The meaning of love is the things, which keep us going, happy and full. The life urge stops where meaning stops, and a giant gap takes its place. We either wrap ourselves up in depression and unhappiness or go in search of adding meaning to life again. Here, having people who can give this support around you is as important as being self-sufficient. If we are able to list the gratitude in our lives, it means we can fill our gaps fast. Another solution is exploring our love sources again. Being itself is a body of meanings. This miraculous journey between birth and death is a full life source. We should let our soul be fed by being.

We Are Each a Story

Today, if you stopped a random person on the street and asked who he or she is, you would hear a long story. That story would have the still-remembered things from what has been lived until then, and the things, which are thought to be okay and which they are not ashamed of. However, the story of that moment and after would not have been written yet. The pen is in your hand. The important thing is what kind of a story you would like to write. Our vision of the world, what we do, our decisions, our thoughts, the environment we choose to live in, all determine our story. In life stories which form on strong ground where we are at peace with ourselves, the very, very joyful moments stay in the mind, whereas the parts which we are ashamed of, would be more or less as if they are not there. Let us write our stories consciously. If we want health, let health be in our stories; if happiness, let happiness be there.

From Jail to Freedom / Journey to becoming an actor in your life

We mentioned that we all write our own stories. Some of those stories are those in which the person builds prison walls for himself or herself. Those never-ending multi-walled prison constructions build up with the meanings that our minds create: Judgements, labelling and assumptions.

We travel into the pit that we deepen with our own effort, think of the same things and are angry about the same things. We declare ourselves the victim and start never-ending complaints. At that point, apart from our own losses, people around us start having losses. Sometimes they come to a state of escaping from us to save themselves. In fact, the only walls in people's lives are our natural boundaries; apart from that, everything unnatural is the walls, we build with bricks that we produce ourselves.

Realising it, when we stop producing new bricks, the existing bricks will disappear without any effort.

Getting Rid of "Tired Me"...

With our worries and the threats that we come across daily (traffic, work stress, being too busy, illness, fears, etc.) our body goes into a constant state of fight or flight. This state has only one priority: Keeping us alive... All healing-renewal processes are held back while in this state. That opens the way to chronic stress and chronic illnesses. If we cannot escape from that dead-end and get stuck inside, the types of exhausting things, such as being fed up, unhappiness, complaining, not enjoying or feeling hopeless, bind us. There is only one escape, and that is accepting life as it is and living in the moment. The prescription is very simple, but applying it is difficult.

In 15 years, through the journey which I started with meditation, I tried all the different ways, like Vipassana, from dialectic behavior therapy to breathing therapy, from walking with your toes open to stopping the brain by raising and lowering the eyebrows. I have learned to establish my awareness by asking the question, "What am I busy with?" 5-10 times a day to raise my awareness and save myself from the whirlpool by asking, "Is this the end of the world?", when some things develop unwilled. I focussed on reducing the number of my relationships materially and spiritually and on raising their quality. When I gave the necessary importance to the people who I keep close to myself and showed them love and respect, I realised that my life got much easier, and people who I did not expect to became angels.

On the other hand, whenever I realised that a person's glass was full of themselves, without forcing too much I preferred to run away by saying "You are right," instead of spilling or overflowing it by trying to add more into the glass. I saw that when I am based on gratitude, even the worst moments of my previous life come to a state of getting closer without hurting or bothering. By seeing beauty, I started to enjoy life. Life turns into a wonderful place with such arrangements, which are small, but difficult to make real. I think everybody must try.

Being a Revolving Door

While life is flowing for all of us, running from one job to another, jumping from one piece of news to another, like watching a tennis match, or from one social media share to another, it turns us into a revolving door. We forget the meaning of our lives and we unconsciously start turning to wherever we are turned, by whomever. Stopping there and asking the question: "What am I doing?" and holding onto life again with awareness is the only solution for us. One of my mind tattoos is the question: "Right now, am I becoming a revolving door?" The one who is not becoming a revolving door lives his or her life agenda, and the things, which he or she believes add meaning to his or her life. Getting lost in the flow is mostly a journey into depression.

Dumping Trash is Forbidden

Being awake while living has a vital importance. At any moment, a friend or a piece of television, social media or newspaper news might dump a bucket full of trash in front of us. If we are not aware and leading a life where we have become a revolving door, our life will pass with us carrying that trash inside our minds. For that reason, by being aware we must learn to say, "Thanks, but no thanks" in the moment of such dumping. We need to be away from a lot of such trash-producing structures. Otherwise, we will be filled with a serious amount of unnecessary negative load, and that turns into a chronic pain dealing with which will get more difficult for us.

Ersin Pamuksüzer

CHAPTER FOUR

FOR MENTAL HEALTH…

- ❖ CORE (ROOT) BELIEF AND FORMS OF BELIEF
- ❖ MINDFULNESS
- ❖ TOLERANCE

"Health is not a condition of matter, but of mind."
Mark Baker Eddy

MENTAL HEALTH

BODY HEART **MIND**

The third component of our health, which we look into integrally, is the mind. Although this component walks arm in arm with emotion most of the time, the most important difference that separates them is consciousness.

Let us define mind like this: Its is a storage, a memory with abilities such as understanding, comprehending, relating, keeping recollections, dreaming, planning, constructing... According to this definition, both logic and consciousness exist somewhere inside this component. Can it be controlled? It depends on what you mean by control. For example, you cannot tell the brain not to think. You cannot say, "Think this, do not think that" either. In this sense, the mind is a component to which entrance is free and uncontrollable, whereas exiting can be directed to an extent. What does this mean? Although the thought enters the mind, it is up to the person to turn it into action, belief, behavior, habit and character, or not... We call this will. It does work which affects emotion when it is merged with the body, and the body when merged with emotion. A decisive and principled state of mind is able to choose not to go into a whirlpool and, by evaluating the body signals better, it is able to start the decision-making mechanism.

In fact, in integrated structures, examining the components one by one is only necessary for analysis. In reality, nothing holistic can be thought of without its components. Despite that, in this chapter, let us bring the mind component one step forward and see what we come across. First, let us talk about unhealthy core beliefs and the subjects of mindfulness and tolerance.

Core (Root) Belief and Forms of Belief

Look at successful people. You cannot see in any of them a mind, which is pessimistic, thinking that it cannot manage, or is hesitant. On the contrary, successful jobs come from people who can think freely, can look from different angles, and have a broad imagination and a bit of courage too. (We must remember patience and hard work in success, also.) Do the opposite. Turn your gaze on the people who are unsuccessful despite having the capacity. You will see that most of them sabotage themselves. What they put there hinders them, they do not believe the step they are taking, and they are pessimistic. You have probably heard the saying, "What I was afraid of has happened." Really, do we write life down with our own pen and then get surprised by it, or what? Have you ever seen anybody who looks at life negatively, constantly complaining, has not managed to close the past accounts yet, and worries about the future all the time, being successful and happy? Let us look for the answers to these together.

Core belief (also called root belief), or in another name "subconscious code," is the sum of our states of mind, which we send to our subconscious from the day we are born. There is no problem when we make the definition in this way, is there? However, if the core belief that we carry is formed by negative codes and affects our lives to a level at which it damages our quality of life, then at that point there is a problem. The specialists say that we avoid what we cannot dare to face; our phobias and prejudices are caused by these.

Our core beliefs are our negative experiences, negative cultural sayings that are pinned in our core without us realising, negative states of mind that we got from family or trusted ones in the close environment, even the words we internalise without thinking too much about, which are repeated constantly in media and in our social surroundings, all of which make a mark in our mind and affect our behaviours and decisions, by silencing that naïve child in our core and forming our timid, hesitant, prejudiced thoughts and sayings. Yet, we need to free that child to be happy.

One of the main functions of the subconscious is to store data. Think about what kind of things we have been sending to that storage since we were born:

"If you don't finish what you have on your plate, it will cry because of you..."

"If you don't finish your food you can't grow..."

"It's a sin."

"It's a good deed."

"God will punish us."

"If you don't work you can't be successful."

"You can't find a husband."

"Nobody will understand you."

"It's just how men are."

"You can't do it as a woman alone."
"He's man enough… He'll do it."
"Men don't cry…"
"Girls don't sit that way…"
"You can't trust people."
"Men cheat."
"I never have luck anyway."
"Bad things always happen to me anyway."
"I need money to be able to manage it."
"Everybody's trying to take advantage of me."
"The world is a bad place."
"Whatever I do, I cannot make him or her happy anyway."
"This is my destiny."
"Dumb blonde…"
"The longer the hair, shorter the intelligence…"
"…"

Don't tell me that, you didn't grow up with these or similar sayings. We might even have heard worse ones. It is good that the new generation has been brought up a bit more consciously. Is that not so?

Without us realising it, our eating, drinking, working, forming relationships, thinking and even believing habits that load a guilty feeling on us, and those which we start to send to the storage together with these meaningful (!) and threatening forms, in fact are nothing more than a bad inheritance from our parents, who actually love us so much, but who were a bit less conscious, relatively speaking. It is also a fact that without analysing why we are doing what, we will not benefit from this inheritance in a positive way either.

Of course, this is not the only way that the core beliefs and subconscious codes form. Usually, the traumas that are lived during the childhood period can cause the occurrence of these codes. For example, let us take someone who has a fear of dogs. We can definitely say that this person has either had a bad experience with dogs or got suggestions like "Watch out! It'll bite…" from his or her parents. Because no child comes into the world being afraid of animals.

It is possible to multiply these examples and even talk about examples that are more tragic. For example, how are the states of core belief moulded of a child who in his or her childhood was raped or turned into a sex slave, do you think? Or would many innocent children, who were forced to beg, used badly, adjusted to drugs and stealing, be able to find the reason to protect the same innocence in their adulthood? Who knows which experiences and belief moulds underlie different reactions, the energiser of which can be things that cannot even be dreamed of. You can guess what a woman who constantly thinks of herself as fat and ugly lived through when she was young. Let alone having lived through something during youth, today, many people who do not fit into the beauty templates that are serviced by the media are in depression.

As long as those who have these traumas do not face their traumas and throw them to the past bad memory bin consciously and willingly, and gather them carefully and repress them, it is not going to be possible to talk about a general state of goodness, because each repressed feeling will come to the surface of the water and damage our life quality.

Our subconscious is like an iceberg; it gathers so much in its tunnels. It is not lazy about holding all the necessary and unnecessary data, and when the time comes it blends it and serves it for our use, and sometimes our own reaction surprises even us. Is it not pretty annoying to know that the life we live is encoded in this data, which is coded in our mind even if we don't want it to be, and in any case is stored by means of our brain's principle of working? From time to time it is necessary to go on a detailed spring cleaning and do a mind detox.

Behavior and Sayings

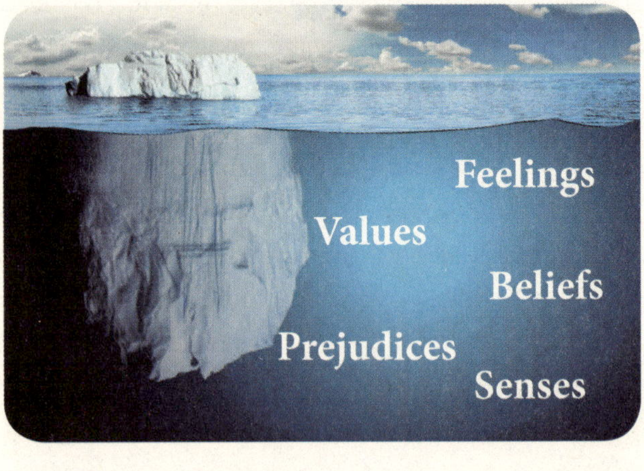

After our genetic codes, what makes all of us what we are today and differentiates us from each other are in fact those codes. The sum of negative states of mind, in other words, core beliefs or Negative Subconscious Codes, which are an important part of our mind structure that determines our decisions, our types of behavior and our position in life, is like a creeper tangled in our subconscious, a bad parasite sabotaging our happiness.

We are going to touch on what we can do about cleaning these unhealthy codes in the "Mind" component of our holistic health and happiness approach. Believe me, it is out of the question for us to live a real state of wellness without cleaning our negative subconscious codes.

How Does Core Belief Appear?

Generally, in childhood and youth, they occur/are caused unwillingly, without knowing what the results would be like. You know they are said, by mistake, just like that... Moreover, by those who love us, and whom we love...

Courage-breakers: The beliefs that are passed on by constantly being told by authority figures like mother, father, teacher, boss and master. They occur with loads like unpleasant, unskilful, unsuccessful and untalented. Even if these loads are not being put on us in some situations, they might cause us to feel guilty and take on the codes. Adults who criticise too much and are too authoritarian might bring up children who are hesitant and avoid expressing themselves. The core belief, "If I speak, I will be criticised" that occurs in the child might become a hindrance, which can appear before him or her all through life. The simplest example: Instead of giving courage to ensure that a child who likes climbing to places constantly or yearns to ride a bicycle and go skateboarding becomes a good sportsperson, constantly hindering him or her with the suggestion "Careful! You'll fall!", and when he or she falls saying, "See, I told you so!" would prevent him or her from achieving success. Brushing off the extreme targets of children with courage-breaking suggestions such as "What is it to you?" or "They shouldn't leave that job to you" will destroy the person's self-confidence. Do not do that to your children!

Direct experience: Some patterns are learned by experience. Children are pretty inclined to catching false beliefs. For example, a child who sees a repressive father or a shouting role model establishing authority at home might internalize shouting, repression and bullying and add them to his or her style of behaviour. A person who has a core belief that being quiet is a weakness and being a loser, and that shouting is power, would embrace this repressive, authoritarian style in his or her family life too and, the bad thing is, would think that he or she is showing proper behavior.

If a child sees that way: A child can embrace something a trusted adult or parent says, without questioning it. Only children? Even adults do that: Accepting whatever their trusted people say without questioning it. And then they write songs like "Cry Me a River..." Joking aside, not even questioning a little bit can bring a person to terrible places. Don't forget, every generation passes its own core beliefs to the next generation too. At some point, this chain must break. Even a simple sentence, which a mother tells her daughter to protect her like, "Good girls do not sit with their legs open" might manifest itself to us later in marriage and sex as a problem. Under many wrong beliefs that were formed in society lie these unconscious sayings, which are accepted without questioning and kept as core beliefs.

Unconscious imitation: Children can take on cultural values, manners of speaking, thinking and reactional styles very easily. For example, the father working and earning money and the mother doing the cleaning at home, cooking and dealing with washing up could take its place as a belief, which is caused by cultural values. Or to a person who constantly codes this lifestyle as the weakness of the woman, the woman doing housework at home can be coded as weakness. Yet, when each of them is examined individually it does not mean anything.

Dread and limitations caused by criticism: While some parts of our beliefs affect our ability and behaviors in a positive way, some parts affect negatively. These sayings that we hear very often, such as, "I don't know what I want", "I'm not clever and smart enough", "I don't have education", "I'm too old", "I'm too small", "I don't have time", "I have no talent", "I have little time left", "I'm short", "I'm tall", "I'm overweight", "I don't know", "What if I cannot manage: Everybody will laugh at me!" are the most common restrictive beliefs. One puts these boundaries on oneself, such as, "I'm not good enough…" Also, fear of being judged, teased and criticised pushes people to failure.

Hopelessness and the feeling of not trusting yourself also feed the feelings of running away and fear. Besides all this, the source of fear of failure is running away from the unknown. One's belief about not reaching his or her target would keep him or her from reaching the target anyway. Research shows that people usually tend to show resistance about changing their beliefs, assumptions and manners. Resistance against any type of change is because of people's unwillingness to take a risk about it. Not wanting to struggle with the unknown... If you realise, many old people find themselves inadequate about learning, especially with electronic innovations. It is easier for them to ask somebody young to do it for them. They do not learn it because they want to protect themselves against the risk of making a mistake. In their subconscious lie beliefs such as that the fixing of the failure would be so difficult and would cause many unwanted things. In other words, they close themselves. However, this should not mean that their beliefs can never be changed. The problem can be solved from its foundation when the dimension of mindfulness is raised.

We can put core beliefs into these three categories:

1. Beliefs about ourselves
2. Beliefs about other people
3. Beliefs about the world

These three categories are often one within the other. Personal beliefs have a very strong effect on the formation of the psychological problem and continuing of its existence, because to a significant extent they decide what the person will think, be aware of, care about and remember.

A strong core belief could close all the doors towards change, and thereby development. Moreover, one who is unaware of his or her core belief, far from trying to change this belief, cannot even stand to hear a new or different thing.

The Cleaning of the Negative Codes of the Subconscious

I guess the biggest hindrance to us being successful and happy in life is falling into the trap of the codes of "I cannot do." A human, in terms of his or her being and nature, should be in harmony with the universe, but because of the factors mentioned above, from time to time he or she can drift away from both himself or herself and nature. In other words, a human who stepped into the world unconditionally and fearlessly learns to be afraid, withdraw, calculate risks, and not to do because of the numberless codes, and learns to be trapped in the surrounding walls of conditioning.

If those who can get over these boundaries are the minority rebels who are heartened, encouraged or automatically question the existing situation, then they are likely to find the power to manage anything. In fact, we wander about somewhere between these two extremes. Let us only pay attention to this: The cleverest thing is to continue our journey, is to lift those blocks which are put in front of us by core beliefs before we stumble and fall down. And that is possible with a kind of mind detox.

Nowadays, many psychotherapists suggest and apply helpful methods to do subconscious cleaning, under the names, "Subconscious Transformation" or "Formatting the Brain." Scores of books have been published on this subject. These are works at the level of the subconscious, ensuring that instead of negative thinking patterns built up over years, positive thinking patterns towards the related subject are obtained, and they aim for the individual to return to his or her nature, thereby catching happiness, wealth and success. This purpose underlies bio-frequency and other subconscious suggestions and raises the individual's quality of life by cleaning the negative subconscious codes with affirmations. The main target of these works is that our mind functions for our own good again, as it did on the day when we were born. In other words, the thing we are looking for is to go back to our default factory settings.

If the same events are happening repeatedly in our lives we areprobably in a vicious circle that is caused by us making the same mistakes due to the effect of these codes. You've probably come across people who say, "I always go and fall in love with the same type of men/women" or, "I experience the same problem in every job I get." You might even be one of them. Be sure that unless we clean that core which underlies repeated mistakes, the results we get are not going to change. We will see that we proceed much faster in life when we find out what hinders us.

You couldn't have not heard this saying:
"Insanity is doing the same thing over and over again and expecting different results."
Albert Einstein

The cleverest man in the world is saying this. Let us escape from the thinking patterns, which pull us down, so that we can get different results.

Probably it would be a cliché to say that when we learn what our core belief is and how to transform it, we draw wealth, happiness and success to ourselves; but some clichés show the right direction to a surprising extent. This does too… First, we must believe that wealth is going to come. Nobody is going to force us to take it; neither will we get it by force; we can only open the paths and change our position so that it flows to us. Thus, the blockages that we live in our relationships will be unblocked. When we learn to act more positively at a much different frequency, then we will attract our surroundings to this frequency too. We will be able to express ourselves as we are, more clearly and honestly. We are not going to live by pretending; we will truly smile and be spreading an energy coming from inside. Because of this, we should understand the reasons for what we've experienced more clearly and pay attention that the same core beliefs are not formed in our children.

Did you know that, although there is not only one core belief of a person, generally all the blockages are still caused by only one dominant core belief? There are branches feeding this core belief. Thus, both the core belief and the branches of the problem should be worked on. After the core belief is realised exactly, then we realise that many of the problems that have happened to us were always caused by that base core belief.

Ok Then, Let's Clean Those Negative Codes!

It is not that easy, dear reader. How can we clean it before finding that disgusting core which has been hidden away since childhood? We can manage to go deep into our own reality and/or can get help from people who are specialised in these subjects. When we reach our core belief, we will need two things to get rid of it:

1. Willingness and determination to change,
2. The ability to think rationally and objectively.

If we have these two things, the only things we have to do are affirmations. Forgiving the ones who settled this belief on us and ourselves is a first step too. Our sentences of affirmation are going to be our new belief.

If we are to give an example:

> *"I think I have a blockage about xxx."*
> *"I think that this blockage is caused by my yyyy core belief."*
> *"I deeply forgive myself and everyone, who caused this core belief of mine."*
> *"I am releasing my core belief about xxx and choose, accept and approve of the plenitude, abundance, energy of love and wealth that will come to my life."*

Although these sentences of affirmation may seem nonsense to you at first, the positive verbs in them such as "I accept", "I approve" and "I forgive" will form a new energy in you and change your perspective. It is essential to want and believe from the heart.

Let us not forget that we summon whatever we believe in life. The things we believe coming to us is a work of frequency. That is why each situation that we resonate happens to us. That is also the explanation of the saying, "What I thought would happen, happened to me," as I mentioned at the beginning.

However, it would be beneficial not to miss one point: As much as we think positively, do whichever affirmations we want, visualise, memorise all the personal development books, and try the new trends, if we have a core pattern which spreads fear energy inside us, then it won't work for anything. I repeat: **Thoughts come true when they are parallel to beliefs**. Wanting from the heart, believing from the heart, etc. These are not empty words. It is not enough just to say, "I believe" or to just make positive talk.

The common properties of core beliefs are that they are very judgmental and critical. Negative thoughts about ourselves can completely sabotage ourselves and make our self-confidence fall unless we change them.

> Do not forget:
> *"Your beliefs become your thoughts, your thoughts become your words, your words become your actions, your actions become your habits, your habits become your values, your values become your destiny."*
> *Mahatma Gandhi*

MINDFULNESS

"Mindfulness" is another subject which is just as important as breaking the patterns.

Mindfulness is one of the subjects, which has taken the attention of philosophy and psychology. It is one of the basic subjects of Buddhist philosophy. From time to time, it is mixed up with a similar word: "Awareness." Awareness is more concerned with attention and consciousness. It is like a radar, placed in the background of consciousness. It constantly checks the inner and external environment and sends signals to the brain. In contrast to awareness and attention, mindfulness also includes remembering. One who often is grateful for his or her condition is in the dimension of mindfulness.

Can we say, "Life should be lived in the moment, and life itself is a sequence which consists of present moments"? Yes, of course, why not? However, from time to time, isn't being in the present moment mentally very difficult for you as well? Don't thoughts escape to the past or to the future? Being in denial is no use: We definitely do this; we do make The Now cloudy with future worries and never-ending vengeance from the past. What we do in fact is, without realising, not being able to live today properly by smearing our present experiences with the prejudices of our assessments about them. While doing this, the fault we fall into is not realising that our assessments are not the same things as experiences. Prejudices, those verdicts starting with "anyway," distance us from objective assessments of the present moment.

Mindfulness is, without judging, managing to gather our attention to be able to focus on the present moment...

Jon Kabat-Zinn

Yes, missing the moment that we live in by living in the past or the future is a very significant mistake that many of us make. Knowing this, are we going to continue repeating the same mistake? When sitting across from a beautiful view, is it not wasting the moment, to be worried about things that are going to happen the next day or to do the accounts of what happened the previous week, while we could be happy, having the pleasure of the atmosphere and enjoying the fact that at that moment we can look at that beauty? We all know the right answer to that perfectly well, but stumble when it comes to applying it. I accept that, it is difficult to find peace without guaranteeing the future. However, what's the problem with today? Maybe the problem will be solved if we are able to gather peaceful and beautiful memories and remember them when the time comes. There is nothing like guaranteeing the future, but there is a term which is "looking to the future with hope," and that is what we need to do. However cloudy it is today…

In fact, living life led by our thoughts, which are wandering inside our brain, our emotions, which develop in connection with them, and living with associative thoughts, is nothing more than being thoughtlessly passive and unable to manage life. There are always going to be (not having them is another subject of stress) bills that need to be paid, taxes, matters that need to be considered, problems that await solution, inconveniences, people that expect attention, jobs. Therefore, missing the moment by constantly thinking about these and ruining the moment that we are in by living in the past or the future cannot be the preference of a clever person.

Many times, we act not according to the things that are happening inside or around us, but to the judgements that we create in our minds. We try to analyse and interpret everything. We look not with our eyes, but with our brains, and even with the judgements, values and experiences formed inside our brains. It might seem to many people that this is how it should be, but the only reason that we stumble on the obstacle of our prejudices is that intensive effort of sense-making. Not managing to see the simple thing causes us not to sense correctly what is happening. Sometimes the fact is as simple and obvious as it looks, but we do not accept this in any way and look for other reasons behind it.

All the things mentioned above are the indicators of not experiencing mindfulness. So, what shall we do?

I guess it is Eckhart Tolle who explained the "Power of Now" best in his books. He says that the most peaceful way of increasing mindfulness and staying in the moment comes from putting the past and the future safely aside. He does not say to neglect the future completely. From time to time, making future plans and, if those plans fail, putting the Plan B into use will definitely work. It is not a bad thing to note the dates of the invoices to be paid in a desk diary, to write down the important days, or to make A, B, and C plans by calculating the possible situations. Moreover, you can plan just to do some planning. Even saying to yourself, "Today, I will spare a certain period of time to make these plans" would constantly prevent you from sparing that moment of yours for the future.

You will be comfortable, if you have a good or a bad plan, not to constantly fictionalise the future in your head (of course, you should be flexible and be open to the possible changes.) However, please do not exaggerate that planning business and make your lives miserable. You cannot plan your every moment. Knowing this, I know you will act cleverly. Buying the plane tickets now for the trips, which you confirmed that you would go on might be sensible if you want to catch a bargain. However, you will come across many situations in which things will not go as planned, and you will fail in those plans. Please though, do not create another subject of stress because things did not go as you planned. ☺ Also, pay attention to the saying, "If you are unsuccessful in planning, then it means you are planning unsuccessfulness!" A successful plan is one which has alternatives and exit doors, and which is flexible.

Let us turn to the past… Who knows what things we've carried from the past to now. Okay, but - we are talking to those who make accounts of the past constantly - is it not necessary that someone should live today, too? That will also pass a little later. Making peace with the past would be the best goodness that you could do for yourself. I am not saying, do not remember, do not think; what I am saying is that we should not be stuck in the past.

In addition, it is a fact that in many situations looking back to the past and taking future decisions accordingly might be necessary. We call this "experience." Experiences are not things to brush aside. Maybe because of this, people have memory: To learn a lesson and not to make the same mistakes repeatedly… You must not do business with someone who cheated you several times, or you must not call back into your life the feelings which made you unhappy; you must know how to say "No!" and even be able to make a clean break. The opposite is valid too: You should give a role in your future life to people who always honored you, supported you and were with you. Do you have memories that you could not manage to solve or make peace with? What can be done rather than brushing them, too, into the litter of the past, and being happy that they do not exist today? Throw them away. Believe me, you do not need a past, which ruins your present day at all. Do not forget, today is the first day of the rest of your life… In other words, "Today is the last day of your past life…" Shut the past down already.

Okay? Deal? Can we now finish with the subject of the past? Yes, definitely, let us close that topic, because if your relationship with the past goes further than that, if you stay there a bit too long, then things become inextricable.

So that is what mindfulness is called: Learn from past, plan the future along the main lines; but at that moment, be right there with all your being…

In other words, "Mindfulness" means being conscious of the experience of now, and accepting that. In the state of mindfulness, the thoughts and feelings are not rejected or judged, and we do not try to repress or avoid them. Positive or negative, all the things being lived in the moment are accepted in their states and set free. This is like a person externally looking at a picture, which he or she sees oneself in, instead of being only inside the picture. In that way, that person's capacity for tolerance of negative emotions like worry, sadness, anxiety and rage also increases. This method is also used in psychotherapy: By focusing on the thoughts, emotions and body in a particular way, it brings a solution to mental disorders like depression, panic attack, phobia, obsession and stress.

Mindfulness is an eastern philosophy, but it is not a philosophy, which exists just in Buddhism. It forms the foundation of existentialism, humanism and even the philosophy of Rumi.

Together with itself, mindfulness also brings the consciousness of being grateful and being grateful causes one to get more pleasure from life; try and see…

Mindfulness and the Immune System

Eckhart Tolle says in his book The Power of Now that "Being in the present moment and in the body strengthens your immune system." Moreover, he also suggests a meditation about being in the body.

The logic is this: Most illnesses creep inside secretly, like a thief who finds the house empty and gets in while we are not in our body (busy with the past or the future). I guess the body is a mischievous structure that is trying to take our attention. And when we give our attention to it, it repays us. This is the reason for focusing on the body and concentrating the attention on each organ separately during meditation.

Being in the body forms an energy shield by increasing the vibration frequency of all our energy space; everything that vibrates at a lower frequency, like fear, rage and depression, stays at a different level of reality and cannot reach us.

The more consciousness you bring to your body,
the stronger your immune system gets.

This is how healing meditation is:

Healing Meditation Focussed on Being in the Body:

Fill up your body with "mindfulness/consciousness," especially before falling asleep at night and before getting out of bed in the morning. Do the exercise below, which will take only a few minutes of your time:

Lie down on your back and close your eyes. Breathe in and out deeply and in a controlled way.

*

Focus your attention on the different parts of your body (your hands, feet, arms, legs, fingers and toes, stomach, chest and head, etc.)

Feel the life energy inside these parts intensely as much as possible. Imagining each centimetre of the body in your mind, scan it for at least for ten seconds.

*

Circulate your attention from feet to head and head to feet a few times like a wave, as if you are filling your mind with your body.

*

After this, feel your inner body as a whole and as the only energy space. Continue this feeling for a few minutes. During this time, be in existence intensely; exist in each cell of your body.

*

Even if your attention breaks from time to time and you find yourself inside a thought, do not mind it and direct your attention again to the inner body. Continue breathing in and out in a controlled way.

*

When you breathe in and out consciously, your concentration will slowly put you in contact with the body again.

*

While your breath goes in and out of your body, follow it. With every breath in and out, feel your abdomen widening and narrowing.

*

If you find visualising easy, close your eyes and imagine that you are surrounded by light. Then take in that light while breathing in.

*

Feel that this light is filling and lightening your body. And then slowly focus on this feeling more.

*

Now you are in your body.

*

Open your eyes and whisper these words to yourself while ending this meditation: "I am in my body, I am aware and I am in the moment…"

Source: The Power of Now, Eckhart Tolle

"When you start the day doing this meditation, at any time that day, whenever you start breathing in and out with control, you will automatically feel yourself in your body again. Your mindfulness will increase, you will stay in the moment and get away from worries."

Interesting; worth trying; what have we got to lose?

Pay Attention while Listening! Do not Waste Your Time and That of the One Speaking…

Most of us do not know how to listen. Do not say, "School life has finished. Never mind the rest." Even though the education period is done, learning is lifelong. In addition, we listen to answers, go forward, do business, communicate and live, not just learn.

Do you know that there are some things sabotaging us while listening? I guess most of our attention is kept by what is going on in our minds. Do you also find yourselves from time to time dealing more with the associations in your mind caused by what is said, than with what the speaker is saying? In that situation, do you sometimes completely miss what was meant to be said? If you ask me, without any exception, we all do it. When we give our attention to the thoughts inside us, we produce questions, cut listening, and focus on our question.

Also, while we are listening to someone else, if we listen and focus on what he or she is saying not just with our mind, but also with all our existence, maybe most of the communication problems that we face today will disappear. If we can silence the inner voice that we carry from the past and which fictionalises with the worry for the future, if we can keep our attention away from associated thoughts and focus, then we create the most appropriate environment for real listening. While we are listening, we should also stay in the moment and we should not decorate and change the thing meant to be told with our own experiences and expectations (with the thoughts of the past and the future.) Mindful listening is such a thing. If we can listen like that, then we can understand what the speaker means to say even more than what he or she is saying. This would both benefit us widely in every type of communication and relation and hinder us from spending our time for nothing.

Relationship Coaching

Have you ever watched those marriage programmes on TV? Everybody criticises them and finds them low quality; they say that they should be taken off and animal documentaries should be put instead of them, but certainly many people watch these programmes. Anyway, this is not the subject. Whoever wants to watch them, let them watch and whoever doesn't, let them not. What I want to point out is this: In those programmes you know that there is the matter of having dinner. Even though it is called having dinner, in fact what is looked at precisely at that point, in other words when the man and the woman are alone and listening to each other at that special moment, is whether there is any chemistry between them or not… You know there is that famous chemistry phenomenon, the one which makes the butterflies flutter in the stomach, makes the mind fly, causes a random encounter to turn into a relationship; yes, that one… What we call chemistry is, in fact, the frequency of the minds… A state of energy, which occurs from mutual interaction… And that formation of mindful mutuality happens because of a type of mindfulness.

In love, which develops naturally, staying in the moment and the level of mindfulness is very high. And when the frequency of the energy that the person spreads matches the other person's, a really strong feeling occurs. It happens by itself. Yes, at that moment everyone is happy. It is assumed that the feeling that we are in causes this happiness. Even though it is correct up to a point, it is not realised that the thing which causes happiness is actually the effect of staying in the moment/mindfulness; in other words, it is forgetting the past and the future and living the moment together with our partners at that frequency level.

When the chaos inside the mind and the communication that this chaos hinders - in other words, non-communication - manage our lives, conflict, struggle and problems are inevitable. NO relationships can develop in that way, and even if they did, after a while splitting up and conflicts would be experienced.

The Management of Emotional Pain

It seems like the pain we suffer from increases as we mentally go away from the moment we live in… So it does. Living in the past is one issue, dealing with the future is another… Better to leave aside dealing with the already lived (past) and that which has not yet happened (future), so that this torture finishes. ☺ Let us be focused on the present time a little.

Oh, by the way, let me say something else: Sometimes there can be a tomorrow that we have to decide on today. That job is today's job, not tomorrow's. We cannot wait until the last day, saying, "We'll take care of it once the time comes." I do not mean this when I say, "Do not constantly live tomorrow in your mind!" Of course, we may have to decide about tomorrow today (in this situation it is today's job, not tomorrow's anyway.) Even if there are uncertainties, let us broaden the alternatives about the decision that we might make, in case the uncertainties become real; let us be flexible, but if we are overwhelmed with worries, continuing to wait for what the unknown might bring at the end of the time that we spared for, this would not be right.

There are people who are a tapestry of so many things. I am sort of one of them, I confess. When there are many points of interest that the person needs to focus on, no subject is unbearable. While I am dealing with the job I have in hand, I get the chance to look at the other one from outside. One is even able to spread the emotional troubles over time in this way. And believe me, life becomes a more joyous place. The only inconvenience of this state is sometimes thinking that you can't catch up and so having the feeling of neglecting some subjects; believe me, even that is an upper-class problem. ☺

Suggestion: Don't get stuck; pass it, and you can come back later…

Psychotherapists also deal with this. Their purpose is to decrease the emotional pain in the person they are giving the therapy to. They know that as much as our attention is spent on mental activity our daily life can be unbearable. Mindfulness provides us with the environment in which we can make more objective comments which helps us to see things clearly by taking us out of our state of "not being able to be in the moment."

Suffering from pain can develop in different ways: Stress, worry, depression, behavioral problems, conflicts between people, confusion… Some of our pains are existential, such as illness, old age and death… We also have more personal pains like our obsessions, which are the main motif of our personality. The difficulties that we experience personally can be caused by past situations, today's conditions, genetic tendency or by other factors which affect each other. Successful therapy is that which can change the point of view of the person about the issue that he or she is suffering from. Of course, if we do not let the problems in our lives make us upset, then our pain will decrease, but isn't this the subject anyway? If we can manage not to allow sadness and pain, then there won't be a problem in any case. Knowing what to do doesn't mean knowing how to do it. People say "Never mind." Okay, I won't ever mind, but how do we do that??

Mindfulness is an ability, which ensures that we are less reactive towards the things happening at that moment. The main approach is about holding back the subject of our pain for a moment in order to be able to stay in the moment.

Mindfulness and Acceptance

Acceptance is the opposite of avoiding, rejecting and refusing. It is the courage to come face to face with reality. Letting the resistance go towards reality is the first step taken to deal with the problem or the subject as it is and searching for ways to fix it.

Acceptance should not be confused with surrender or giving in. Seeing the existing situation as it is, is important for the problem to be defined correctly. First, the problem should be defined, and its existence accepted so that the solution can be focused on. This is the logic of it.

In many psychological illnesses, people come across thoughts and emotions which they have difficulty accepting. Apart from the inner life, such as thoughts and emotions, physical illnesses, death, economic difficulties and problems in work or family life can also become sources of stress, which are difficult to accept. It can take time. However, it is impossible to get to the solution without acceptance.

Often people think that the only way to escape the discomfort that thoughts and other stress sources give is to demolish them. Unfortunately, many of these stress sources occur because of conditions, which are not under people's own control. Disregarding the things that we cannot eliminate is nothing more than deceiving ourselves, like assuming that the things we do not see do not exist. Mindfulness involves approaching and accepting sadness, worry, anxiety and fear, rather than avoiding them. Accepting does not mean appreciating the unpleasant things or having a passive attitude against everything. On the contrary, accepting means making space for unpleasant incidents, people, situations and emotions, and coming to reconciliation with them, even if it causes discomfort.

We observe that the people who have a tendency to accept reality, problems, success and defeats as they are, are the people who can manage to stay in the moment and develop mindfulness, and who do not postpone their problems but prefer to solve them. This is a healthy and conscious mental act. Mindfulness is perhaps the first condition of living.

The sources that we suggest you watch:

Spiritual ascension.

The speech that Anita Moorjani made in TEDxBayArena: Anita is a cancer patient, who went into a coma in 2006. Anita's story about consciousness, mindfulness, love and smiling, which tells about the astral journey she went through while in a coma.

Source: In a part of this chapter, I benefitted from Matthew McKay, Jeffrey C. Wood and Jeffrey Brantley's Dialectic Behavioural Therapy Ability Teaching and Eckhart Tolle's book named The Power of Now.

TOLERANCE

There must be some among you who have read Victor Hugo's Les Misérables. In the story there lies an unforgettable lesson about the subject of tolerance. You may remember the incident of Jean Valjean, who becomes a galley slave because of stealing bread and spends years in misery, and who then steals the silver candelabras of a bishop who had taken him in and given him a place to sleep and food; when he gets caught however, the bishop saves him from the guards by saying that he himself gave the candelabras to Jean Valjean. It is a great example of tolerance. The bishop forgives and tolerates him, despite the fact that Jean Valjean actually had stolen the silver candelabras... Here there is an unbelievable lesson! The bishop is an experienced and reasonable person who knows that what pushes a person to evil and mistakes can be the unfairness that the person has come across in life. This story gives us messages about evaluating, using initiative, forgiving, generosity, wisdom and tolerance. Of course, I am not saying let us forgive all the thieves, but there are such incidents in which tolerance can rehabilitate people much more than criminalisation. The tolerance in this story turned Jean Valjean into a grateful person. If he had been convicted again, that great story which makes you read the rest of the book may not have existed at all. What happened next? I say you should read it.

I have an anecdote like this: I guess I was seven or eight. My mom had bought me a bagel and I was walking, holding her hand and eating it. I had taken just one or two bites when someone who was passing by grabbed the bagel and went. I was holding it so tight that a part of it was left in my hand. In my child's mind, I was so angry at that seizure. My mom said, "I wish you had left all of it to them." I didn't understand what she was trying to tell me then... I couldn't understand such hunger that makes someone grab the bagel of a child from his or her hand...

Tolerance is not shutting your eyes and not caring or accepting. Maybe we can say that it is forgiving by understanding the underlying cause of some events, which are difficult to accept. Yes, tolerance is trying to understand and respond to what happened with forbearance. This term is such a friendly word, which contains within it forgiveness, positive values, hope, generosity and trust. Sometimes there is no need to object to things which we are convinced are not harmful. We can decide for ourselves with our own free will. This, of course, does not clear the offence nor make it acceptable, but we can have a heart when we are judging. Let us take children who make noise when they are playing. If there is nobody around who is ill or sleeping, then there is not much need to upset or try to silence those children; we can show tolerance, can we not? As I said, showing tolerance does not mean accepting everything that is happening. On the contrary, it is being result-focused by seeing the facts, being aware of the situation for better or worse, and not being stuck on small details.

Have you ever seen a wise person who is furious and makes angry statements: Divisive, negative, speaking in high-pitched frequencies and shouting? Okay, I accept, I could first ask if you have ever seen a wise person before at all! Putting the joke aside, you at least know some people who have an image of being wise from books; for example, Buddha… Can you even think of the experienced and sensitive wise people, who came to the world to spread beauty, knowledge and love, in fact being the ones who are wrathful, divisive and who make angry statements? No, these two - I mean wisdom and rage - are two terms, which cannot stand beside each other and are irreconcilable. On the contrary, whatever happens, a wise person's image contains calmness, simplicity, tranquillity and love. We can bet that the common direction of those people who show a path to humanity with their words and philosophies is that, whatever they say, the first thing to come to mind would be "tolerance." Tolerance is their natural way of life. In fact, maybe this term, which should be taken as an example and leaves everyone with inner peace, requires us to behave more in the way of forgiving, rather than not seeing the mistakes.

Anger is the heaviest load that a person can carry. And forgiveness is the type of behavior that takes off the weight off one's own shoulders… So, tolerance is an approach which has the ability to always forgive, and which opens its arms calmly to incidents, issues, and even mistakes, and searches for solutions.

Tolerance is not a term about not seeing the mistakes, but about forgiving the mistakes that you see.

Tolerance is not forgiving or giving permission all the time either. It is not denying the incidents and facts. In fact, it is not an action. In fact, it is possible to say that it is an inaction, because it does not require any work. Intolerance, which is the complete opposite, is an action. An action of competing and proving your rightfulness... It is possible to say that an intolerant person strives far more.

Intolerance destroys the properties of human beings, who are social beings, living together and dealing with differences on common ground. It hinders communication, which is the greatest ability of humans. Approaching any event with intolerance is also against nature and the universe. Nothing can be denied completely. Even the strictest rules have exceptions.

Tolerance is a choice...

We have to say that, in fact, we should also approach intolerance with tolerance. Because whatever the incident, thought, thing, subject or behavior is, we should be able to tolerate it. We do not have to accept it. However, this is also a fact:

> *If we extend unlimited tolerance even to those who are intolerant, if we are not prepared to defend a tolerant society against the onslaught of the intolerant, then the tolerant will be destroyed, and tolerance with them.*
>
> *K. R. Popper*

Tolerance is a type of a philosophy, thought and action. Generally, it is inherent in easy-going people with a lot of experience. It is a property of people who have been around, rather than those who are at the beginning of their life and still just learning everything, and it is definitely contagious. It is an approach, which comes from family. It is also seen in children who are brought up by tolerant parents.

> *Conflict is one's greatest disease, whereas tolerance is one's greatest remedy.*
>
> *Voltaire*

Putting up with different ideas and being able to listen to them is also an act of tolerance. We do not have to agree with the idea, but it is appropriate for a civilised person to be able to point that out in a calm style. Democracy is a type of governance, which started entirely from this philosophy. It requires toleration of different people's opinions.

> *In order to have faith in his own path, one does not need to prove that someone else's path is wrong.*
>
> *Paulo Coelho*

I repeat: If we use tolerance with the meaning of bearing even the incidents that you do not accept, then that will be our biggest mistake. We should either remove the unacceptable subjects from our lives or solve them. Otherwise:

> *After a while, you deserve the thing you tolerated ...*

This is a universal rule: Intolerance is the first sign of a lack of education.

> *An ill-educated person behaves with arrogant impatience, whereas truly profound education breeds humility.*
>
> *Aleksandr Solzhenitsyn*

We are individuals who live with our decisions and with behaviors, which occur according to these decisions. We are society. If one makes a mistake, we all suffer the punishment; if one behaves rightly, we take the reward together. Being tolerant is also a behavior that is an example to society, but there is a sensitive point: We should also now say "Stop!" to the same extent.

> *Keeping in mind that what we face is just our own stupidity, fault and evil, sometimes we should approach every stupidity, fault and evil with tolerance.*
>
> *Arthur Schopenhauer*

One of those subjects that needs to be shown tolerance is religious beliefs, as befits the name "belief." If it was something proved, then its name would be "knowledge." We should respect and be tolerant towards the believer, as long as he/she does not exaggerate and does his/her worship with respect to others' limits.

Religion is like a pair of shoes. Find a pair suiting you and put them on. However, do not try to make me wear your shoes.

George Carlin

If we are to carry out a mind detox, then we cannot leave out tolerance.

Different People of the Same World

Sometimes, seeing what different worlds people who share the same places with great pleasure belong to is in fact stimulating, and explains these nonsensical goings on in the world. Recently, on a Sunday, while I was walking between the Istanbul districts of Emirgan and Kuruçeşme, I observed thousands of different types of people and reflections of lifestyles. Of course, this mosaic condemns us to very different views. While some of us do not throw trash on the ground, some of us throw it into the sea, which is more difficult to clean, and when you warn them they can say, "What's the problem? I haven't thrown it on the ground, but into the sea." Or a young girl who attentively covered herself can be the object of her boyfriend's loving caresses in front of everybody. This colourfulness is the best side of life; but to endure that, you need to be either mature or apathetic. Those who care live through serious inner storms, and their life quality decreases with the hard hits. I personally am one of the ones who chooses to observe and just say "Okay" comfortably, because I am not attached to evaluating or judging.

Ersin Pamuksüzer

CHAPTER FIVE

ESSENTIAL SOURCES OF LIFE

- ❖ WATER
- ❖ SUN
- ❖ SLEEP
- ❖ BREATH
- ❖ LOVE
- ❖ SEX LIFE
- ❖ BIRTH
- ❖ MOVEMENT
- ❖ SMILING
- ❖ FEEDING
- ❖ AVOID GMO

WATER…

"There is nothing softer or more fluid than water,
and yet it is so strong that it can drag and
tear apart anything that comes in its way."
Lao Tzu

Water is our Most Valuable Nutrition: H2O

While there is a Magical Formula like H2O…

If approximately 70% of the human body is water, then a human's renewal must be by water too. Pour away the dirty water and continue your life with clean, clear water. What a hopeful, healing promise… In fact, this is true : While a newly born baby's body is approximately 74% water, as we get older, this ratio decreases to about 60%. So, we lose our water as the years pass. Just like nature itself… If I start with "Our sources of natural water…", then the subject goes in another direction. So, better to go back to water inside the human body. ☺

None of the tea, coffee or other drinks replace water. However much liquid we take into our body, we have to consume water separately, and just as "water." Maybe mineral water or spring water can replace water partly.

So how much shall we consume? Everybody says something different… The right answer to that question is this: It depends on the situation. More or less 40 ml. per kilogram. Water is our normal daily need. Therefore, if someone who is 50 kilograms drinks 2 lt. of water a day, it is beneficial. However, there are times of sport, detox, illness, etc.… I mean, there are situations in which the need for water increases or decreases. Well, the best way is to make sure you recognise your body and figure out the amount of water you need for yourself. Do not go under 40 ml. per kilo, and the upper limit is up to you. Well, I should mention that drinking too much water is fatal… Remember that if you drink too much, you will not leave any mineral in your body and the kidneys will be in shock.

There is also this method: Look at the colour of your urine. Light-colored, water-like and non-smelly urine will tell you that you drink enough water, whereas dark yellow and unpleasant smelling urine is a warning sign to "Drink water!" - don't forget.

Why Water?

In the body, water is mostly in the blood and then in the muscle tissue. Well, be careful, because even 3% water loss means health-threatening dehydration. As well as preparing the ground for getting ill, it hinders healing too. If the correct daily amount of water is not consumed, the density of the blood will increase, and its fluidity will decrease; this will hinder the transportation of oxygen and nutrition to the organs, increase the acid ratio in the body and invite all the illnesses created by those acidic environments that we mentioned at the beginning of the book.

On the other hand, in a body, which consumes enough water, everything will run relatively like clockwork. Transferring nutritious substances to tissues, digestion of these, the functioning of the kidneys, occurrence of the smooth structure of joints, getting rid of toxins; in short, water is the most basic and essential nutrient that we need for all our vital organs to function.

"We never know the worth of water till the well is dry."
Thomas Fuller

The Magical Formula of Life

People who consulted Anuj Srivastava, an Indian-origin cardiologist living in the United States of America, insisted that he give them a mantra. So, he gave this mantra as a magic formula:

"If you do this thing that I tell you, you will visit a doctor very few times all your life, maybe never..."

1. As you wake up in the morning, drink about a litre of warm water so that your body becomes alkaline. It isn't even important whether you brushed your teeth or not; drink the water...

2. 40 minutes after your meals, drink hot water, because some of the fats in the body dissolve in hot water.

3. Always drink your water sitting down... Otherwise, you treat your joints badly.

After saying these, our dear doctor mentions the pH value of the water that you should drink. He says that the pH value of the water you drink should be 8.5-9.5. However, wait a minute here -He is suggesting this, but some other doctors' approaches are completely the opposite. For example, they do not find drinking a litre of water in the morning realistic as they believe it is a bit of a strain on the body to drink so much first thing in the morning Secondly, a pH value at this level would ruin the flora of the stomach and make digestion difficult. Therefore, most doctors support lightly alkaline waters (7.4 - 8.0) and water consumption without exaggeration, spread out through the day. To be honest, this is the most logical and the easiest way...

There are Flawed Views…

Well, our doctor says that, but if you are not a sportsperson and if you are not without water in a desert (if you are, never do this anyway), instead of drinking a lot of water at once, spread the amount of water you need to drink throughout the day. This is a lot healthier. We should not exhaust our body with too much of anything.

Okay, I accept that there is a logic in drinking plenty of water as soon as you wake up, and forty minutes before you go to bed, and forty minutes after dinner. As soon as you wake up to alkalise the body, which has been without water all night; before going to bed to support the body, which will be without water all night; thirty minutes before meals so that the digestive system works more comfortably, and forty minutes after meals so that food can be digested in the stomach acid comfortably… However, this should not mean exaggerating.

Does such a question as "The body is a wonderful mechanism, it will remind us that we are thirsty anyway, so why should we make a schedule for drinking water?" come to your mind? If not, it is better to know: Yes, we need to bring drinking water to a conscious and controlled state, because specialists say that the feeling of lacking water does not work very healthily for people who do not have a habit of drinking water. They say, "Because of the consumption of tea, the body will think that the thirst is gone, so it will be late in giving us the signal of thirst, and this will leave us extremely thirsty. Thirst is a body signal given by reflex; however, the body could forget to give this reflex. So, we should have the habit of drinking water even if we are not thirsty."

Magical Liquid

The benefits of water do not finish there. Look what kind of things I came across while researching the subject of water:

- It's very good for headaches because the underlying reasons for many pains is dehydration.
- Water is important for the hands and feet, which do not get warm. It speeds up circulation and provides warmth.

- It is good for cracked skin, dryness and hair. A moisturised skin will keep its youthful look.
- It is good for intestine and kidney functions.
- It helps in getting rid of toxins.
- It is good for allergies; getting rid of extra toxins helps in getting rid of allergen substances.
- It helps in getting rid of oedema from the body.
- Knowing you are doing theright thing for the body also gives comfort psychologically.
- It postpones ageing.
- It keeps the body full.
- During summer, it is easier for the body to get rid of toxins by sweating and it's actually good for the skin as it keeps it moistured.
- What else do you want? ☺

Important note: Water might not always be our life source. In situations (renal failure, cirrhosis, heart failure…) where the organs, affected by oedema and extra acid in the body, gather water, the amount of water we consume should be arranged under the control of a doctor.

What is Alkaline Water?

pH is a unit of measure, which describes the degree of acidity and alkali of a solution. It is measured on a scale from zero to fourteen. In full, it means "Power of Hydrogen"… The term pH was defined by a Danish chemist called Søren Peder Lauritz Sørensen in Carlsberg Laboratory in 1909.

The descriptions in chemistry, on the other hand, is like this: "Alkalis are bases which dissolve in water. The amount of Hydrogen (H+) and Hydroxyl (OH-), which ionise inside water define acid and alkali. If H+ ions are more, the water is called acidic; if OH- ions are more, it is called alkaline. When they are balanced, then it is called neutral."

The pH scale is between the measurements of 1 and14.

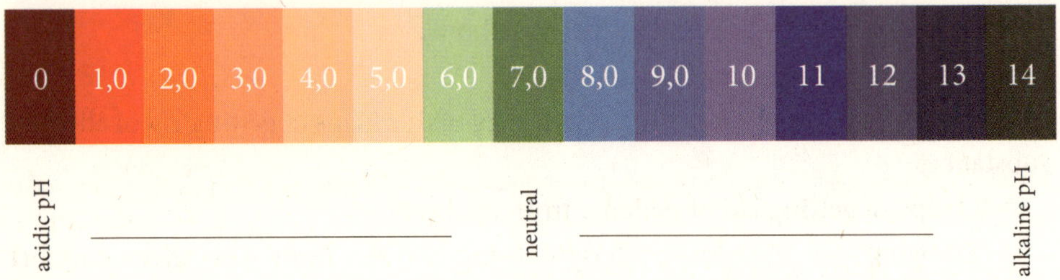

Specialists suggest that we choose waters with a pH level of 7.7 - 8.0. They say that more than that would affect the stomach acids and postpone the process of digestion. Let us remember that we cannot be free from all body acids by just drinking alkaline water. (I remind you that the pH value for the vital fluids of our body function at their best is 7.35 - 7.45.) Therefore, sorry Indian-origin cardiologist Anuj Srivastava, but that is the one that makes sense for me too.

The Philosophy Created from Water is not a Lame Philosophy!

Our life-source, water, has inspired many thinkers. These words, in fact, guide us about life too; water contributes not just to our body's health, but also to our emotional and mental health… It is very difficult to think of a life without it. Here are some of those words…

There is always an exit, a solution:

> *"Take some water in your hand and tightly close all the gaps around your palm. Make it a fist. That one drop of water would find a gap to get out despite all your care and precautions. Human should be like water in life. He/she should be versatile and dynamic about always finding a practical and alternative exit against danger and despair. The mind should flow like water."*
>
> *Bruce Lee*

The human soul's need is not just at one time. It requires permanent solutions, not palliatives…

"If the water source does not erupt from your own soul,
you cannot get rid of your thirst."
Goethe

It is how we look at things, which brings us to deadlock. We fall into difficulty not because there is a problem, but because we cannot deal with it…

"You don't drown by falling in the water; you drown by staying there."
Edwin Louise Cole

The same thing may change according to the place and situation…

"Water becomes a river if it flows, a waterfall if it falls,
and a lake if it stops."
İbrahim Sediyani

Being humble will not decrease your value…
"The virtuous person follows and forms his/her life as in the example of flowing water. Water gives life to all beings without exception; water is always in low areas; nobody searches for it in high lands. Therefore, the path of water sets an example for the accomplishment of spiritual virtue."
Lao Tzu

It Is Very Easy to Make Alkaline Water at Home

Nowadays, everybody knows these methods and applies them, but let us remind you. You can use these methods to make alkaline water at home:

1. Add lemon slices to your water!

The reaction of lemon, which is an anionic fruit, together with water, creates an alkaline effect.

A whole washed and sliced lemon is ideal for two litres of water. So, one slice of lemon is all you need.

2. Add bicarbonate to your water!

You can add a ¼ teaspoon of bicarbonate to a glass of water.

Attention: If you are on a sodium diet, doctors do not recommend this.

3. Use Alkali Drops!

You can buy alkali drops from a pharmacy. Two drops are enough for a glass of water. Ask your pharmacist what this drop contains because it may be a substance, which can increase sodium.

Important Note: I researched this question, which immediately comes to mind about lemon: "Okay, it is known that lemon contains citric acid and beneficial nutrition in vitamin C. However, how does it happen that by adding acid to water we are able to make it alkaline?" I would be surprised if you did not ask this question. The easy answer to that question is this: Nutrition being acidic or alkaline is nothing to do with the effect it leaves in the body after it is digested!!! ☺ It means chemical reaction. At this point, I should go into what anion and cation are, how they get into the reaction and transfer an electron to each other, and what is "ash-analysis technique"[17]; however, do not torture me with this. I have already passed my limit! ☺

17. **Ash-Analysis Technique:** A technique, which shows, after being burnt, what kind of components nutrition produces.

SUN...

"Who looks at the sun cannot see the shadows."
A Brazilian saying

Do not Shoot at the Sun

A guy, being bored of the sun, takes his gun out and bang bang, shoots at the sun twice. Not a joke: This apparently happened. I hope it is some different kind of humor. Of course, it must be, what else can it be? ☺

I did not want to pass the subject without pointing out that our other most valuable nutrition is the sun. It is our joy of life. A catalyst of some vitamins becoming beneficial for our body... A source that gives health and beauty... Of course, when it is taken properly and sensibly...

While writing about the ways to get rid of depression, I said, "For the sun to work we need to take vitamin D. The opposite is valid too: We need the sun for the vitamin D we take to work." Now I want to widen this subject a bit more: Sun is a factor that brings vitamin D in the body to an active state. Only together with the sun does this vitamin become a part of our happiness. Just like for a plant to be able to photosynthesise, the definite rule is sunlight, it is of course not surprising that the source of our life plays the main role in making living creatures' body-functions work.

So, let us have a look at whether we get the right amount of sun. Since cancer cases have increased, who tells us to protect ourselves against the sun and provides sun-creams, in a range of factors, to the market? Yes, correct answer: The Medical Industry... As well as already having malnutrition, we've also started to see the sun as an ogre. Well, are they wrong? Of course, not. The only thing we must do is be careful how much time we spend in the sun....

Lying down in the sun for hours, if we stay until our skin is blistered, crinkled, shedding and permanent blemishes have occurred, then we get the harm of the sun rather than the benefit of it. However, it is good to know that we need our life-source, the sun, for at least twenty minutes a day, and direct sun too, without any protective cream, when the sunbeams are at their straightest angle, and when our shadow is shorter than our height... Why? Because those UVB beams, which play a role in the synthesis of vitamin D, occur at that straightest time; that is why... However, if UVA beams, which occur when the sunbeams come horizontally, are taken for too long, that is carcinogenic. Therefore, we can cover ourselves with protective creams before we are exposed to those beams.

The protective creams that we put on our body are barriers to getting vitamin D. Vitamin D, which dissolves in oil, goes away when you have a shower. We will have tired our body for nothing.

We need the life-source, the sun, for at least 20 minutes in a day,
and direct sun too, without any protective cream,
when the sunbeams are at their straightest angle,
and when our shadow is shorter than our height...
But, that's it... More is harm, a lot of harm too...

SLEEP…

"No small art is it to sleep:
it is necessary for that purpose to keep awake all day."
Friedrich Nietzsche

Here is another essential nutrition source for health: Sleep… Have you ever paid attention to the fact that children who are bad-tempered and causing trouble put their fingers to their mouths, rub their eyes and look for a place to snuggle down after a while? The trouble they cause would increase if sleeplessness continued. Do you think that itis different for adults?

Think about the pleasure you would get from a comfortable, uninterrupted, quality sleep. When you wake up, the world and the colors look more beautiful; many problems that are bothering you are smaller, offenses become meaningless and troubles are lighter. Why? In fact, everything is the same as before you went to sleep; what changed is your rested mind and point of view. Isn't it because of that that they say "Before your important decisions, definitely sleep on it for a night and then decide"?

Do you remember, at some point, on TV, during the time when those game shows went really crazy, there was a show, something like a stamina contest? People were standing for hours while touching somewhere, and the one who gave in was out of the competition. Speaking was allowed; sleeping or sitting was not. Hours passed, a whole day even, and another day… The longer the hours went, the more the nerves stretched and the level of talking nonsense increased. Oh, the fights happened between them… Then you saw whatever you were looking for: People crying, going into depression… The programme had greatratings. Result? The last person standing was the winner, despite the fact that they may have been hallucinating, having a nervous breakdown with dark circles under their eyes and had many cells erased from the brain. Are you asking what he/she won? Well, if you ask me, in return for losing health in that way, there cannot be an achievement, but I think there was a money award at the end. Anyway, okay, these shows are fine, but is it worth destroying the brain cells of this many people just for ratings? ☺

Suffering from lack of sleep all the time is a problem, which needs treatment. Not sleeping enough affects the brain so negatively that we become terrible mentally, physically and emotionally. Sleep is needed for the healing and the functioning of the body. Like a mobile phone without any charge, living creatures also renew their life batteries by sleeping. The more regularly they do it and not break this habit, the more advantage they get in life.

Lack of sleep can badly damage us, far more than we expect. It may make us take the worst decisions, may cause hallucinations, takes the ability to fight against life away from us, makes the immune system weak, causes anxiety, and is the trigger of some mood state disorders. (Example: Bipolar disorder.)

It is said that the average sleeping time an adult requires in a night is 7-9 hours on average. There are people who are okay with less and can get used to it, as well as the ones who cannot come round in under ten hours. If it is assumed that each body has a rhythm of its own, then troubles begin when someone slips down in his/her own rhythm. It is like the body starts an alarm mechanism and opens the door to every type of illness. Brain functions do not work as they should. Concentration ability decreases. It lowers the performance, as it slows down learning. Moreover, the next day, when starting the day, the blood pressure of the person is higher than normal. One gets angry much more easily,sense ability decreases, and the tendency to think negatively increases. Pessimism, and even depression, always come together with sleeplessness. Youngsters who study all nightand go into an exam are not doing a very good thing either. I know a person who fell asleep during an exam because of not sleeping enough. Exceptions do not break the rule, and we cannot avoid the exceptions. In fact, sleep should be examined according to each person, too. The need for sleep can differ a lot from person to person and in different periods of the same person's life. There are people who always sleep for a short time or for a long time. A habitual amount of sleep is important because, in research, no difference was seen in the situations of people who sleep a lot (for example more than 9-10 hours a day) and people who sleep little (for example, less than 4-5 hours a day). It seems like the definition of enough sleep should be defined according to the habits of the person.

We know that the brain secretes many hormones during sleep, like getting taller and growth hormones in kids, and digestion and appetite hormones in grownups... The interruption in development of people who do not sleep enough is not surprising at all and, in parallel to that, the digestive system getting slower and also the increase in appetite caused by the need for energy. If youare not able to sleep, you are tired and angry, and on top of that, you are hungry as hell, too. Therefore, when you find food, you eat like a small hippopotamus. You put on weight, you are still annoyed, and your brain does not work efficiently. You have a stupid face from sleeplessness. You misunderstand everybody. You are in a fight with yourself. Your eyes lose their brightness. Emotional life is terrible and there is no sexual life left at all anyway... Is it worth it? Put your head somewhere and sleep... We loved it when we were young. The sentences "Let's not sleep tonight..." or "I was up all night again" were very popular in our college years. Funny...

Believe me, the brain keeps an account of sleeplessness in some way. If you lived through a period, which required less sleep, then there must be days like a payback when you sleep a lot so that both your body and nervous system rest and calm down. People, who are angry, rushing and living as if somebody pressed the panic button, should be recommended healthy sleep before any tranquiliser or antidepressant.

Suggested average sleeping times according to age:

- Newborn babies: 16-18 hours.
- Between 3-11 months: 14-15 hours.
- Ages 1-3: 12-14 hours.
- Ages 3-5: 11-13 hours.
- Ages 5-10: 10-11 hours.
- Ages 10-17: 8.5-9 hours.
- Adults: 7-9 hours.

In fact, the sleep duration is about the quality of sleep. Even a half hour snooze during the day can save the rest of the day. Many business people I know snooze on the couch in their offices after lunch; it is well-done. It would be great if everybody had that opportunity and snoozed 20-30 minutes during the day...

Much research done on anti-aging talks about the benefits of the melatonin hormone, which is secreted during regular and quality sleep. It is stated that because quality and regular sleep rests the body, it takes the brainwaves to the theta level and provides healing that can postpone ageing. It is sensible when you think that the body recovers in sleep… Now the tale of Sleeping Beauty came to my mind. How easy was it for that princess, who slept about a hundred years and lost nothing of her beauty to find a man who was a hundred years younger… And a prince too… ☺

When the sunlight gets less towards the evening hours, our body produces the sleep hormone known as melatonin. The secretion of the other hormones inside our body slows down and our body temperature starts decreasing. It is good to create an environment for the transition to sleep when melatonin starts to be secreted. The benefits of sleeping without missing the secretion of that melatonin are too many to list. Moreover, if possible it would be very good if the teeth are brushed and one goes to bed at the same time every night, because not missing the natural sleeping process is important for quality sleep(Milk and a mom's kiss? A kiss would not hurt, of course.) ☺ I don't know if you ever read a couple pages of a book, or play one last game on your phone before you go to bed, but then when you put your head on the pillow, if your eyes are closing, lucky you! (While sleeping, I suggest switching your phone off completely. If you say that there is an alarm and you won't be able to wake up the next morning, then put it on flight mode at least. We should at least be away from radiation while sleeping.) ☺

Let me mention "Circadian Rhythm"[18] a bit. It is a name given to people's biological clock, which runs in a 24-hour cycle. It is affected by factors such as light and body temperature. It affects body temperature, renewal of cells, hormone secretion, appetite, physical and mental fitness, and the quality of sleep. Our circadian clock, which is placed in a part of our brain, is stimulated by the light coming from the retina and sets itself. Thus, our body starts moving with the information it gets from our circadian clock and secreting more serotonin, adrenalin and cortisone hormones in daylight. Acts like waking up in the morning and starting to move are possible simply because of these hormones. People who

---

18. **Circadian Rhythm** is all of the biochemical and psychological behaviours of plants, animals, funguses and cyanobacteria in a 24-hour period. As a term, "circadian" is said by Franz Halberg to derive from the Latin word circa. Circa means (often preceding a date) "approximately."

have been on a journey with a big time difference will know that their sleeping clock as a messed up stage while trying to adapt to the place's lightness or darkness. Known as "Jet lag" - tiredness, sleeplessness, change in the eating routine, balance disorder and disruptions in the digestive system - it postpones the adaptation to daily life and tires out the body unnecessarily. In such situations, perhaps, with the help of melatonin pills, a conscious sleep arrangement can be made according to the sleeping order of the time zone you will go to. For example, if you are traveling to a country with a 12 hours' time difference, with these pills you can arrange that you get sleepy in the sleeping hours of the geography you will be in.

When I learned the effect of sleep on our digestive system, I started sleeping more happily. While sleeping we are doing a very big favor to ourselves. Why? Because particular immune cells increase during sleep, and also because the sleep hormone melatonin is a perfect antioxidant that fights free radicals and other toxins.

We should also mention the effect of getting up early on our health and development. Specialists suggest waking up early so that sleep can be healthy and we can rest enough. The ancients say, "Do not let the sun rise on you," and they advise us to get up before sunrise. We should listen to these ancient people; they knew something, so they said it. Moreover, research shows that sleeping again after waking up in the morning to some extent damages the repair that had been made through the night. It means sleeping too much can be as harmful as sleeping too little. The harm it brings are lethargy and slowness in blood circulation which can also cause eating problems. If we listen to our biological clock and obey the directives it gives us, when feeling tired if we do not resist, and when we wake up if we get up and provide the body with its vital needs such as eating, moving, etc., then we will be doing good things for our body's health in natural ways. Let us listen to our body's messages.

The belief is that sleep is a time-period that is needed for the brain to rest. On the contrary, sleep is the time when the body is busy with resting and repairing, not the brain. The research done on the electrical structure of the brain show that, during sleep, our mind works at least as intensely as when we are awake. The only difference is that the tasks performed during day and night are different. However, the brain does not need to stop to rest; it needs to relax. The thoughts being free… So, we can say that sleep is a kind of brain detox.

In the past, when we were younger, we thought that sleeping late, even not sleeping at all on some special days (such as New Year's Eve Night) was a good thing. As if that was not enough, when ending the evening, here in Turkey we regarded going to a tripe soup restaurant and gulping down a sheep's head followed by sheep's head and foot soup as a ritual. In our circle of friends, there would even be those who ate eggs with sausage. Simply: Youth. We learned later that the actual name for eggs with sausage eaten at that time was "***go to bed and die,***" the name of the head was "***come out dead tomorrow***" and, in Turkish, tripe (işkembe) soup already sounds like "***torture (işkence) soup***"... ☺ Do we need to say that it is dangerous to sleep just after eating at night? It is an important reason for waking up tired. When we sleep with a full stomach, although the body should be in resting mode, because the digestive system cannot work properly it will not be able to digest the food enough, and this will cause toxin production. Moreover, will the brain send the command to work to the digestive system or the command to rest to the body? It will be baffled and run into a contradiction. Neither will the body rest enough, nor will any good come from that digestion. In short, before sleeping, our digestion process should be finished already.

We should sleep hungry...

Are You Suffering from Insomnia?

Here is a simple recipe for you:

Lavender + Rose + Melissa + Linden + Sage + Camomile + Mint +...

While passing a herbalist, buy these ingredients and have them in your kitchen. When necessary, make tea with them. It gives such a sweet sleep that you cannot open your eyes, I promise... ☺

P.S: Also, do not forget after reading this book that herbalists should be our best friends, the second place that we go often… The first one? I don't know either. ☺

Keeping the Rhythm of Sleep

It is possible to provide the rhythm of sleep and to keep it as follows:

- Sunlight is effective on our circadian rhythm. We can set the natural rhythm according to that and benefit from sunlight.
- Let us sleep in darkness as much as possible. Sleep hormones like darkness.
- It is said that for a good sleep the best time is 10:00 pm. Do not believe it. ☺ Nowadays, not even children go to bed at that time. However, it is still good to apply this: Especially if our working hours are specified and we do not have a chance to sleep during travel, we should allow ourselves eight hours of sleeping time. We should do this favor to ourselves for our daily performance. It wouldn't be bad to start life with an advantage of 1-0 in the office over the people who slept less, would it?
- If we are careful about sleeping at the same time every night and waking up at the same time in the mornings, and keeping evening meals light, we will not have either weight or sleeping problems… You know I said that while sleeping our digestive system gets slower? Well, sleeping just after eating also increases the risk of reflux, I'm telling you.
- I have experienced something in my life: Whatever I listen to or watch before sleeping stays in my mind. If I listened to nice music, I wake up humming it; if I watched a stressful TV programme, I find myself busy with that. You know, the brain does not stop. If the last thing I watched will continue in my brain as a dream, knowing this, why am I doing this harm to myself? Who needs those zombies during a beautiful sleep?
- Allow yourself to start the day beautifully: Starting every new day opening our curtains and taking in the sun.. If we have the opportunity, we should do a few stretching exercises while taking fresh air outside for a few minutes. Before having your morning tea have a nice stretch. ☺

If we are resisting sleep, read and see what kind of things we are sending invitations to:

- Stress
- Brain shrinkage
- Weight gain
- Insulin resistance
- Maybe diabetes
- Premature ageing
- Alzheimer's
- And even cancer…

Quality sleep provides a quality wakeful period…

BREATH…

"There isn't another thing respected among people like royalty. Royalty isn't worth as much as a healthy breath in this world."
Sultan Süleyman the Magnificent

If the purpose is to stay in Alfa brain waves, living happily and in peace, reaching that hormone that we look for in our natural healing environment and getting pleasure from life, then here is the simplest method: Breath…

Breath, which is known as "Nefesh" in Jewish mysticism and "Nefis" in Sufi tradition, has been a subject for all religions and mystical disciplines.

I have emphasized the benefits of breathing for our health in different places of the book. We say that it will increase the oxygen's access to the cells and that by calming us down it will take our excitement and stress under control. But how?

Specialists say, "The description of proper breathing is baby breathing." Breath, apparently, should be deep, flowing and holistic, like a baby's breath. In addition, it is said that breath should be both in the abdomen and chest. When looking at a baby sleeping in peace, oblivious to the world, one says to oneself, "Definitely there must be something that they do right and we cannot manage. Otherwise, we could sleep that comfortably too." In this case, we do not breathe properly…

If we look at the subject from that point of view then we can say, "Proper breathing is baby breathing: Let's do what they do," and then leave the subject. Yes, babies breathe in directly into their abdomens and do not wait while breathing in and out. Their breathing starts first in the abdomen and then spreads out through the body like a wave in an ocean. Well then, can we do it, and should we? If you like, let us look into what the breath is, and then decide…

What is Diaphragm?

The diaphragm is a name given to the thin and wide group of muscles, which separate the abdominal cavity and chest cavity from each other and is placed between them. If you wonder what it looks like, here it is:

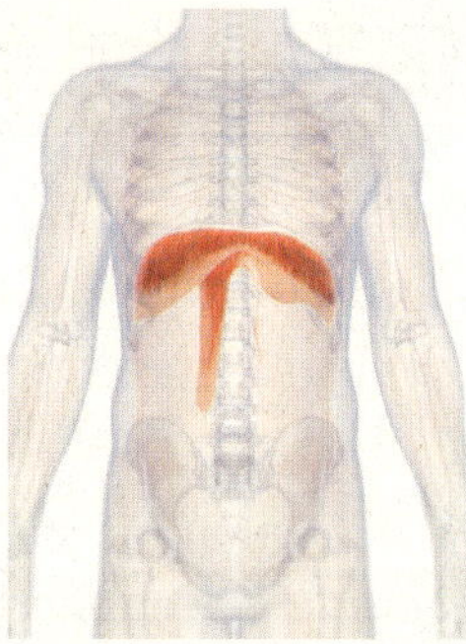

I said to myself to open the high school first-grade book and look what kind of a thing that breath is... The book says, "The respiratory system is a system which lets carbon dioxide (CO_2) gas in the blood change place with oxygen gas (O_2). In the respiratory system, the oxygen in the air, which is taken from outside with the help of the nose and mouth, comes to the lungs after passing the pharynx, larynx and trachea, respectively." Then this question comes to my mind immediately: Okay, fine; while this many organs take part in respiration, why is there a group of people who talk about the importance of breathing, insisting on "diaphragm breathing" and, as in every subject, why are doctors and breath therapists up against each other, why is everybody busy throwing mud at each other, and who is going to tell us the facts about this subject?

Showing no laziness, I attended a few seminars. All of them were by valuable people in their areas. They have books on this subject and talk in seminars; they explain the importance of breath to your body. However, to me, the most acceptable among them was what Tuğçe Tuna, a lecturer in one of the main art branches of Performing Arts (and head of department) in the Social Sciences Institute of Mimar Sinan University of Fine Arts, said about breath and diaphragm.

I am presenting my own understanding and summary of the seminar:

What! Diaphragm Breath? What Other Breath Can There Be Anyway? ☺

First, let us be clear about this subject: There is not a separate kind of a breath called diaphragm breath, because what we call breath is already something which occurs with the contraction and relaxation of the diaphragm muscle. Without the diaphragm, there would be no breath. The diaphragm muscle is a group of muscles just under the lungs. In recent years, tpeople have refered to it as an organ but it doesn't matter what you call it.. If we have such an understanding, we should correct it immediately: We do not breathe for the diaphragm, we breathe because of the diaphragm. It is our choice to just circulate it inside the lungs and let it out or to make it reach the abdominal area too. When we breathe more deeply, together with these muscles' movements, the abdominal area of our body fills with air too.

When the diaphragm contracts, it has the effect of a pump and lets air go into the lungs. In that area, expansion in the muscles among the vertebrae also occurs. These are the muscles, which are quadratic helpers to breathing. The diaphragm is also important in the functions of the neck muscles. How we use the diaphragm can cause situations in which we cannot use the full capacity of the lungs and our energy in daily life. In the breathing process, when diaphragm muscles, spine muscles, and neck muscles are used at full function, if the lungs are allowed to fill with air completely, then it means good breathing has taken place. It means, when we breath through the diaphragm consciously, we ensure it works properly and let the lungs fill with air completely.

Tuna says, "In fact, our body knows what way it should breathe." For example, in evasion and escape mode, or when we force the body's performance, when we run and we need more breath, then our breathing quickens. It would be nonsense to make the count of taking that breath at that moment into the diaphragm in eight goes and let it out in however many goes. The body already knows to arrange the breath according to circumstances. We can only talk about calming down our body and bringing it to rest mode, and while doing that to make it easier by benefitting from breathing.

In fact, the purpose is to balance our inner pressure by breathing in a more effective way. To change that, we must first know where we spoil the breath. You know we were saying that all of us breathed properly when we were born? Well, I will touch on that now; babies live in Alpha mode. Because they are constantly in a resting state, their breathing is calm and deep. In them, there is not any mental or emotional hindrance to spoil the breath. That happens in time. Whatever happened to us happened when we were around 2-3 years old; the mind started working. We met with authority. We started to spoil our breath because of our parents' breathing habits, their impositions, our experiences, the belief systems that we produced, the meanings that we ascribed to those beliefs and mindscapes;

in short, together with pollution. Well, what can we do from now on? If we can manage to put thoughts that are more constructive in the place of belief systems and negative mindscapes, and by increasing the capacity to breathe, if we learn to breathe properly and apply it, then can we make our breathing flow properly again and enjoy the comfort it brings? What is proper breathing anyway?

I think proper breath is the breath, which is most beneficial for the body. If you want, instead of "proper breath," we shall call it "the most beneficial breath," because there is no such thing as wrong breath. The body is a miracle that can provide what it needs automatically from outside, so how can it make a mistake? Only the mind makes faults. This is my definition. Being in the state of consciousness, when is the body in the position of resting and recovering itself best? The answer: At low frequencies (the conscious is closed in Theta and Delta) of the Alpha mode… Therefore, we can do the most beneficial breathing for our body (it means the calm and deep kind of breathing by which we can send oxygen all through the lungs) in Alpha mode, by meditating and in such deepness of breath as when the diaphragm can circulate it inside the stomach and lungs. When we say proper breathing, in fact, we look for is this condition…

When we disconnect consciousness while breathing, we generally keep the breath shallow and in the chest area. Because we cannot use the diaphragm muscle consciously, we either know the benefit of using it or do not believe it, whereas when we learn to use the diaphragm muscle, we do not just massage all the organs in the diaphragm area, but also relax our nervous system because of it. That is why they recommend breathing using the diaphragm muscles to people who are nervous and carrying out nerve-control in that way.

Singers, dancers, performance artists (especially theatre performers) and sports people know the importance of using the diaphragm muscles effectively. By means of these muscles, with a little effort they can use their voice in a more effective and powerful way. Moreover, conscious breathing relaxes the heart and moves our life energy. There are also articles saying that this kind of breath supports the digestive system and excretion. In addition, it is confirmed that it activates the serotonin hormone. Therefore, this directs us towards a more positive and constructive emotional state than the state of negative emotions and thoughts. Do you not breathe in deeply and let it out when you are bored?

In summary, being in the condition in which we take the most beneficial breath is already the name of the thing we try to catch in life… I call it meditation mode.

Catching the calmness and peace in that mode and breathing deeply and in control is one of the methods by which we can feel stronger, more energetic, clearer, calmer and more decisive.

I even reached the information that the kinds of cancer, which are common nowadays have a connection with breathing, in such a way that, in fact, cancer finds the right environment for itself in situations where the oxygen level in the body is very low. When we also count stress, malnutrition, immobility, alcohol, cigarettes, fast food and environmental pollution - do we think a life that invites cancer is a good one, or what?

So How is Beneficial Breath Taken?

1. While breathing, first the diaphragm together with the stomach, then the lungs will fill with breath.
2. Although breathing in and out starts consciously at first, later it will become automatic and be deep and constant.
3. Together with breath, we should change our belief structures, think positively and support this therapy psychologically too. We should not allow the energy flow to cut thoughts in our minds, to control us. That affects our breath directly.

It is said that this mentioned breath (whatever you want to call it: Proper breath or beneficial breath) also affects sexual life in a positive way. With point-pressure and affirmations applied together with the breath, taken into the abdomen, activating the root chakra, which is the energy source of the physical body that lets us have healthier relations sexually. This is the logic of it.

In fact, it seems like with proper breathing it is possible to become able to deal with every kind of trouble: Health, work problems, losing weight, being relaxed psychologically, being able to use your voice properly, sorting out your love life, keeping energetic and young, detox, psychoanalysis, fear and anxiety problems, lack of sexual desire and whatever comes to your mind... This actually is not a miracle; it is just because breath exercise is a holistic therapy. As I said, when creating the conditions of meditation and consciousness together with one's suggestion ability, they get stronger and the feelings that are tiring and upsetting for the body can be left behind with breath therapies. It means, in short, the purpose is to gather the right conditions together. To breath alone is not enough. The purpose is just to raise your mindfulness level by focusing on the breath and getting lighter by affirmations.

Hiccups are a regulatory reaction for the breath. Do not try to cut the hiccups. When your inner pressure is recovered, they will leave you. Sneezing is the same… Never explode yourselves by closing your ears and nose! ☺

Everything is Everything: How did They Break Away From Each Other?

When we look at life, we come across the fact that everything in the world is connected more or less, from somewhere. As a man who took a systems engineering lesson at one time, I never have forgotten, "The effect of the butterfly which flapped its wings in Hong Kong on the Frankfurt Stock Market," which was told in the first lesson. In short, we are creatures who live together with (including the ones we like and do not like) nature, birds, bugs and each other. While living, without forgetting this, we should think, "From which corner of each thing we do, where are we nudged? And what happens there?" Some bonds are strong, such as family, workplace, friendship, and national feelings. However, some are weak, such as the bond of one of our citizens, working in nature in a rural area, to the American Dollar. One of the strongest bonds in the body is between breath and emotions. It is very strong and has an immediate effect, because in fight or flight oxygen is necessary energy production at the cellular level. For that reason, generally, on the way to mindfulness, the easiest success comes with the following of the breath. Living everything, the moment and the breath, with a holistic approach, is a quality that we would want our God to have destined for all of us. In recent years, I put myself in training to be "constantly mindful." Godspeed my way. I also recommend it to everyone. A mindful life is lived fully.

Someone without mindfulness and Wise-Mind abilities in his/her pocket, by being very sensitive, touchy etc. and living negatively, can drag himself/herself to a crash.

Ersin Pamuksüzer

LOVE

"When the power of love overcomes
the love of power the world will know peace."
Jimi Hendrix

I said to my daughter, "There cannot be a living thing that love cannot connect to life in the world... Wait, this is a good sentence, I will write it in the book."

"This may not be valid for all living creatures, mom. Love a shark and see then if you can be connected to life?"

"Even if I don't, the shark may get more connected to life because I love it; how do you know? I can be a good dinner for it. Moreover, loving a living creature doesn't have to be about touching it." ☺

"Well then, to connect a depressed shark to life, what do you think the love you show it should be like?"

"Hahaha! Okay, fine, I cannot be as quick as you with words. You're right; I think it's better if we don't touch some living creatures while showing them our love." ☺

This conversation with my daughter continued for a while. The subject had come up because of the badly conditioned (broken leg, dirty and timid) street dog that she took from an animal shelter and turned into a happy animal by loving it. She loved it, fed it, protected it and did everything for it to get well. I always objected to its sleeping with her in her bed and the fur it shed in the house, but now, I approach even these with such understanding... The fur around can be sorted by just switching on the hoover, however, there is no value like my daughter giving happiness and receiving it back. ☺

P.S.: I observe the peace and happiness of the love that she has towards animals in her life. My respect for all kinds love is big. Now, I only object to her desire to bring home every street dog she sees, but I do not think that my objection will be very effective one day, and I will find myself trying to live with an army of animals in our home, which will be turned into Noah's Ark. ☺

Crouch Down and Spare Time to Stroke a Cat!

A child does that; a child who has been brought up by her family with love towards animals starts life loving animals, people, and nature. Until he/she has been frightened, is harmed and his/her love is abused… We adults simply want to regain that love-state and that feeling of being unprejudiced, carefree and in a secure environment.

What kind of a phenomenon is love that it leaves an endless energy to every type of living? What kind of a source that it adds all physical, psychological and divine vibrations to our constitution? What kind of a healer that it mends all wounds? Would there be any reason to live in this world without it?

If we call love a frequency, then there is no point in explaining it to someone who has not experienced it before; in words, it is not possible anyway. Even if you do not verbalise it, love is a dimension that you feel. Expressing your love to a living being can only be reinforcing the love you can show to them. The words "I love you" are only valuable together with acts and the frequency that has been felt or someone made to feel. On the contrary, it is ordinary…

Love is freely willed and unconditional. To love someone or something, that person or thing does not have to love you back. Even if you cannot name it, in the base of the love you feel there will be something that your body chemicals know. There may be many factors underlying it: Liking, pleasure, trust, warmth, satisfaction, etc. However, the feeling of love does not need a description by itself. Everything living or lifeless that you can feel this feeling towards are your precious things.

Love is the most powerful healing power. It raises the bond with life and gives the joy of life. We should not restrain our love, just like our smile and touch. In addition, not to lose our love, we should look after our loved-values and protect them. Love, which is taken for granted and for which we have lost mindfulness is like the flowers that have not been watered, used badly and been wasted. Each love which we water and nurture, flowers.

We wrote at the beginning, *"Those who had loads of love when they were kids are lucky, because the most valuable nutrition a child can get when growing up is LOVE. In fact, it is the most valuable nutrition that any living thing can have. Love teaches people tolerance. Giving without expecting anything in return, attention, patience, too… It's not a coincidence that a lack of love underlies the individuals who create conflicted societies today."*

Love is perhaps the reason that the world is turning (no, I'm exaggerating, but not that much.) ☺ Think about it: How empty and meaningless everything would be without it. Unfortunately, in the daily hustle, how little time we spare for the main thing we should spend time on. How many are we who can show their love by crouching down for a kitten and reaching a hand without being afraid of getting scratched or dirty? How much time do we spare for a baby, flower, nature, lover, mom, dad or child? Well, that is another subject that we should raise our mindfulness towards if we want to live the healing, beautifying and pleasing pleasures of love and be bonded to life more; then what we have to do is to be mindful towards it and protect it.

Love is our source of freedom, our shield that gives power. Nobody can take it from our hands; only we can leave it. If we have love, we can burn down all the connections that limit our acts.

Love is our heaven. It is the only value that increases the more we share. Lack of it feels cold, fades all the colors and quiets all the sounds. Lack of love leaves one without protection against the powers filled by negativity, such as fear, sadness, illness, and hate.

Although love is an emotion strong enough to connect all people and create a brand new culture, why do we behave in the world as if we have forgotten this term? While love can bring all creatures to a vast harmony together, instead why do we act with rage and hate, which are a lot more tiring and separating? Is rage easier for us? Does it need less effort? Maybe because we have lost our mindfulness, instead of approaching with love we prefer other ways. Many matters push us to feel negative feelings for the one across from us. Getting angry, we take the easy way and expect a quick solution. The difficult thing is to approach even a fault with love and affection and to fix it. Love brings life a perfect unity. It causes us to perform informative behaviors and exemplary acts.

Look at people who are serene, calm, self-confident, worry-free, at peace, trusting, at ease, positive, sociable, free and happy. You will see that among their common traits there is the holding of the energy of love.

There is an important reason that I include the energy of "love" in the essential sources of life. In our search for holistic health, this energy, which has both emotional, mental and physical healing properties, is in fact our essence. In fact, it may be the most precious term that adds meaning to life…

SEX LIFE...

"Making love is the sensual and spiritual dance of female and male..."

Making love is the sensual and spiritual dance of female and male... When there is emotion in it, pleasure becomes more and increases. Although the reason for that is psychological, the result is holistic. The opposite is valid too... It means good sexuality will increase the feelings towards the partner.

Let us have a look at what sexuality brings us to our holistic health approach. This natural phenomenon, which all living creatures do with an instinct for reproduction and the continuation of the bloodline, is also a pleasure source for humans (and some animals.) Moreover, this phenomenon of pleasure has been standing out so much in people that we can say that sexuality has gone far beyond its basic reproductive purpose.

According to the holistic approach, sexuality being able to have psychological and physiological integrity can only be possible if it is lived together with a partner to whom you have positive emotional feelings. "Making love" is a reciprocal act. At its roots lies the verb "love." What I mean by "healthy sexuality" is a natural thing which sex generates from mutual love and attraction. I'm not talking about a one-sided deception.

Yes, sexuality is good for health both hormonally and psychologically, and as a movement. As follows:

Hormonal Benefits

- Because of the pleasure-giving endorphin, which is secreted during sex, worries disappear. Endorphin is known as the natural morphine of the body and terminates the problem of sleeplessness.

• In addition, oxytocin, which is a happiness-giving hormone, is one of the basic hormones related to sex. This hormone, which causes contraction of the uterus, rises to five times more than its normal level during orgasm.

• It improves the sense of smell. Prolactin hormone, which is secreted during orgasm, stimulates the smell-center of the brain and so, after regular sex, the sense of smell will be improved.

• It postpones aging by regulating the hormonal levels.

• It keeps the immune system strong, again because of hormones.

• Aches decrease because of the endorphin secretion (natural morphine) during orgasm.

• The testosterone hormone that is secreted during sex has positive effects on the bones.

• It decreases period pain. It also regulates period times.

• It increases libido. After sex, the testosterone hormone, which raises the libido, increases. So, this hormone stimulates the sexual drive again.

• According to research, it decreases the risk of prostate cancer in men.

• The DHEA hormone, which is secreted during the whole process of sex, is a derivative of an androgen hormone, which is secreted by the adrenal gland and which decreases both in women and men in relation to aging. DHEA increases the sexual desire, postpones ageing, protects from depression and strengthens the muscle and skeletal structure. This hormone goes up to five times its normal level during ejaculation and orgasm.

• Even the sexuality of the couples, who had a good sex life before can have a hitch for a while. The reason for this is mostly the prolactin hormone. Women who have given birth withdraw from their partners for a while via the force of their hormones and concentrate on the baby. The sexual desire, which has been lost after the birth can be brought back to its previous state with a regular sexual approach.

• It decreases vaginal dryness.

Blood Circulation and Movement Benefits

• Sexuality lived with love is good for the whole body. It is an activity; it is plenitude.☺ Regular sex prevents weight gain. When you take into account that a half hour of bedroom pleasure burns 200-250 calories, is there a more joyous sport than that?

• It decreases the risk of stroke and protects heart and vein health. Research shows that the risk of heart attack falls by half for men who have sex regularly every week.

• With regular sex, because of vaginal and pelvis vein circulation developing well, the problem of vaginal dryness, which occurs especially after the menopause, decreases in prevalence, because vaginal wetness occurs from the vagina's own vascular structure.

• It regulates body warmth and tension.

• It causes wounds to heal quicker.

• It puts the body in shape. During sex, many muscles of our body and our skeletal system work in coordination and do intensive exercise.

• It heartens the body. Strengthens the pelvic muscles. During sex, many muscles situated in the pelvic area work in coordination. In that way, bladder, uterus and intestine prolapse, which are generally seen in women after menopause, decrease. During sex and orgasm, the rise in the blood-build-up in the pelvis area causes the tubes and ovaries to function healthily.

Psychological Benefits

• Decreases depression.

• Increases feelings of love and bonding.

• Increases our self-confidence. Satisfying our loved partner physically and emotionally makes us happy and causes self-confidence in ourselves. In that way, you start loving yourself more.

• Happy sex reflects on people's whole lives, emotions, and thoughts. Sharing pleasure and the joyous state that the hormones give makes us happy for a long time.

Except for these benefits, there can be many psychological benefits; sexuality with a disliked person against one's will, would destroy the human psychology.

Sexuality is a completely natural phenomenon that needs to be lived according to its natural flow, together with respect, love, and empathy towards the partner's preferences, too.

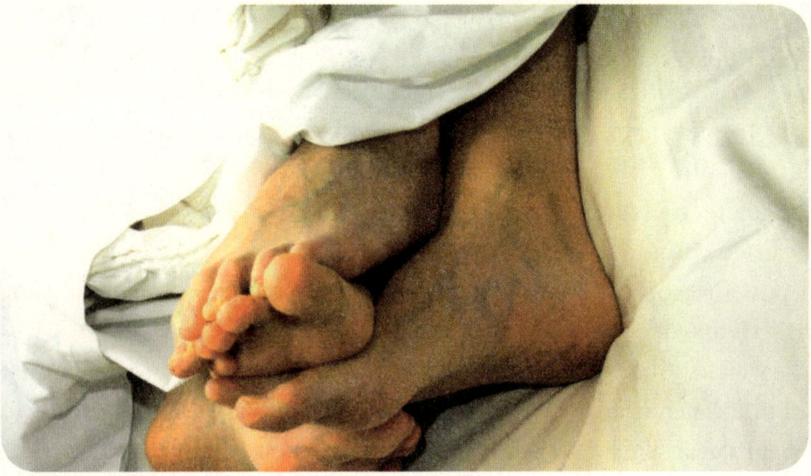

If you have a partner, live the joy of togetherness for your health, happiness, and strength… I guarantee that you will not lighten the troubles of life by talking, shouting or sulking, but by going into your bedroom and closing the door. ☺

The hanky-panky that you have with your lover, is the most beneficial and pleasing wonder of the world. Live sexuality with pleasure.

***

Years ago, I used to write for a magazine named Capital Brave. Looking through the archive, I found one of my writings:

DO NOT HAVE SEX WITH SOMEONE YOU DO NOT WANT TO BE LIKE...
(Tibetan Philosophy)

Have you heard about Tibetan medicine? Or have you ever come across a specialist who diagnoses and treats according to Tibetan Philosophy? I have. Believe me, I do not know how it happened, but I saw what I will write now with my own eyes; read it and you will be surprised.

Years ago, a ringing in my ear that showed itself even in quieter environments occurred. First, I paid no attention to it, thinking water must have leaked in, sleeplessness must have affected it, that it must be from stress, etc. Realising that it was not going away, I went to an otorhinolaryngology (ear, nose and throat) specialist. After checking my various parts, he directed me to a neurology doctor. Well, that doctor, may he live well, after his inspection told me that I would need to go into all the magnetic diagnosing machines (MR, Tomography, X-Ray...) that there were. I did what he told me. I spent a lot of money. Result? A huge zero. The heartbeat inside my ear was just the same: Bonk! Bonk! Bonk!

In the whole process, as well as not having a result which would be worth all that money that was spent, those great, great professors believing not me but those hi-tech devices, and because they could not see the symptoms, saying, "There is nothing wrong," hurt my feelings. The philosophy of "if the device says so, then it is so," must be a Western medicine thing. The more I said, "Don't say that though, there is something," the more they counselled me to see a psychiatrist. I listened to the advice. I went there too. As you can guess, the doctor prescribed me an antidepressant. "Well, so what, I will try it too," I said to myself, and used it in despair. Ooohhh, I felt so comfortable and beautiful...You cannot even guess. My feeling of worry disappeared. Although watching the world from behind a smoke curtain, I had become a sweet person who did not get angry.

What about the ringing in the ear? It stayed the same. Bonk! Bonk! Bonk!

Just when I was saying to myself, "There is nothing left to do, I must get used to living with it," I came across one of my musician friends, who by a miracle had met with Tibetan medicine while face to face with a risk of going deaf, and had recovered. He introduced me to the doctor who had made him well (I'm not giving details: it would be an advert. ☺)

It happened just like this:

I went in. The doctor was sitting at a table and he invited me to just beside him. On the table there were two models, one showed a woman's and the other a man's anatomy, a white paper, and a pen. He/she did not even ask what my discomfort was. He/she held my wrist and started to scribble something, which I guessed to be Chinese, on the paper in front of him. (P.S: Until that moment, I had neither filled in a form, nor given information to anybody except my name and surname while making an appointment.)

He wrote on that paper my blood group (and that was right), the illnesses I had had before (and he knew all of them even as far as at which age I had had them) and everything happening in my body at that moment and started reading them to me. Before I told him, he told me that the reason I had gone there was the ringing in my ear. Saying to me, "One of the veins to the brain is blocked, but there are other things that we need to sort out before that," he wrote a detailed prescription for me. Apparently, I was underweight and this and that was lacking in my body… He did not even discourse on the subject of ringing in the ear; he just wrote a prescription for that too.

Well, saying prescription, it was nothing like acetylsalicylic acid; it was things like eggs that were put in olive oil, cloves of garlic that were crushed, vinegar that was applied to the head that we call folk remedy… Had I done all that? No. Had the ringing been continuing? Yes.

I had got used to living with the ringing. 6-7 years had passed since then. I said to myself that I wished I had listened to him. What could have happened if I had gone to bed, applying that garlicky liquid to my head for three months, as he suggested… My kids and family, my colleagues and social environment would have got used to the smell coming from me anyway… ☺ So, I decided to go to that doctor again. I made an appointment.

When he/she saw me, he said softly to me, "Because you did not do what I told you to, here you are again, aren't you?" I was shocked. He had recognised me after all those years. He gave me the same prescription again. "I cannot charge you," he said. "However, if you do not do what I say again, do not come near my sight again…"

I tried to do what he said for a while, but could not bear it for more than three days. My musician friend applied the treatment that was given to him and was healed, but me… Ear ringing? It continues as before… Bonk! Bonk! Bonk!

In fact, the things I am going to explain are not these. I have made this introduction just so that I can explain how extraordinary but real the diagnosis and treatment with Tibetan philosophy is. I do not know what its secret is, but I believe in Eastern medicine with all my heart (I do not apply some prescriptions, but that's different. ☺)

Now, let us come to the business: Tibetan philosophy says, do not have sex with someone that you do not want to be like… Do you know what your private energy causes during sex? Have you heard that like two cables full of energy tied to each other, your aura and your partner's are tied, and you experience an energy flow during it? If you are unaware of the level of the physical or mental fussiness of the person that you are integrating with, accept the risk of the big trash of a psychological breakdown that it will leave on you. In other words, if you do not know the personal things of the person that you have a fling with, the kind of people who see this as a score or hunting may leave you an emotional wreck, instead of giving sexual satisfaction or pleasure, be careful! The reason that the people who set their sexual lives on polygamy carry mess, pollution, untidiness and no peace in their auras is that.

Your frequency of having sex means having a deeper and a stronger bond with your partner's aura. Having each other's energy in time will cause you to have similarities, not only emotionally, but physically too. This can be both in a good way and in a bad. Imagine the confusion of someone who has polygamous relations, carrying the spiritual properties of everybody he/she is together with within his/her aura, and transforms in fact to everything and everyone except his/her own higher self. Choose your partner well if you do not want to grow older as a person whose karma is messed up without realising it and who experiences a decline in every moral and material aspect, because all the negative energies (emotion, thought, belief) that he/she received are getting in his/her way, with a polluted aura, and with a ruined life energy.

I am not the one who says this; Tibetan philosophy does. ☺ The inference is: Do not have sex with the person you do not want to be like!

Love,

Selda Terek

P.S: The part in this writing "Do not have sex with the person you do not want to be like" is inspired by the site Spiritual Quantum and www.instagram.com/dusunenakil

Sex and The Relation of Man & Woman

Although allegedly I do not understand much about sex and emotional relationships, I am showing the courage to write my opinions about it. Man and woman are very different structurally. Man is a hunter in his nature and woman, although there are some points of view that do not accept it, is a provider in her nature. One is annoyed if there is an issue that he could not solve, whereas the other talks about an issue just to share, not so that it is solved. The man who does not understand this will throw himself into the solution pit and be branded with, "you do not understand," and rightly so. On the other hand, when the hunter comes home, he wants to hide and cool down. However, a shopping list may be waiting for him at home. Avoiding it with "Yeah, yeah… Whatever…" is another death pit. If couples understand each other's needs and adapt to these, then they create successful relationships. The book Venus/Mars is an old but a good source on this subject.

For sex, lately, they say that sex that is robotic and when not dressed up with emotions, is not very good for health. It means, when the subject is sex, the parties should approach each other willingly and filled with love. Of course, the term "love," in my usage, means unconditional love, but it should be interpreted in the frame of absolute "wise mind." Unconditional love without any verification many times ends with disappointment, and mostly this is true for the person who wants to be protected.

In addition, there are hormonal urges. Man is the champion of testosterone, the more he solves and wins, the more his joy hits the peak. On the contrary, the woman is poor in testosterone, and instead of winning, giving life, sustaining life and everybody living well makes her joy hit the peak. In short, in this chaotic world, it is difficult to have a healthy relationship; may it be easy for us all.

Ersin Pamuksüzer

BIRTH

"Miracle..."

I think birth is the most surprising issue in this miracles lark. Of course, science explains what happens and how, but it is impossible not to be surprised each time, looking at the miracles that science explains by its acrobatic manoeuvres, and not to admire the balance of nature.

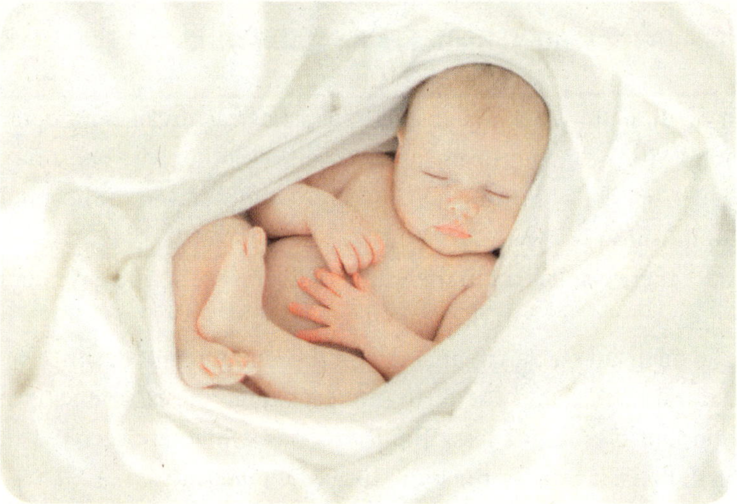

I won't waste time with explanations such as, "To continue the bloodline, by the means of the sperm of the male meeting with the female's egg..." etc. etc. They taught us something in biology lessons and we all know how a baby comes to exist... Science can explain how one living being comes to exist through another, and the subject of the incredible love towards that being and the bond with protective links; however, what I actually wonder is what is the reason for this madness? Anyway, not going in those aspects at all, once more raising my hat to these miracles, I would like to continue my words.

In a holistic health approach, while explaining that everything natural is good, I would like to talk about the benefits of being born and giving birth in a natural way, too.

Natural Birth in the Miracle Land, Earth...

What is a natural birth? It is, after the process of 38-42 weeks of pregnancy, together with automatic contractions, the baby coming to the world through the vaginal route. The alternative and the unnatural one is the operation that we know as caesarean.

Natural birth has benefits for the mother and the baby. Such as:

The Benefits of Natural Birth for the Mother:

- First of all, natural birth is an event, whereas caesarean is an operation. So, when you take the healing process into account, a mother who had a natural birth can go back to her daily life more quickly. She does not stay in the hospital for long. The risk of infection is lower.
- Because there is not a cut in the womb of the mothers who gave natural birth, they can give natural birth in the second pregnancy too, whereas it is a big risk to give natural birth after a caesarean. A rip in the womb might occur.
- In natural births, after the birth, the probability of experiencing risks such as infection and bleeding is less. The hormones, which are secreted during the natural birth make it easy for the mum to accept maternity.
- Problems like post-natal pain are far less compared to caesarean for women who give natural birth.
- The "death ratio" is less for mothers who give natural birth.
- Even the pain of contractions during a natural birth is important to understand the birth. It also provides hormone secretion.
- Straining during natural birth makes the pelvic muscles stronger.

The Benefits of Natural Birth for the Baby:

- Natural birth is an ability granted to women from nature. It is a process, which is natural but fragile, painful but brilliant. After natural birth, the mother heals faster compared to after a caesarean operation. Because she returns to her daily life faster, she does not go into patient psychology. Both psychologically and physically she is in a state to deal with her baby more.
- In natural birth, the risk of breathing problems is less for babies. The reason for this situation is that while the baby is passing through the birth canal, the tight environment that the baby comes across is a natural mechanism that uses pressure to eject the amniotic fluid in its lungs.
- During a natural birth, the various bacteria that the baby touches with its mouth while passing through the vaginal channel are actually highly beneficial for the baby's immune system. Nowadays, even in caesarean birth, this fluid is touched to the baby's mouth. If the doctor does not forget, of course. ☺
- In the process of natural birth, the baby secretes endorphin, which is the hormone of happiness. This hormone is a pain reliever at the same time. These hormones cause the baby to adapt to the world more easily.
- Statistics show that babies who are born naturally go into intensive care less than caesarean ones.
- Because no anaesthetic is used during natural birth, there is no risk of anaesthetic going into the baby, and not thorough milk either, whereas this risk is high in caesarean operations.

MOVEMENT

"A rolling stone gathers no moss."

The unhappiest people I see are the ones who are not active... The ones retired to a corner just moaning and sitting with dark clouds above their heads should stop moaning over nothing. They themselves are summoning the unhappiness.

Motion, exercise or sport, whatever you call it... Being active is a must for health. Moving is as beneficial as immobility is harmful... Why? Because when an active body calms, it can get a real rest; it heals and renews itself, whereas when immobility tires a person it cannot be rested and tiredness causes unhappiness.

In addition, mobility:

1. Accelerates breathing and blood circulation. It provides more oxygen and blood to the tissues. And this causes the tissues to feed, to become lively.
2. It gives skin a healthy and a lively beauty.
3. Causes calorie burn and melts fat.
4. Accelerates metabolism.
5. Together with healthy nutrition, provides weight loss and keeping in shape.
6. Protects muscle mass and helps fat burning.
7. Increases flexibility, ability to move, balance and coordination.
8. Strengthens the bones and protects them against osteoporosis.
9. Decreases the level of harmful cholesterol (LDL) and triglyceride and increases the level of good cholesterol (HDL).
10. By causing secretion of "happiness hormones" from the brain, it decreases stress.
11. Increases sexual performance.
12. Keeps away depression.
13. Keeps mental functions alive.

14. Helps to regulate blood pressure.

15. Protects against cardiovascular disease.

16. Provides protection against cancer.

17. Makes ageing slower.

18. Keeps the person spry psychologically.

19. Increases the sensitivity of muscles to insulin hormone. Breaks the insulin resistance, balances the level of blood sugar and insulin.

Believe me, it is not possible to get this much benefit from any diet or medicine.

How is yoga effective for diabetes? The link below will be helpful to you:

http://www.ba-bamail.com/content.aspx?emailid=20330

There is a sport appropriate for everyone's age and condition. Walking may be the most practical one of them all; swimming is just the job for the muscles. Find the type of exercise that suits you most and try to do it at least 30 minutes every day.

If you are on a diet or detoxing, do not forget that if you do not move you cannot reach a healthy form just by diet alone.

Being active must be a part of our lifestyles. In fact, it is so easy; we can start by not missing the opportunities to exercise in every day life. By walking short distances instead of going by car, by taking the steps instead of the , , by cleaning our own homes, etc., we would be doing such good for our bodies. Working sitting down all day, a life with minimum movement, causes weakening of the waist, back and stomach muscles and hernias. If you experience any of these symptons even a cough or a sneeze can cause the formation of a hernia.

If we are conscious to start the day with stretching exercises, of course, it is even better (be careful not to ignore warming up first.) Warming up the body only takes 2-3 minutes , but do not overestimate it. Before you start to stretch your neck, arms and legs, even 2-3 minutes of running on the spot, on the very spot you are, will provide blood circulation and warm you up. After regular stretching exercises daily you will see the benefits and your body will get used to them....

We are talking about such difficult movements. Here are some examples for you:

Don't say, I did stretching so it is okay now, I will sit around and enjoy myself until the evening. Warming-up and stretching should only be movements to start the day. As long as movement is not integrated into life, the benefit will be short term. Whatever your age, do your housework yourself. Don't be lazy. Shall I count even the things that bring you the most joy and pleasure? Spend time, money and effort on this job. Then you will make it more valuable. How? You could be a member of a sports club, for example. Seeing people who are making an effort on their body will motivate you more. That way, you can even exercise in the company of a professional and join in with sports activities which were previously not on your radar, with equipment or without, such as yoga, Zumba, cycling, pilates, aqua gym, and dancing. Don't you want to spend money? Then every aspect ofnature is at your command. Don't forget that the healthiest sport is walking. Put your comfortable sports shoes on and go where your heart leads you. ☺ I mean, do not get comfortable being immobile.

If you definitely expect a sports suggestion, then I can suggest yoga, which has movements to stimulate and satisfy both your body and spirit, to move and open the energy centers. Yoga, in fact, is not a sports activity; it is a life philosophy. Underlying every yoga movement is a purpose and an intellectual target. Yoga Asanas are different than physical exercises. The meaning of "Asana" in Sanskrit is "Sitira Sukha." Sitira means "mindfulness," and sukha means "unwind." By being mindful to unwind, being calm but spry…

While applying Asanas, stretching needs to be done in a mindful state. After doing Asanas for fotry-five minutes, relaxation on the basal metabolism is provided.

With this method, our sympathetic nervous system relaxes. It is not possible to have this relaxation with other physical activities. In addition, with stretching exercises, all the stress and tension in the body disappear. While applying Asanas, if we give ourselves the command to stretch too, our work will be even more productive and put us into a peaceful mindfulness.

Movements, which Activate the Energy Centres

Yoga Asanas

Asanas are one of the parts of the yoga path. They separate into parts within themselves.

Surya Namaskara - Salute to the Sun

Surya Namaskara, which is a set of twelve Asanas done one after another as one stance, provides perfect flexibility to our body. It is suggested that it be done at sunrise and sunset.

Surya Namaskara

Pranamasana Hasta

Uttanasana

Pada Hastasana

Ashva Sanchalanasana

Parvatasana

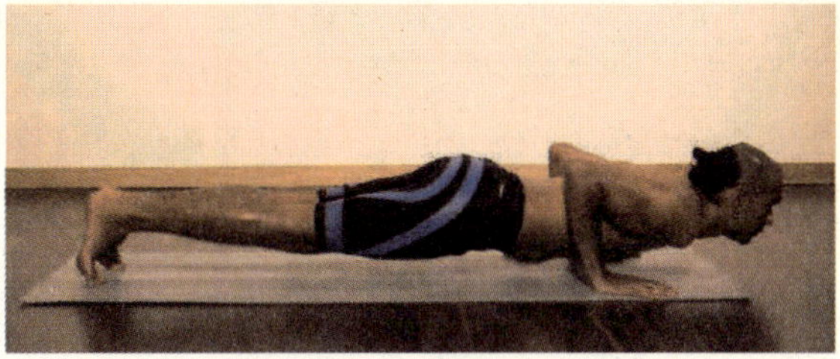

Ashtanga Namaskara

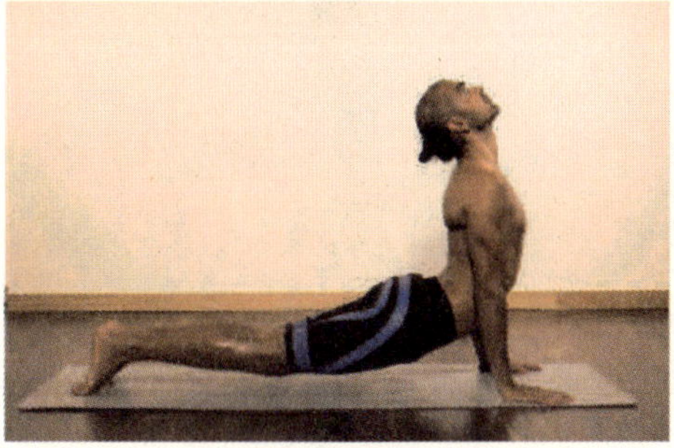

Buhujangasana

Parvatasana

Ashva Sanchalanasana

Pada Hastasana

Hasta Uttanasana

Pranamasana

The Benefits of Surya Namaskara:

– Strengthens the memory.

– Gets rid of psychological strain. Strengthens digestive system.

– Freshens the skin. Hinders skin breakdowns.

– Gets rid of constipation and indigestion.

– Strengthens the stomach muscles.

– Exercises the lungs and causes plenty of oxygen to go into the blood.

– Activates the endocrine secretion glands and returns them to a normal state – especially the thyroid glands.

– Stimulates the secretion glands.

– Strengthens the nervous system.

– Keeps the muscles flexible.

– Works the chest muscles, especially in women, prevents flexibility loss, stimulates secretion glands.

– Widens the chest and shapes the arms.

– Makes the spine and back flexible.

– Regulates sleep.

Who Should Do Surya Namaskara?

- Pregnant women starting from three months.
- Hernia patients.
- Hypertension patients.
- Women during menstruation.
- People who have back problems.

The Asanas and the Names

Standing Poses:	
Ardha Kati Chakrasana:	Half Waist Wheel Pose
Padahastasana:	Hands-to-Feet Pose
Ardha Chakrasana:	Half Wheel Pose
Trikonasana:	Triangle Pose
Virabhadrasana:	Warrior Pose
Parsvakonasana:	Side Angle Pose
Vrksasana:	Tree Pose

Sitting Down Poses:	
Vajrasana:	Diamond Pose
Virasana:	Hero Pose
Shashankasana:	Hare Pose
Ustrasana:	Camel Pose
Supta Vajrasana:	Lying Diamond Pose
Supta Virasana:	Reclining Hero Pose
Paschimottanasana:	Seated Forward Bend Pose

Padmasana:	Lotus Pose
Yoga Mudra:	Yoga Pose
Vakrasana:	Twisted Pose
Ardha Matsyendrasana:	Half Lord of the Fishes Pose
Maricarasana:	Marica's Pose
Sirsasana:	Headstand
Gomukhasana:	Cow Face Pose

Face Down Poses:

Bhujangasana:	Cobra Pose
Salabhasana:	Locust Pose
Dhanurasana:	Bow Pose
Mayurasana:	Peacock Pose

Face Up Poses:

Viparita Karani:	Legs-Up-the-Wall Pose
Sarvangasana:	Shoulder Stand Pose
Matsyasana:	Fish Pose
Halasana:	Plough Pose
Sethubandasana:	Bridge Pose
Chakrasana:	Wheel Pose
Savasana:	Corpse Pose
Hamsasana:	Swan Pose

Some Special Postures and Names:

Hasta Uttanasana

Hasta Uttanasana

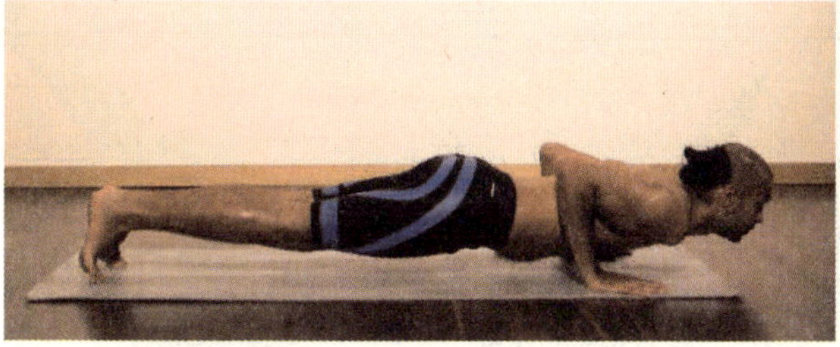

Chaturanga dandasana

Chakrasana

Garbha Pindasana

Halasana

Hasta Padangusthasana

Bakasana

Kukkutasana

Karna Pidasana

Padmasana

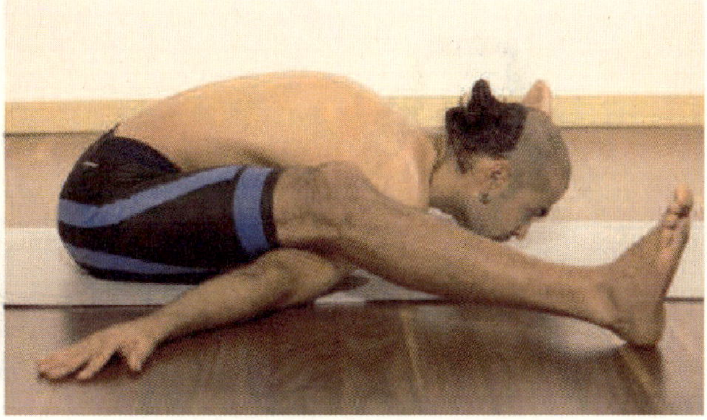

Padmasana Kurmasana

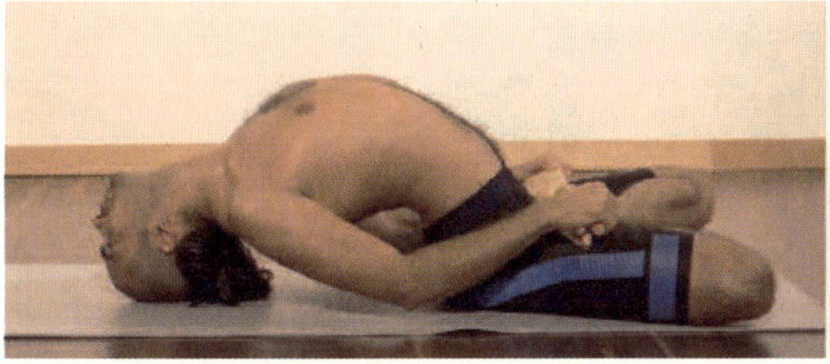

Matsyasana

Pindasana

Parsvakonasana

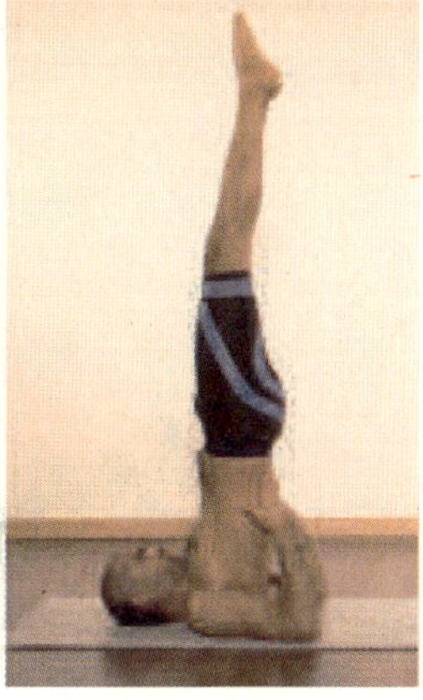

Saruangasana

Prasarita Padottanasana

Sethubandasana

Sirsasana

Purvottanasana

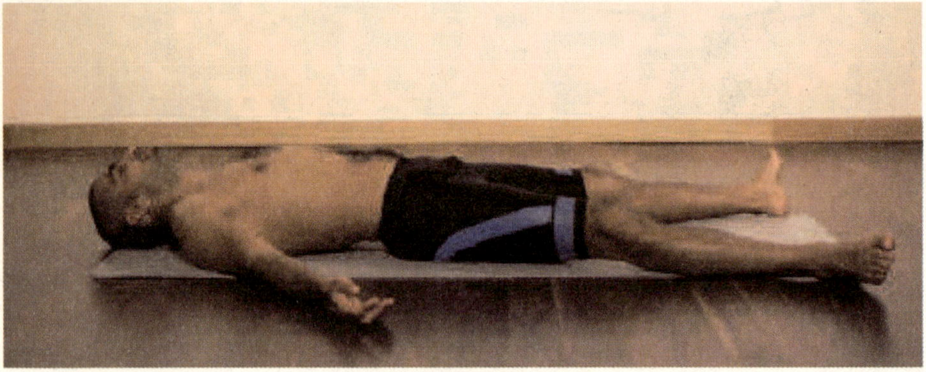

Savasana

Shashankasana

Trikonasana

Vriksana

Supta Parsva Sahita

Upavistha Konasana

Utpluthih

Uttana Padasana

Urthava Dandasana

Virabhadrasana-1

Virabhadrasana-2

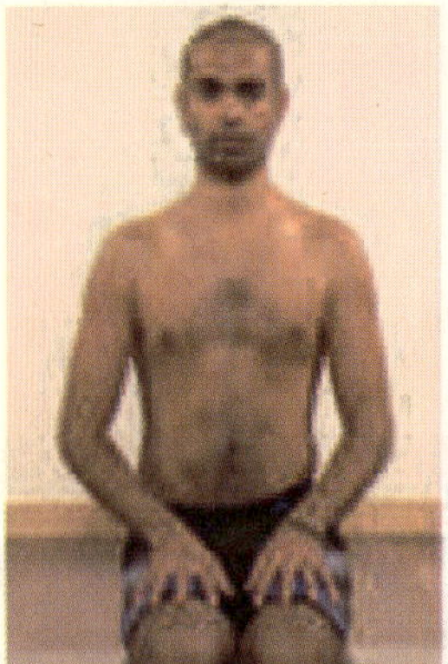

Virasana

Buddha Konasana

An important reminder:

- Please do not start yoga Asanas by yourself. First, learn them in the company of an instructor, because an Asana done wrong can cause you serious injury. After learning the right ways of doing the poses, you are free. While doing these exercises, you must work while protecting your back and spine.
- You must have had eaten at least an hour before you start your exercise.
- You should always wear loose clothing and ideally bare feet.
- The environment you do these exercises in should be calm. There should be nothing to bother or attract your attention (noise, too much light, a bad smell, too much wind, too hot, too cold.) Nowadays you can find some very pleasant yoga music online that can help you relax and unwind..
- Moreover, while you are exercising, you can burn some incense or relax with essential oils, especially lavender.
- For the continuation of the effects of the hormones secreted during yoga on the body, a weight or cardio workout or eating is not suggested straight after a yoga session.
- Try not to wear any scents or perfume as this will stimulate your senses.

Each chakra in our body has its place in the centers of the neural network. Yoga Asanas stimulate our neural network centers and secretion glands. In that way, the emotions that those chakra's affect are stimulated too, and they relax… It would be good to look into the subject of chakras in detail.

P.S: The energy centers are a subject to look at widely; their effects on the body, etc. In this book, I just want to confine myself by saying what the chakras and energy channels are and leave it there, because it is a very deep subject for another book… A part of the writing below is an excerpt. The source link is added.

Chakras and Energy Channels

Eastern philosophies say that besides our existing body we also have an energy body. In addition, the same philosophies say there is a neural network inside each of us that affects our mind, emotions and body, and that forms the exterior physical world inside us and responds. We have another body in secret, which looks after our holistic being, and where three channels (nadi) and seven energy centers (chakra) exist.

There are situations, which those three channels you see above correspond to: For example, the blue channel represents the past, emotions and desires. It is thought to be the place which carries our desire energy and where memories, habits and conditionings are stored. It is named "superego" in psychology. The left channel in Sanskrit (the ancient Hindu language) is called "**IDA NADI**," Moon Channel.

On the other hand, the yellow channel corresponds to behaviours, plans, and mental activities. It reminds us of the idea of our being apart from the world and being "me." In psychology, it is named "ego." The right channel, in the Sanskrit language, is "**PINGALA NADI**," Sun Channel... This channel carries the active energy and contains mental performance.

The channel placed in the middle is the Center Channel, where the chakras are. In Sanskrit, it is named Middle Way, "**SUSHUMNA NADI**." The energy channel that exists now, not in the past or the future. The chakras, I mean the energy centres of the body, are positioned on it.

Source: For detailed information...
http://www.sahajameditation.com/what-is-the-subtle-system

When the emotional conditions and spiritual quality that all seven chakras correspond to exist, and the kundalini* energy that sleeps inside us wakes up, then it is believed that these qualities occur by themselves and start expressing themselves inside our lives. It is known that Meditation and Yoga are the processes, which activate this sleeping energy and feed the chakras.

Chakra is a word in Sanskrit, meaning "tyre" or "wheel" when we look at the dictionary meaning. In many old texts or holy books, it is explained with different names too. The symbol of the wheel reminds us of the spiral turns of the energy.

Each chakra is the entrance of an energy at a different frequency. These energy channels circulate the life energy inside the human body and balance the energy flow. Whenever a blockage occurs to one of these doors, the body's receiving of energy becomes difficult. Problems start in this way, because the energy current, which feeds the body is limited. When chakras do not work properly, the body will have difficulties in protecting its health.

The life energy provides circulation inside the body via chakras. Chakras work at minimal levels in many people. If there is a regular energy exchange, our consciousness will go up to a more mindful level.

In that way, physics balances and regulates the body functions, and we have a healthy body that works with a higher quality life energy. In the case of a situation of any physical unbalance/functioning disorder, the related chakra is affected by this imbalance and, just the same, a functioning disorder in a particular chakra can cause a connected physical problem.

* **Kundalini:** In Sanskrit, the word Kundalini means "mysterious." Being the mysterious evolution energy that exists in the human body, it is in a state of immobile potential energy that sleeps in the human organism.

1st CHAKRA (Root Chakra – Innocence)

Color: Red
Note: A
Element: Earth
Sense: Smell

It is located at the end of the coccyx. It represents a connection with the world. All the hard parts of the body such as spine, bones, teeth, nails, as well as anus, large intestines and prostate are the organs, which this chakra is in interaction with.

Lack of energy around that area causes a feeling of physical weakness. Anxiety and lack of trust show themselves.

2nd CHAKRA (Sacral Chakra - Creativity)

Color: Orange
Note: D
Element: Water
Sense: Taste

It is located under the belly button. Gonads, prostate... It controls both sexual and creative energy. It is one's own residence. This chakra does not wake up until adolescence. It is affected by how the feelings are shown or repressed during childhood. It is related to the feelings of fear and excitement. Pelvic arc bones, reproductive organs, kidneys, bladder, blood, lymph, gastric juices and fluids such as sperm are the related areas of this chakra in the body. During the balanced energy level, it causes open natural behaviour towards others and the opposite sex and feeling friendly, in the case of energy lack, lack of self-confidence, apathy, and sexual frigidity occur.

3rd CHAKRA - Stomach Chakra (Solar Plexus - Serenity)

Color: Yellow
Note: E
Element: Fire
Sense: Vision

It is located in the navel area. It is an exit door, where our emotional energy drains. For an average person, it is the center of personality. It is related to the subjects of self-confidence and braveness. Lower back, belly, digestive system, stomach, liver, spleen, gall bladder, autonomic nervous system, are the related areas in the body. At the balanced energy level, it creates serenity and inner balance. Accepting yourself and caring for others; in the case of lacking, introversion, numbness, lack of appetite and unusual eating habits can be seen. If it is not in harmony with the heart chakra, this causes neurological illnesses. Losing the ability to fight.

4th CHAKRA - (Heart Chakra – Love and Affection)

Color: Green-Pink
Note: F sharp
Element: Air
Sense: Touch

It is located in the heart area. It is the centre of Love and Attention. If the chakra is in balance, then in life you will pass barriers to love. The source of all divine and human love is here. The related areas in the body are the heart-circulation system, lungs-breathing system, immune system, arms and hands and skin. At a balanced energy level, you will be affectionate, in empathy, humane, positive, sociable and sentimental, whereas in the case of lack, you will be oversensitive and a dependent personality, have a paranoid nature, indecisiveness, be scared to let things drift, and be distant.

5th CHAKRA - (Throat Chakra – Communication)

Color: Blue-Turquoise
Note: G sharp
Element: Ether
Sense: Hearing

It is the center of the expression of a person. This center is a bridge from the physical world to the spiritual world. As this enter develops, the ability for telepathy increases. We express everything alive inside us through this chakra (laughing, crying, love, worry, aggression, desire, thought, etc.) Neck, throat, jaw, ears, noise and windpipe, bronchia, gullet and arms are the related areas in the body. In the case of balanced energy, ability to express yourself without fear, and to show your power, the feeling of integrity, however in the case of an unbalanced energy, a scared, timid, quiet, changeable personality, and even stammering can be seen.

6th CHAKRA - (Third-Eye Chakra – Forgiveness)

Color: Indigo-Purple
Note: A
Element: Electrical or Telepathic Energy
Sense: Thought

It is the center of psychic powers or high senses. Via this chakra, you can take guidance. It is related to seeing directly. It is the center of concentration in meditation. This is a door opening to high worlds. Eyes, nose, ears, sinuses, brain, cerebellum and the central nervous system are the related areas. In the state of balanced energy, the fear of death disappears, substance-addiction stops, and you do not need anybody else to complete yourself. You can reach inner mindfulness and realise the energies directly. In the case of energy lack, an undisciplined and schizophrenic nature, which is too sensitive to others occurs. You only sense what you see and reject spiritual facts. You become forgetful. Material feelings, physical needs and secret feelings fill your life.

7th CHAKRA - (Crown Chakra – Integrity)

Color: White-Purple
Note: B
Element: Cosmic Energy
Sense: 7th Sense

It is the chakra with the highest vibration while active. It becomes the channel for the energy flowing from high levels. It is connected with high consciousness. The nervous system and brain are the related areas in the body. In the case of balanced energy, the consciousness is completely open, and you are calm. You get the answers to your questions easily. The only thing you do is direct your attention to the subject. In the case of lack of energy, a joyless and catatonic state, feeling of unclearness, purposelessness and fear of death are common. A superficial lifestyle and limiting the ego, stress, worry, hysteria, imbalance of the right-left brain, headache, and depression can show themselves.

Source: http://www.sakintaekwondo.com/taek-giris/yazar/yazi27.htm

In addition, you can benefit from the sources below on the subject of the chakras and yoga:

- https://www.goodreads.com/book/show/576362.Eastern_Body_Western_Mind
- https://www.goodreads.com/book/show/192993.Chakra_Clearing
- https://www.goodreads.com/book/show/618639.The_Chakra_Bible
- https://www.goodreads.com/book/show/832543.Anatomy_of_the_Spirit
- https://www.goodreads.com/book/show/961417.The_Sevenfold_Journey?ac=1&from_search=true

Let's Get Active

In my old world, I used to activate my physical world in the sports center that I visited 2-3 times a week. In the new world of mine, I have arranged myself a set of exercises of being born to the day, starting the day. This set is composed of the TurboSonic and trampoline, which I use at home. TurboSonic is a device which makes vibrations with sound waves and works out the whole body. Passing totally thirty minutes together with those, and then after doing ten minutes of the yoga poses that I have chosen, I start the day. If I am on a journey, a series of exercises: plank (three minutes) that I do with my own body weight, squat (forty times) and dynamic meditation, swinging your body wherever you are and then finishing with the body turning to both sides such that it creates a full circle, inspired by chi-kung. In short, I became self-sufficient and able to do sports when I do not have any equipment at all, too. At home, putting aside the classic equipment, I do exercises like trampolining, which provides a more natural flow to the body. Now I do not have any excuses. If I have a one or two-meter square space, I can keep my body working. There is no need to be a member of a sports center, or for things like being stuck in the traffic. Another easy training method is "interval training," which is going up and down thirty steps fast, ninty steps slow on the stairs and repeating it eight times.

Ersin Pamuksüzer

SMILING…

"We do not laugh because we are happy, we are happy because we laugh…"
William James

There is a very nice saying of Anton Chekhov, "If life does not make you laugh, it means you have not got the joke…" ☺

There is neither a tax on laughing, nor any other cost to it… It's magical nutrition too, and exists more or less everywhere… I'm talking about real laughing, being sincere… Not pretending that you are laughing, grinning… Not at all annoyingly, mockingly showing your teeth to everything. Let us remember that in nature showing the teeth is aggression. ☺

If you want, let's have a trial right now. You'll be surprised. The thing you will do is this: While reading these lines, smile and let people passing ask you, "Well, are you reading a funny thing?" Tell them why you are smiling and suggest that they do the same thing. Even if you are alone, smile. There is no need for someone to ask something. Let that smile stay on your face. You will see that you are feeling better after a while. Repeat that frequently. And, ladies and gentlemen, I'll tell you a secret: This is a method of a natural Botox. ☺ When you do this, your rage muscles do not work; on the contrary, your forehead area is stretching. Try it if you don't believe me; I economise in a lot with this method.

While talking on the phone, place a smile on your lips; this will reflect in your voice and your words automatically. Or if you are a debater on a panel, place a well-dosed smile on your expression. This will cause you to sense and understand the opposite side more positively. So, what then? If I make a sentence like, "Smile, and the world smiles with you…", believe me it will not be wrong, but this is not what I really want to do. Life smiling at you is only one of the benefits that smiling will offer you. However, look, how many more there are:

• When you smile, the muscles on your face stretch. This makes your expression nicer and more attractive. Only if you are not annoying and fake…

• Smiling creates such a psychological effect that you realise, without willing, you look positively and see, think, speak, and behave positively.

• You communicate more easily. Outsiders will not be shy or scared to speak to you. What holds people back from communication is fear of being rejected and rebuffed. It is thought that a person with a smiling expression would not show this disrespectfulness.

• Being able to smile even works during an argument. Keeping silent for a while, say, "Never mind" and look into the eyes of the person that you were arguing with, with a smile. You will be providing that person with such an environment that he/she starts questioning himself/herself. Saying this, you actually say, "If you want, you can weigh your words and thoughts a bit." Of course, before doing this, you must have already talked and defended your own argument. You wouldn't start an argument saying, "Whatever." Yes, it is a difficult method to apply and you should get your anger completely under control while doing it and should never have a mocking attitude either. However, it definitely works.

• If you continue smiling, after a while, there won't be anybody in front of you who is scowling. You manage to create a space of positive energy. The ones who want to be included in that energy space will come to the same frequency as you. It means they'll be smiling people too.

• Humans, in fact all living creatures, tend to run away from worry and direct themselves to pleasure. Laughing, smiling environments are always attractive. Humans try to be a part of these kinds of groups.

• Communication is healthier in a group of smiling people. An environment, which is sincere and has a high level of humor is joyful and creative. This gains you positive returns in both your work and social life and keeps you away from stress.

• A smiling face is the most powerful source of attraction. Your circle widens and the number of people who approach you with sympathy increases. This is a must to look beautiful. A healthy person will prefer a flawed beauty that gives serenity over a sulky repulsiveness with beautiful lines.

• The effect of your smile is in proportion to the sincerity of it. You cannot deceive yourself or others with a fake smile. For that reason, put a serious reason behind your smile; do not smile just through your face lines, but through your brain. Think of a funny incident and concentrate on the nice things in the environment… Smiling starts in the brain and opens up on your face.

• Smiling creates positive energy in both the brain and the body. It more or less opens every door. If there is a door, which a real smile cannot open, then let that door stay closed.

• Smiling creates a more powerful orbit than an established authority via rage. It is charismatic, mysterious and attractive, and is necessary for self-confidence.

• When a constantly sulky person is angry, that does not attract attention very much, but when a generally smiling person sulks or gets angry it takes more attention and creates surprise. That person can get help more quickly from people.

• Smiling is the most positive and beneficial thing you can do in your life and friends will enjoy your company and want to be around you.

• It is important for your image too. Smiling is a sign of health, calmness, power, and joy.

• You cannot buy a smile, you only give or take it willingly which makes it more valuable.

• Besides communicating with other people, contributing to your relationships and developing these, smiling causes you to be at peace with yourself. This, in fact, is the most important thing of them all.

• Generosity, smiling and tolerance work arm in arm with each other. Generously smiling wakens up the feelings of trust and cooperation. People who smile more are accepted as being more generous and extroverted.

• Smiling is the facial expression of successful, calm people who are aware of their place and experienced. Anxiety, panic, and anger are the signs of being without control.

• Will it work if someone who has done a bad thing smiles? According to research done in 1995, it might. When we see people, who violate the rules later, while smiling, we can become more tolerant. This smile being or not being a false one, a painful looking one or a real one, does not change anything. In any situation, it gives a chance to the person who violates the rules.

• Smiling compensates for the mistakes in society. Accidental flatulence or burping can happen. Be comfortable and laugh at yourself! Others will laugh at you too. Otherwise, you will be the target of awkward looks or stares. Well, take the trouble to say "sorry" too. ☺

• Smiling should also be the first step of compensating for a fault. Especially, smiles together with shyness might get the faults that we committed in front of society to be forgiven easily. If you expect tolerance from the other person, first you should give that tolerance in the manner of your appearance and energy.

• Everything aside, smiling makes us feel good. It makes us interpret life in a more beautiful way and see our glass full instead of empty.

• Smiling motivates the person opposite us too. For example, if you match the efforts of your child, who is trying to make you appreciate him/her with a smile, you will bring up a more extroverted and happy child. If you criticise constantly, then your child will be shy. You should create a smiling environment for him/her so that his/her creativity increases.

• One of the ways to decrease the stress in a bad situation is smiling. Psychologists call this "the facial feedback hypothesis." In other words, sometimes, even forcing ourselves to smile can heal our psychology later on.

• Smiling adds inner-sight. When we are angry or tense, we have difficulty focusing and may not realise what goes on around us. At such times, in being able to gain inner-sight against the troubles you are facing, the power of smiling is undebatable. Smiling helps both with feeling good and with increasing the flexibility of your attention.

• Smiling makes you sexier. It is always said that women smiling has a magical effect on men. They investigated, within the scope of a study, how men approach women, and it was determined that if a woman makes eye-contact with a man opposite her they get close to twenty percent less time, and when the women smile at the man this amount increases up to sixty. I'm just saying. ☺

• When men smile at women, a similar effect is seen but the power of the effect is less. On the other hand, it is known that the appearance of shyness in men has a bigger effect on women.

• Sometimes we do not want to give away a secret. Smiling helps you to hide your real thoughts. What I'm talking about is not a fake smile, it is a smile of camouflage… However, be careful; it might also cause antipathy.

• Smiling can cause you to earn more money. Yes! Especially if you are working in the service industry, because of your smile you might get more customers because you will be preferred. Even the tip for a smiling waiter or bellboy will be more.

Anyway, in any case, do this smiling business at its right amount. Smiling at a very wrong moment might cause you to lose all the positive affects you have made. While smiling by force, you might be whiny, repulsive and weird. ☺

You Should Laugh, Be Happy and Most Importantly Be Satisfied…

Laughing is a sign of joy and happiness. In other words, we laugh if we are experiencing pleasure and happiness. In a long-running piece of research done at Harvard University, it has been found that at the base of happiness, lies people feeling good in their relations and being satisfied. The second most important basic keystone is the person being glad about all of his/her being. In short, it is not enough just to feel good in relationships; to be at peace and glad about everything in our lives and mind carries us to happiness and pleasure. As long as a person keeps himself/herself in a contented, satisfied state, everything will become straight and life will flow more easily. This is an art.

Ersin Pamuksüzer

FEEDING…

"Do not dig your grave with your own fork and knife"
British Proverb

Do you know what "La Vache Qui Rit" is? My favourite cheese brand. It is not the brand of my favourite cheese… I mean, I like the brand. The cheese is not bad either. The meaning is "The Cow that Smiles." A cow smiling is a good thing; happy cows mean happy nutrition. My God, what am I saying! Animal lovers will attack me… I would also like to talk about happy leeks and happy carrots, but as long as meat is in our nutrition chain, do not take offence, please.

While I am going up to sea level with my bike in Holland, I pass by incredible fields. Cows spread in the middle of green… Some sitting in groups, gazing around with their significant looks. Others eating continuously with their heads down, ruminating. Although they are living the happiness of eating, some from here and there, you cannot see a cow jumping with joy. The cow itself is a stable animal. ☺ That black and white one, how she is looking into my eyes, indifferently… Is she trying to say something, I wonder? These are my feelings in that environment. Simply, they are smiling, healthy animals in their own environment.

It is possible to see a similar scene in Switzerland too. The same year, the state of a farm I saw in my dear country made me pretty upset. Numberless cattle in barns, jammed and overwhelmed by heat. They squeezed water over them so that they did not get completely stupefied… ☹ I was sad. You cannot keep yourself from thinking, "Ah! Where are those animals spread around in a field, the fish swimming in the sea and the chickens walking around in nature?" The animals are in the barns nose to tail; if you ask about fish, they are in the nets of fish farms, the chicken had hormones so that they grow as soon as possible, and are waiting to be cut…

I'm telling you again: Animal lovers, please do not get upset with me. I wish we could only feed with greens. However, if we will talk about animal products too, then we should start by putting reality in front of us. In fact, if we think that in a world in which even the adrenaline of the animal which suffers fear before being cut is calculated for, the nutrition that comes to our plates from a system where animals cannot feed peacefully and happily, cannot move, and are brought up on hormones is not so good for us.

So, what is the situation with grain? Do you know that they have manipulated the codes of our nutrition? Yes, that is the situation. In the name of improvement, their genetics have been changed. Our nutrition is full of chemical additives. While the lifetime and the taste of these products containing chemicals have seriously increased, what happened has happened to people. Obesity has arrived; diabetes, cancer and chronic illnesses have increased, and allergic reactions are nearly accepted as normal. And what about the psychological problems that we have because of nutrition?

It is not easy not to be upset. Putting ourselves aside, it looks like the new generation will not see any nutrition which will not be genetically manipulated or bloated by hormones.

In this part, I would like to have a few clichés:

- An approach like, "Don't leave it on the plate, it's a pity!" should become, "Okay, I am full and too much is harmful." Of course, food can be left on the plate. It does not have to end up in the waste; it can go to Dyson or the kitty.
- Nowadays, obesity has hit a peak. The reason: Ready-to-eat food, fast food restaurants, eating badly and too much, and the additives in food...
- Fats! How many more times will they poke it into our eyes and we still will not learn? There are some fats that we really should avoid,these are trans fats[19], margarine, corn oil, vegetable oil, etc.... These are bad for our health. On the other hand, fish oil, the fat from meat, and olive oil (preferably extra virgin) are good and even necessary for the body. The things that cause cholesterol in the body are not fat, but sugar and stress... It is necessary to consume these fats and oils without exaggerating. How many more times do we have to hear that?
- What has Hippocrates said? "If you can heal a patient with food, then there is no need for medicine..." In that case, instead of the medicines made up of chemicals, we should try to get our remedies from natural nutrition. For that, we should have a varied diet. All kinds of vegetables... We need to make all sorts of vegetables and spices which we have not heard the names of before a part of our

19. Transfatty, trans-isomer (E-isomer) are the names given to the unsaturated fatty acids. Because the term refers to double carbon - the configuration of the carbon bonds, the Transfatties can sometimes be monounsaturated and sometimes polyunsaturated. Transfatties are the fatty acids that are necessary.

lives. The substances we need are in them. Making magical mixtures-pastes out of spices, we can create our own life secret. I have mentioned it before; each of us should have an herbalist friend.

• I love tomatoes. I have found out that the substance called lycopene in them is very beneficial, and if it is cooked a little, it is even better. They say not to peel a tomato because that lycopene gathers just under the peel. Between us, I would eat my belt if I put this sauce over it ☺: The trio of tomato + garlic + olive oil cooked in a pan for 4-5 minutes…

• It is said that buying okra, green beans, artichoke and shell beans in their seasons and freezing them is better than buying them out of season.

• Tomatoes too. It is good if we buy them in summer and preserve them in the jars.

• Why do we think Turkish cuisine is special? I will tell you the answer; because of yoghurt, kefir, pickles, vinegar, and offal. ☺ These are foods spread to the world from us. The benefits are not up for discussion. I ask, which burger in the world can take the place of Sultanahmet meatballs?

• We mentioned eating a variety of vegetables, but I think we forgot to say that we should not cook them too much, so that we do not lose their vitamins and minerals. It is even better to eat the ones we can raw.

• I remember my grandmother with God's grace and with longing. I understand now, at this age, her efforts to make me eat bone marrow. No comment.

• It is not necessary to fear offal, but we should consume it in controlled amounts. Liver, kidney, etc. are sources of protein and minerals. However, I should point out that I do not feel happy with a cow head that is looking at me with its frozen eyes from my plate. Thinking about the rest of them depresses me, so I'm not going to write about them. ☺

• I wish there were a farm where we could buy our meat and milk. That we could see the goats eating thyme, drink their milk and buy butter from that farm. A few chickens walking around and their eggs…

• I like bread a lot but it does not like me. This is a one-sided love. Gluten! Let us keep away. I said it before. We are face to face with genetically disordered grain.

• Fruit? Of course it can be eaten but within a limit. You know evil is hidden in the detail; the evil in fruit is fructose. In other words, the tastiest sugar in the world…

• As much as we say eat mostly vegetables, vitamin B 12 is only found in animal products. Alternatively, from the corner pharmacy. Make your choice. ☺

What is Super Food?

The thing we call superfood has in recent years been the most popular nutrition; antioxidant and giving high sustenance... These are both tasty and beneficial. It is necessary to consume plenty; however, now, because they are imported and very popular, their prices are high; be informed. I wish they could be produced more in our own country.

1) Cranberry

It contains valuable substances, which have an important role in fighting against cardiovascular illnesses, ulcers, hypertension, cholesterol and cancer. The potassium content is extremely high.

2) Pulse and Wholegrain Groups

Pulses, which are a source of low-calorie protein, are quite rich in fibre. These fibres help in decreasing the cholesterol and providing weight control by creating a feeling of fullness.

3) Chia Seed

These little black seeds that we have started to come across very often contain vegetable-sourced omega-3 fatty acid. They have the property of becoming jelly. While a spoonful of chia-seed at breakfast covers most of the daily recommended protein, it also helps you to feel full for longer...

4) Cocoa

Is it possible that there is someone who does not like chocolate? Cocoa contains serotonin, the happiness hormone; however, they say that it is necessary to consume this wonderful product pure… Maybe we can prefer products that contain 70% cacao and above.

5) Avocado

In its content, there is oleic acid, vitamin E, lutein, and folate. It protects, keeps us young, feeds and is very tasty too.

P.S: 100 g. of avocado covers 28% of daily fibre need.

6) Dried Nuts

Yes, too many causes weight gain, but they protect our skin, organs, hair and nail health, brain and psychology with the valuable fats they contain. We should consume them.

P.S: It is healthier to consume nuts like almonds, walnuts, hazelnuts and peanuts raw.

7) Salmon

This is a fish rich in omega-3. Delicious,It would be a mistake not to eat this wonderful fish.

30 "SUPER FOODS" THAT DR. FURHMAN SUGGESTS

	Nutrition/Calorie Index	Sodium (mg)	Calories
Leaf Cabbage, Mustard plant, Russian turnip plant	1000	46	74
Kale	1000	45	55
Watercress	1000	28	45
Bok choy (Chinese cabbage)	824	87	31
Spinach	739	118	34
Brussels sprouts	672	49	84
Chard	670	470	52
Roka	559	27	25
Rocket	554	11	4
Cabbage	481	18	50
Bean sprouts	444	11	53
Red pepper	420	4	58
Lettuce	389	22	48
Broccoli	376	44	45
Carrot Juice	344	126	75
Tomato and tomato paste	190-300	26	43
Cauliflower	295	28	43
Strawberry	212	2	69
Pomegranate juice	193	10	150
Blackberry	178	2	93
Plumb	157	0	114
Raspberry	145	2	96
Cranberry	130	2	123
Papaya	118	6	82
Brazil Nut	116	1	230
Orange	109	0	62
Tofu	86	9	69
Any kind of beans, which are not canned	55-70	11	269
Seeds: Linseed, sunflower, sesam	45	1	186
Walnut	29	1	196

THE RIGHT MONTHS FOR FRUIT AND VEGETABLES

JANUARY: Brussels sprouts, leek, celery, chard, purslane, pomegranate, grapefruit, banana

FEBRUARY: Leek, red turnip, cabbage, onion, celery, chard, asparagus, rocket, chestnut, hazelnut, mandarin, banana, green almond.

MARCH: Beetroot, lemon, asparagus, turnip, broad bean, reddish shell bean, cauliflower, leek, spinach, baby carrot, mandarin, strawberry.

APRIL: Artichoke, carrot, peas, tomato, bell pepper, celery, cabbage, broccoli, baby carrot, cherry, green almond.

MAY: Aubergine, tomato, shallot, reddish shell bean, lettuce, baby carrot, white asparagus, watermelon, strawberry, cherry, plumb.

JUNE: Artichoke, fresh potatoes, lettuce, green beans, bell pepper, okra, sweetcorn, carrot, cucumber, cherry, peach, damson plum, green plum, strawberry.

JULY: Artichoke, peas, corn, lettuce, green garlic, cherry, watermelon, apricot, melon, grape, blackberry, fig, fresh walnut, mulberry, red plum.

AUGUST: Okra, shelled broad beans, iceberg lettuce, fresh walnut, fresh hazelnut, damson plum, grape, mulberry, fig, cherry.

SEPTEMBER: Okra, leek, cauliflower, tomato, black-eyed pea, fresh walnut, fresh hazelnut, chestnut, pomegranate, quince, watermelon.

OCTOBER: Leek, cauliflower, celery, spinach, cabbage, courgette, pepper, aubergine, pear, pomegranate, apple, mandarin, fresh walnut, fig, grape.

NOVEMBER: Cabbage, Brussels sprout, radish, butternut squash, orange, mandarin, quince.

DECEMBER: Chard, leek, celery, rocket, chestnut, butternut squash, pear.

GMO

We said to our son, "Go and study genetics, it is the job of the future."; he studied, then messed the food up…

GMO (Genetically Modified Organism) is the name of something odd which has occurred with our food getting away from being natural, because of human beings botching things by sticking their noses into everything.

I'm not saying that I wish humans would not use their brains, but I can't help getting annoyed when they destroy something and leave it while meaning to improve it.

New agricultural and animal products occurred because plants' and animals' genetic specifications have been changed by scientists in laboratory environments. We call them GMO. In fact, GMO studies did not have a bad purpose. GMO studies were just a beginning, the end of which was not guessable. Today, the point we have come to is this: When weird nutrition transforms into weird living creatures' bodies, then we remember those scientists with love(!) and respect(!).

The real purposes of GMO studies were these:

- So that plants and animals could reproduce and grow in places apart from their natural habitat… Thus, producing different foods in different geographies and terminating hunger and the world that was feeding better were the purposes.
- By creating an artificial climate to be able to grow every product without depending on the place or time.
- To provide resistance against bugs and illnesses.
- To be able to get higher yields.
- To increase the flavor in fruit and vegetables, to brighten the color and increase the attraction.
- To develop more resistant and nutritious specious.
- To lengthen the shelf life of fruit and vegetables.

• To provide a commercial and economic advantage to some people... That simply did not fit! Maybe because of that, it was not possible to say "Stop!" to the course of events.

Okay, we can delete the last item from the records. No scientist works day and night so that some people gain a competitive advantage; they work out of curiosity and for the passion of science... However, capital's intersection with curiosity: GMO is born.

The techniques of GMO are also used to place genes into a plant or an animal's DNA or extract genes from these DNAs. Look what works genetic engineering, which is a pretty popular and a promising future job of our era, does: They answer our needs for tomatoes, which have antifreeze fish genes and endurance against cold weather, or corn, which has the bacteria gene that endures against the pesticide used to kill the weed. Okay, all good, but what about the side-effects of this business? To lengthen the shelf life of fruit and vegetables, what state do the lives of people have to come to? What kind of logic can it be to inject the gene of bacteria known as Bacillus Thuringiensis to the DNA of corn? Okay, the Bacillus Thuringiensis gene may be carrying a protein that kills bugs, but if you transfer it to corn so as not to have to spray pesticide on it, how are we going to eat that corn?

Just because I'm saying this, do not think that I'm very against GMO. Of course, the natural options and produce that grow in their own climate are better. However, while science has been showing so much improvement, should we not have taken the insulin gene from pigs and transferred it to bacteria so that we provide insulin to diabetic patients, or found the hepatitis B vaccine, or sweetener (aspartamine)? So, the genetic engineers who find these are good, but the nutrition GMOswhich create strange reactions in humans and animals are bad, aren't they? I guess so...

Here are the Possible Harms of DNA Change:

The transaction of placing a gene in a plant's DNA might be experience-worthy research that is attractive to scientists, however, if this job continues with today's logic of "Whatever happens, happens," if the scientists do not have foresight about where the gene is leading to, then we have a problem. If the products with GMOs will harm the other genes, will cause them to produce non-existing proteins in nutrition, to cause allergies, to produce toxins and destroy the balance of nature, then may they not exist. I would not like to think and talk in a bigoted way, but uncontrolled science that goes to the extreme can be our end.

What are the Possible Harms of GMOs?

- Causing disorder in body systems.
- Cannot be eliminated from the body.
- Increase in chronic illnesses.
- Increases of unforeseen risks.
- Damaging the ecosystem.

According to the statistics published by the World Health Association since 1996, health problems in the USA have increased. This comes in the same years as GMO studies have intensified. The proportion of Americans who have chronic illnesses increased from 7% to 13% in only nine years. Food allergies have shown a sudden rise and illnesses like autism have increased. Even more are the reproduction, digestion and immune system problems… In the research done both on animals and humans, it has been determined that the products with GMOs cause organ damage, digestion problems, immune system illnesses, disorders, speeds upageing, and can cause infertility. Among the things, which have been determined is that some of the proteins with GMOs and chemicals, in the case of a failure to digest, can be stuck inside the body. For example, while a gene, which was injected into soya beans may transfer to some DNA of the bacteria which live inside our body, the bug-killing substance which is produced through corn with GMO showed itself in the yet-unborn fetuses of pregnant women.

In short, genetic engineering exposes the world to a serious of transactions, which are impossible to compensate for. So then, what should be done before new toxins, allergens, carcinogens and nutritional weakness give more harm to birds, bugs, amphibians, sea ecosystems and the organisms on the earth, and before chemicals decrease biodiversity and pollute the water sources? Well, in fact I passed over humans, but before humans destroy the world, something has to be done…

The products with GMO are more common than we think. Here is a list of the most common products with GMO: Soya beans, corn, cotton, milk, sugar, aspartamine, canola oil, courgette... Apart from these eight products, a lot more of them can take their place on the shop selves without us knowing.

In short, whatever good intention they had when starting with GMO-products, of which the control has been lost, they are a factor that threatens not only the properties of humans, but all of nature's too. Whichever living thing, an animal, bacteria or virus, that the GMO-products harm, will definitely affect people in this ecological system. It is not for nothing that the people who are conscious of the possible harms of GMO-products dream of living on their own farm and looking after chickens in their hutches and tomatoes in their gardens.

Antioxidant Sources

We definitely suggest you read:
Vitamin B17 – ENOANT + apricot stone + WG
http://www.healthyfoodhouse.com/pharmacy-doesnt-want-you-to-knowabout-this-cheap-and-natural-remedy-against-one-of-the-deadliest-disease

The Nutrition That Causes Acid	The Nutrition That Causes Alkali
High Acid:	**High Alkali:**
Meat	Lemon
Cheese, butter, yoghurt	Melon
Egg	Dark green vegetables
Bread, pasta, cake,	All raw vegetables
White sugar	Sea vegetables
Sweeteners	Seeds
Deserts, chocolate	Almond
Ketchup, mayonnaise	Peas
Fizzy drinks	Spices
Tea, coffee, alcohol	
Low Acid:	**Low Alkali:**
Cooked broad bean	Steam-cooked green vegetables
Modified soya, tofu mushroom	Ripe fruits
Potatoes, corn	Quinoa
Cooked oils	Millet
Commercial fruit juices	Sunflower seed
Vinegar	Extra virgin olive oil (cold-pressed)
Honey	Spices
Dried fruits	Fermented food
All nuts except fresh almond	
Acid Minerals:	**Alkali Minerals:**
Phosphorous	Calcium
Chlorine	Magnesium
Iodine	Potassium
Nitrogen	Sodium
Sulphur	Silicone
	Iron
	Manganese

CHAPTER SIX

TIPS FOR THIS AND THAT

"If you want to be healthy, do not eat much,
If you want to be respected, do not speak much..."
Uzbek Proverb

Tips are important. How would it be if you had a handy notebook where you write down the tips you come across throughout tyour life and write down the practical suggestions that you find interesting? Believe me, it is a very joyful thing to do.. I suggest that you try it as it strengthens people's interest and increases the awareness towards this type of subject.

Tips for Healthy Life

• Start the day with an easy-to-digest type of food. The best breakfast is a liquid drink that does not need digestion.

• Include apple vinegar in your life. Apple vinegar added to water that you drink every morning and evening is a very good balance for the body chemistry.

• Naturalise getting nutrition, not eating food. Eat food for pleasure and get nutrition for your health.

• Let fermented foods be a part of your life. For example, the pickles that you make at home are a rich source of probiotics.

• Do not see milk products as nutrition. Eat them for pleasure and in a measured way.

• Get flour-based food out of your lives or eat it for pleasure and in a measured way.

• Always have a section on your plate that is at least 50% dark greens.

• Do not drink fizzy drinks - evaluate them in the same category as alcohol. Drink very little and just for pleasure.

• Keep away from animal products. If you eat them limit your intake and keep it to a minimum just for indulgence.

• Change coffee and tea with such harmless alternatives as herbal tea or turmeric latte, wild pistachio coffee, or drink caffeine solely for pleasure.

• Get into the habit of putting your knife and fork down between bites and try not to rush while eating.

• Do not drink water while eating. Use it only to rinse your mouth or clear your palette.

• Do not talk while eating and do not do anything else at the same time, just focus on eating. Make sure you chew each piece of food 30-40 times in order to experience the fulltaste, also try closing your eyes from time to time too.

• Do not go to bed with a full stomach, while the digestion process is continuing.

• Eat dinner early. If you are eating late, eat light and only easy-to-digest food.

• Do not judge people; accept them as they are. Even if it is not right for you, think in the way that for that moment that is their preference.

• Do not spend more effort than necessary to change people. Be content with how it is and review your relationship again. Do not carry toxic emotions.

• Do not naturalize anything to the level that you cannot separate from it. Everything is transient; live according to the book.

• Find out what is bothering you and ask yourself if that is the end of the world or not. If it is not, then do everything you can to return to your usual life.

• Each life is a story. To write a good story, be careful to have good people around you and know their value.

• Every person has a good side. By seeing their good sides, let them make your story richer.

• Approach life in integration. Do not attempt to understand anything by separating it into parts. Think of all the parts as if they are connected to each other. Do not forget that your liver with your stomach secretions, and your breath with blood circulation, are parts of a whole.

• Be the actor, do not be the victim. Take responsibility; do whatever you can; do not waste your life by complaining.

• Detox your friendships and leave problematic relationships behind.

• To reflect your potential in your story at the maximum level, put your priorities in order and be focused on them.

• Make plans, but do not fall in love with your plans. When necessary, be able to change the plan immediately. Be open to changes all the time.

• Plan your risks,mistakes are not the end of the world. Have pleasure from taking responsibility and trying some things, but do not make mistakes as a habit.

• Buy an air ionizer for your bedroom for fresh air.

• Drink clean, alkaline and ionized water. Invest in this and get an alkali water device.

• Take precautions against electromagnetic pollution. At least purify your bedroom. Carry protectors like q-link on yourselves.

• Create a moment in which you integrate with nature. Swim, step on earth, smell flowers and touch leaves and trees. Listen to nature, birds, and the wind. Feel rain and grab the snow.

• Do not wear new clothes without washing.

• Live with a few necessary clothes. While buying some things, question if you really need them or not.

• Have a clear-out at home from time to time. Do a home detox.

• The more things you have, the more responsible you are. Do not carry unnecessary responsibilities.

• Approach the things that have been left natural with respect. Take care of children, spend time with animals and get the pleasure of their naturalness.

• When you get the opportunity, walk, run. Get on to a vehicle only when you have to.

• Create action into your lives. In the mornings and a few times during the day, do stretching exercises.

• If you want to do sports with a device, try a trampoline so that all your muscles work.

• By turning upside down in the inversion device, move the lymphatic system.

• Naturalise working with your own body weight. Do planking (parallel to the floor, carrying the body weight with the forearm, elbows and toe-tips) for three minutes and have brilliant stomach muscles.

• Do squats (crouching and getting up by bending the knees) so that your legs get stronger. Do this forty times after eating to keep you in shape.

• Have active friends who meet to do sports activities, rather than to eat.

Tips for Nutrition

• For nutrition, if possible choose foods, which are produced naturally, do not include any artificial additives or genetically modified foods.

• Reduce animal products from your diet and increase your intake of plant based foods.

• Instead of processedproducts opt for fresh fruit and vegetables coming directly from their source.

• Use cold pressed oils such as olive oil, sesame, sunflower and hazelnut, etc.

• Reduce your animal fat intake from your diet and eliminate cooked fats, which include a lot of free radicals that cause serious harm to your health.

• Reduce caffeine intake and drink more herbal teas.

• Try to eat more vibrant colorful vegetables as these are rich in antioxidants.

• If you drink sociably opt for a quality wine over beer or spirits.

• Always make sure your fruit and vegetables are ripe.

• Make sure you drink enough water and remember that recommended water intake varies from person to person.

• Change your relation with food and remember that food is a fuel for your body, which prevents you from getting illnesses and improves healing.

• Try to increase the consumption of raw and natural foods. Remember that during cooking, a lot of nutritional value is lost.

• Choose natural grains instead of treated white options. Grain is never white in nature; it turns white when treated.

• Opt for dark green and wild leaves.

• Instead of table salt, which has been iodized and treated use sun-dried, sea or Himalayan salt,

• Choose freshly squeezed juice and quality drinks that are tinned, pasteurized, bottled or carbonated.

• Use sauces that you have prepared yourself with ingredients such as lemon, oil, and spices to add to your salads instead of ready-made dressings.

• Avoid eating fried food such as chips and over junk foods.

• Always drink alkaline water.

• Make sure you eat sea vegetables. Those are the richest sources of organic minerals.

• Your diet should consist of mainly fruit and vegetables. Vegetables contain less sugar compared to fruits and they provide more organic minerals that have a vital importance to our body's optimal functioning. Instead of using sugar, prefer date, raisin or maple syrup.

• Increase your intake of green vegetables as they contain a high amount of Chlorophyll, which is the green pigment in plants- nature's way of turning sun-energy to oxygen. Eating a green-vegetable dense diet will improve your health and energy levels.

• Do not forget, each thought and emotion are physical molecules sothere is a direct connection between our diet and mental health.

• The more you chew and break down your food the better it will be for your digestive system.

Tips for a Healthy Kitchen

• The kitchen is the heart of any home so make sure you make it a joyful place with a design you like filled with lots of fresh, organic, healthy foods.

• Do not forget that the healthiest products are the ones in season and locally produced..

• Keep dried nuts and fruits in the freezer, in covered containers. If you keep them in the fridge make sure you use them within three days as the taste and nutritional value decreases afterwards.To maintain freshness make sure cooked food is stored in covered containers.

• Avoid keeping tomato-based products in plastic containers.

• Do not chill tomatoes straight away. Keep them in a cool, dry place such as the kitchen surface in a bowl with the stem left on. When they have reached the required ripeness they are then ready to be chilled.

• If you keep chopped garlic in the fridge soak it in olive oil.

• Keep the oil you use out of the sun in a cool dry place. When deciding which oils to buy choose the ones in dark bottles.

• To ripen avocados or tomatoes fast store them in a bowl with apples - as apples spread ethylene gas and speed up the ripening process.,

• Cutting green salad leaves with a knife may cause color change and empurpling. Tearing the leaves lightly will give a better result. In addition, fresh herbs and leafy plants that are chopped on a cutting board will lose a lot of the natural essential oils that they carry. Instead, it is suggested that you break the leaves apart with your hands.

• To prevent cooling and taste change wash green leafy vegetables with cold water. Drain the water off and dry well in a salad spinner. Wrap them inside a paper roll, place them in plastic bags, and keep them in the vegetable part of your fridge.

Tips for Nutrients

• To keep vegetables fresh, remove fresh leaves from packaging, rinse, dry and keep in damp towels. If you don't remove roots/stalked dip the roots in sweet water and keep them in the fridge.

• Keep grains and spices in covered containers.

• Consume cooked food within three days at the most. At the end of three days, the tastes and the quality will start changing.

• Nutrients are healthier when stored in closable glass containers. But avoid keeping tomato-based nutrients in plastic containers.

• To be able to have fresh herbs during cold seasons, vacuum-close them and store in the freezer.

• When buying ginger make sure it is fresh – it should be firm and tight, avoid pieces with have wrinkles and soft stains. Ginger is great for boosting your immune system.

• To speed up the ripening process of fruit put it in a paper bag.

• The best time to eat bananas is when they are really ripe and covered with brown dots, they taste much sweeter and tastier.

• You can keep strawberries fresh by cooling them between layers of kitchen paper layers and placing inside an airtight container.

• When adding sweet cherries, grapes or tomatoes to a marinated salad, make holes in them carefully with a fork. The marinade is absorbed better and they are tastier.

• If you pour lemon juice on sliced avocados or apples, you will see that they keep their color.

• To stop apple slices from turning brown pour a little lemon juice over them.

• When buying fresh mushrooms, instead of a plastic bag, always use a brown paper bag. It keeps them fresh twice as long as asa plastic bag.

• Be careful washing mushrooms, instead wipe or brush them to clean and get rid of dirt.

• Keep lemon, orange and grapefruit peels in the freezer; grate the necessary amount for a tart, cake or cookies, etc

Tips for Healthy Self-Care

• If you have an allergic structure, you can make your own deodorant. With jojoba oil, jasmine oil and a bit of carbonate of soda will make a highly natural and useful underarm deodorant.

• Keep your feet comfortable; do not wear tight, pinching shoes or heels that are too high. . How can you be comfortable and have a good head on you if your feet are in pain.

• Brush your teeth with carbonate at least once a day. For white teeth and a healthy mouth…

• You can make your own body lotion as well using a mixture of coconut oil, vitamin E ampule, aloe vera and bepanthen.

• Vinegar is great for skin health. It is good for psoriasis and decreases skin blemishes which is why it is used commonly in facial masks.

• Mix a bit of apple vinegar with the juice of a cucumber and apply it to your skin. This will clean the skin as well as tightening it.

• Mix a small teaspoon of vinegar with two small teaspoons of honey and apply it to your skin as a mask. Continue this for a week, It helps improve skin making it feel soft and smooth.

• Mix a glass of cold water with half a Turkish coffee cup of apple vinegar and cool it in the fridge for a while. Apply it to your skin with cotton wool a few times a day. It will help get rid of the blemishes and wrinkles.

• Mix baking powder with vinegar and apply it to your hair. This application will both allow you to get rid of dandruff and to have healthy looking hair. This mixture can be an alternative to shampoo.

• It is possible to use vinegar also for foot health; Add a glass of vinegar to a basin of water and place your feet inside for twenty minutes. This application will both get rid of foot odour and rest your feet..

• You can make your own toothpaste. Add to carbonate of soda and coconut oil 10-15 drops (mint, orange, strawberry…) to of one of your favorite scents. Mix all the ingredients until they become a paste. Keep it in a jar and use it with your mind at peace.

• The base for many face peelings is carbonate of soda, because of both its bacteria-killing structure and that it melts easily in water. Wet your face and hands and pour some carbonate of soda on your palms by rubbing your hands on each other, until it forms to a paste consistency. Place it on your face with circular movements and wash it after a few minutes and it will leave yourface feeling shiny and soft.

• The best remedy to get rid of itchy fly stings is a mixture of a few drops of water and carbonate. When you apply this mixture to the infected area, the itching will stop in a few minutes..

CHAPTER SEVEN

DETOX
EXPERIENCES

- ❖ PHYSICAL DETOX EXPERIENCES
- ❖ MENTAL and EMOTIONAL DETOX EXPERIENCES

"If you are not using the knowledge, having it will not benefit you ..."

The Story of M…'s Losing Weight

Woman, 42 years old

I have always loved eating and that has always had the main role in my life. I guess I'm one of those who lives for food. I loved watching my mom while cooking, our conversations in the kitchen, and the cooking programmes on TV. I still like it. When I was in my adolescence, I used to bake and decorate a cake and photograph it. And in weight, I was always full-figured. My weight and height were nearly the same. I wore size 40-42. If I over-ate a bit, I immediately became size 44 and even more. Only then would I go to a dietitian or a center and lose about 10-20 kg quickly and drop down to size 38. However, because of my eating habits, I would go back to size 40-42 very quickly, because I never stuck to the weight-protection periods after losing weight. Apparently, the entire secret lay there…

If you ask what I ate: pastries, cake, pasta, rice, patisserie products, milk products, junk food, crisps, pizza, hamburger, cok,e etc. I could live on cheese and bread. Instead of water, I used to drink three liters of cola (or other fizzy drinks.) There was nearly nothing healthy in my nutrition system. I had had bronchitis when I was six and I had allergies when I was thirty-five. I won't even mention the gas and intestine problems. Of course, later, I learned that the problems were caused by my eating habits.

That process was like a war. I was tired of losing and gaining weight at the ages of 33-35 and I gave it up as a bad job. This avoidance carried me to over 100 kg. Unfortunately, for the first time in my life, there was a process that I could not stop.

→

Actually, when I look back to see at which times I put on weight, I realized that I always attacked food in the periods of not being happy, when I lived with uncertainty for the future or I felt emptiness. I mean, not from hunger, just to get rid of gloom…

It took a long time to realize that I could not get rid of my distressed feelings by blowing myself up. Just at a time when I was thinking "It is too late now," I met detox and alkaline nourishment. It was like a revolution in my life. I was eating and losing weight at the same time. I had only changed the contents of what I was eating. I lost exactly fifty kilos with this method. Ten of that fifty kg passed with two detoxes, one for each week, and the rest by changing my nutrition style to alkaline. Nutrition based on vegetables, greenery, pulses, fish, nuts, herbal teas, spices, herbs, and water. I started to eat greenery and vegetables for the first time, in a health center abroad based on raw nutrition, and I got an education in healthy nutrition. In addition, I took online education on the psychology of eating.

Suggestion:

I guess becoming conscious about nutrition is an opportunity for us to understand the harm we are doing to ourselves and to fix it. This is what I can suggest to everybody: Find out what is going on in your body, and also where nutrition can take us to too… Then, you naturally stop doing that evil to yourself.

K.N.'s Story

Woman, 30 Years Old

I grew up with sentences like, "Your face is like an angel, but your weight messes up everything." 1.73 height and 120 kilos… Yes, obesity… Pasta, fried aubergine sandwiches, chips, ketchup, hamburger, pizza… A lot of TV, no exercise… You will be surprised, but I still did not have any difficulty in finding a boyfriend. I guess having nicely colored eyes and a decently shaped face work, however much your weight is; but for some reason, my relationships would not last very long. I started to blame myself. I did not know where I had made a mistake. While thinking and being upset that the ones who come to the beauty of my face leave because of my waist (and always following wrong methods to lose weight) I realized a completely different fact. All my boyfriends who left me (it was hurtful being first in the lists of "to be dumped" or "to be called from time to time") always said the same cliché: "You are a very good girl but…." I realized that none of them introduced me to his friends as his girlfriend. I was not stupid. I was aware of that. I blamed my weight. When they were alone with me they became boyfriends, but they were ashamed of my physical self when with other people. That was obvious; I'm not a fool.

My life was passing by on diets; I was not able to meet the success I wanted to. I started to go from doctor to doctor. They looked at my thyroid hormones. It was determined that I had hypothyroid. Apparently, that was the fact underlying my problem of not being able to lose weight. After my thyroid was taken under control under a doctor's watch, with the discipline of detox and alkaline nutrition, not only my weight but also my perspective of looking at life changed. I understood three things: Unless I made my eating habits my lifestyle, the fat cells, which are willing to increase in my body, would not leave me in peace; there was, of course, a relation between my self-confidence and my body, but first of all, I had to be at peace with my feelings and, finally, if there was a desire, then the way to it could definitely be found.

→

In two years, I dropped down to 70 kilos from 120. If I lost five more kilos, I was going to find my ideal weight. By the way, there were moments when I loosened my diet and rewarded myself. When I really wanted, I took a forkful of dessert or had other little escapades… However, I worked fearlessly to reach my target.

The detox center that I went to suggested a holistic approach. I mean, only physical purification was not enough. I should be calm psychologically, too. I started to do yoga regularly. Of course, meditation was a part of it as well.

Now, I am between 65 and 67.5 kilos. When I put on a little weight, I immediately pay attention and get rid of the extra kilos. I eat vegetable-based food. I am also happy with my emotional life. Without exception, all the boyfriends I had before wanted to come back. I just told them this: "You are a very nice person, but…"

There is no such thing as impossible in this world. As long as we are strong-willed…

Love.

C.B.'s Story

Man, 60 years old (from the notes he took in 2012)

Y.D. came to Turkey from America for his relative's funeral. He had become exactly 130 kilos. "A very close friend invited me to a health center in Bodrum; please come and keep me company and don't leave me to go there alone." He insisted so much that I thought he would not speak to me ever again if I did not go with him. TheLifeCo journey started this way. On November 4th, 2012, Sunday, I went into the records as 96 kilos.

Until then, I had surrendered myself to many systems. To hospitals, doctors, sports clubs, dietitians... I lost weight with each of them. Then, I went back to even more weight than before. I smoked 2.5 packets of cigarettes and drank tons of ouzo and wine.

Now, I am 60 years old. Going this way, according to calculations made over ten years including cancer, I will catch various illnesses and have operations. Then, spend the rest of the years taking pills in care homes and hospitals. My close people will appear and disappear at regular intervals. And one day, like every mortal, I will pass away from this life.

My purpose is not to gush about this organisation. It is to curse at my own mind and to come to terms with the torture that I did to my body... To realize the stupidity of not being able to see the picture of my family and my ancestors... My dad died of a heart attack at the age of 67. My mom is living with 30 cm of platinum in her lower back at the age of 88. She is healthy, and her memory is better than mine. The difference is: My dad always ate and drank, my mom never ever overate. She said eating too much is a sin. She always ate in a birdlike way; tiny bits. I realized this fact again in TheLifeCo. I, who could eat nine people's food at one go, am now trying to learn water fasting.

I have learned that it is not at all necessary to eat 3-5 times a day. I should only eat when I get hungry. I should not eat everything that comes in front of me. I should leave the rest to my body.

→

I have learned that my body talks to me all the time and sends me signals. However, I have not ever even tried to listen to it.

I have learned that all the meats I'm eating are actually not my food, they are carnivores' food and, the more I keep eating them, finally, I will get cancer.

I have learned that having a position and money, for the purposes of my life, is not beneficial to betterment. All the successes I have had until now were temporary. In nature, if I cannot be myself, I'm lost anyway.

I have learned that, while I'm teasing myself with feeding, I'm actually stuffing myself. This stuffing converts into illnesses in my body.

Today is December, 21th, 2012; the longest night of the year. The last day of the Mayan calendar. And I am 83.5 kilos, spending joyful and healthy days.

I looked at the laboratory results of the tests I had had done. There are nearly fifty headings, and nearly all of them are within the limits. The year's results are just beside them:

PSA from 3.4 to 1.8, LDL Cholesterol from 161.6 to 89, Cholesterol from 232 to 168,

Triglyceride from 107 to 54, Glico went down to 70, Urea from 36.38 to 14.98. Unbelievable change. What more can a person want for their health?

I have learned that there is nobody else who can help my body and me apart from myself. My visit to this world can last a long time.

I want to thank Y.D thousands of times for persuading me to go to TheLifeCo with him, and also to thank everybody who made an effort for me.

With love

C.B.

M.T.'s Story

Man, 55 years old

The World Health Organisation, WHO, defines health as an emotional, mental, physical and social "state of goodness."

Well, also a bit of answering is necessary to the question of how will we manage our subconscious and conscious existence and keep our joy for life dynamic in a sustainable way!

Being a simple Caucasian-origin person, when you also take the quality of aging into account, the time we spend in the world is about ninty years...

The suggestions we get, starting from our childhood and the fact that the evolution of humanity has not been completed yet, decrease our life quality and make us ill!

For health, peace, and joy of life, a completely different philosophy should be developed for life... We haven't even come close to that philosophy! When we look into history, mythologies, religions, disciplines, and doctrines, they cannot help us. Because none of them are preventative; that's not realistic!

Living in Istanbul until 55 years old, a retired senior executive in chemical engineering, I spent a full year in an Aegean town, which I escaped to because of the chronic silica cough and my allergies, which occurred because of the gentrification of Fenerbahçe in Istanbul, which had become torture. During that time, I benefited from all of the techniques that I know and, of course, from the information on TheLifeCo's website! At the end of that one year, despite the anxiety and worries in the world, in our country and my family: Zero coughs, zero allergies.... My hypothyroid has healed significantly!

Our efforts at creating a philosophy, producing ideas and creating a realistic guide for living in the world are so valuable!

Of course, they will find a solution to death, but to enjoy life, meet with the taste of it, and live in joy, I still do not have a word to say or a formula or a pill to suggest! We are in trying with patience, ambition, and determination... Continue researching....

Yours sincerely,

M.T

X.'s Story

Man, 42 years old

I do not want to give my name, but my story is this: I had been living with serious stress at that time. I am very ashamed to say this, but I was in love with my closest friend's wife, and she with me too. We were having a secret affair, and I had to meet with my friend often too. I am ashamed to even say it now. That is the biggest mistake of my life and the most important lesson that I have learned.

My face itched. Partially... Especially the points where it meets with my hair... I was going crazy. I had a stubbly beard (still have), and it was itchy too... My jawbone and especially, my chin... But it was not a simple thing, it was an itch that you cannot imagine. However, when looked at from outside, there was no lesion that showed itself. I scratched them until the blood came. There was not a doctor left that I had not been to. The dermatologist gave me a lot of skin pomades; for nothing. I felt two-faced and dishonorable. Maybe the thing I was trying to get rid of and extirpate was one of these faces.

I started to have other health problems too. The doctors were not able to find a solution to my troubles. It was like an emotional toxin was gathered inside me and I could not throw it out.

→

This relationship went on for a whole year. I could neither confess the situation to my friend, nor escape from the love. I had that trouble for a year and itched all the time. Then, the woman I loved left me. She left me just like that. And went back to her husband. I could not believe it. I thought that she loved me very much. I do not know if it was because the thing I experienced was so sudden, or the fact that I was wrong about her love; I was destroyed. I did not see them for a while, but avoiding them had started to draw attention. I spoke with the psychologists, but I could not even talk to them out of shame. Then, a psychologist found out herself. She said: "Focus on the problem that you think you cannot explain to me. Whatever it is, it hinders you from being at peace with yourself. Stop accusing yourself..." I needed it so much that I started blurting it all out. I told everything as it was. The psychologist listened to me without judging. She asked me what I was going to do next. I focused on the moment by stopping, for the first time, challenging the past that I could not manage to come to terms with. And, we found out that I had to get rid of that feeling. The therapies went on for about six months. Every session I came out happier. I realized that, from the moment I accepted the fact and made the decision to get rid of the feeling, the itch on my face was gone. I had had a bad experience from every perspective, but I had had my lesson too. I decided: from that time on, as a principled person, I was not going to go down the paths that I thought were wrong.

They and I started to see each other again. The weird thing was, she was now just my friend's wife to me; I had no feelings left for her anymore. It was like we had never lived the things that we had lived before. Their relationship was sorted as well. They were even closer than before. The good thing was: That closeness made me happy.

Being able to speak, accepting, getting rid of feelings which were toxifying me from inside, and knowing what not to do from this time on, healed me. And, I saw that psychological causes have direct effects on the body.

Yours sincerely,

X.

V...'s Story

Woman, 38 years old

My partner was cheating on me. It had been months since I realised that, but I couldn't say a word. I was scared that he would leave me and go. I couldn't imagine separating from him. However, it was so difficult to live, knowing that he was with somebody else... I was suffering. I was constantly thinking about the past, how we got married loving each other... And I also thought about the future, how much I would miss him if we split up...

I couldn't speak to anybody. I just lived that distress inside myself. It felt like I had a lump in my throat. I went to the doctor and he said I should have an endoscopy. Result: Gastritis caused by stress. They gave me medicines. I used them, but I got worse. My partner was sorry about my situation and trying to support me during my illness. He was showing me love as a person, but as a woman, he wasn't touching me at all. I was aware that he was suffering too.

We have a daughter. She was 14 then. She is a very sentient child who can show empathy. One day she came next to me and said: "Mum, I may be young, but I'm not blind. If you don't find a solution to this situation, you'll get ill..." She looked me in the eyes and went to her room. I threw myself into the bathroom and cried in the shower for many long minutes. By the time I came out of the bathroom, I had decided.

On Friday, my daughter was going to stay at her friend's. I decided to talk to my partner. He said to me that he was going out, that he had a job to do. Again, he had made up a business meeting. "I know you have a job to do," I said. He was surprised. "What I will say is short, it won't take much of your time, but it would be good if we talked face to face," I said.

→

I'm not a person who can argue. Also, I would never want to shout at my husband, nor cry in front of him. I gathered my courage. We sat opposite each other. I had even made coffee. I only said this to him:

"I'm aware of everything, where you are going tonight and the unreal things that you tell me all the time, but you think that if you told me the truth it would hurt me so much and that would upset you, too. I know that you think what you're living completes some things that you can't find in our relationship and you take the chance to hurt me because of it. I love you, and I know that you love me, even if it's not like before. However, I think, in this condition, I mean while you're together with us, you won't be able to make a healthy decision. If you want, leave home for a while. Or, I can leave, but it would be better for our daughter to be with me at this time. Make your decision as a free person. If you decide to come back, I'll try to forget this issue, but if your decision is to set up a new life, I'll respect that too... Just save yourself and me from this fragmented situation. This is the most logical solution I can think of just now."

He didn't answer at all, he just held me and pressed my head to his chest. "You're right. I'm sorry for everything I put you through," he said.

I couldn't imagine that I could have acted this strongly towards my husband, and that while I was saying all that I was neither able to get angry nor to start crying. So, after all, it is possible to decide to be strong.

He left home that night. Then I cried for hours. I was suffering so much... My hand kept going to the phone, but I never called him. My word was my word. I had to stand by it.

I explained the situation to our daughter. She looked at me and said: "You did so well mum, I'm proud of you."

Our separation took about a year. During that period, my partner didn't neglect the household needs or our daughter, but I never saw him. We needed to talk on the phone once or twice. He phoned. I suffered so much. In that year, I had very sad days and nights, but I was always honest towards myself, my daughter and the people around me.

→

I didn't deny being sad, but weirdly my gastritis was gone, I had got my health back. I was doing sports. I found very old friends through social media. I was going out with them and sparing time for my hobbies and sport.

Exactly one year later, I got a phone call from my husband. He wanted to talk to me face to face. We met outside. I went stylishly, but simply. My heart felt like it would burst from excitement. We went to a restaurant that I had never known about. When I saw him, I realised that he had lost weight. He didn't seem very healthy. His face looked sunken. I couldn't say that he looked well. On the other hand, he kept saying how well he thought I looked.

"How are you?" I asked, looking into his eyes. I genuinely wondered how he was. He said that he was well. I didn't ask if he had made up his mind or not, I waited for him to say it. However, he wasn't interested in that. He was only saying how much he had missed me. Then I asked, "Have you made up your mind? Are you coming back?" He said that he couldn't decide yet. To be honest, I hadn't expected an answer like that. I had thought that if he wanted to meet me, he wanted to come back. So, I smiled at him and said, "So, let's carry out my decision then." It wasn't something that I had planned. It just came out of my mouth. He was surprised. Maybe he was right to be surprised. He wasn't the one who had given me time to make a decision. It was obvious that he thought of me as the person who would always wait for him. It had never occurred to him that I could make a decision or have a desire.

"Of course, I'm listening to you," he said. I told him politely that divorce would be the best decision. "No, it's not possible!" he said. Even funnier was him asking me, "Do you have someone in your life?"

It was the first true laugh that I'd had for a long time. He understood that I had done everything because of my love towards him. He wasn't going to get the point, as long as I didn't express my feelings and kept on being the one who waits, ready as a substitute. "No, there isn't anybody else, but there might be one day," I said.

→

We got divorced. He didn't want to; he even told me that he wanted to come back, but I had already decided that I really didn't want it.

Now, my ex-partner feels like a close relative to me, like my uncle's son or something... He, on the other hand, keeps telling me that whenever I want, he wants to set up a life with me again. I still don't want it.

I can tell you this: Being strong and managing to let go are really about deciding. And pain is a really valuable feeling, to those who know the value of it... We cannot ignore the problems in our lives. We should produce solutions for them and carry on, and not get stuck in an unhealthy life because we have problems. Not in the past or future, we should live in the now, and be happy. In separation, I chose to do sports, eat well, be honest, accept and be happy with myself. Now, I am happy. Without needing anybody, happy...

With love and respect.

H.'s Story

Man, 46 years old

Until my mom died, I lived in denial of the fact that everybody had always known. I am a homosexual. You cannot know how difficult it was not to be able to admit that, and to put on a mask for years. I thought if mom had heard this when she was alive and well, she would have killed me right there. Well, even if she had not heard, did she not know what everybody knew? However, from the fact that she did not acknowledge this, it is obvious that she was ashamed... I had also grown up to learn that it was a shameful situation.

On the other hand, I was living what my hormones, my mind, and my feelings were telling me; there was nothing to it that could have been changed by social values and other people's points of views. The fact that I was feeling different from others should not have locked me inside the limits of feeling I was unacceptable.

I lost my mom four years ago. We had lived together. I have aunts and cousins who still live, and a big sister... There was no situation in which I needed to avoid showing who I was. So, I began to tell the fact, which everybody had known but could not say out loud, to my family first, and then my friends. It is impossible for me to tell you how much of a burden was lifted from me. It was like, after every confession, my blood circulation quickened; I felt more robust and happier. I guess the name of that was becoming at peace with myself and being able to be myself.

I realized that when I explained my situation to people as a self-confident person who knows what she/he is doing, there was not even one person who did not want to accept it. I would have nothing to do with the ones who blame, criticise and laugh at me behind my back anyway. This is a situation of how my hormones from birth make me feel. I do not have to make anyone accept me. It is enough that I can accept myself. Now, I feel completely happy and free. Radical acceptance... Whatever you are, you are. You should continue life being happy with yourself. First, you should accept yourself, before you expect others to accept you.

Love,

H.

X.Y.Z.'s Story

Woman, 48 years old

I have never had an orgasm when I was with a man up to this day. I was overweight. Since my childhood, it had always been suggested by my family and friends that I should lose some weight. Some said: "Nobody would take you like this." The ages when I said, "Let them not take me then!" were past. I had not managed to have a decent relationship and I thought that the reason was my weight.

I lost weight about ten years ago. Until then, I had had boyfriends and sexual experiences with them, but I had never experienced orgasm. This experience that I could have by myself, I could not have with men. I thought that after I lost weight I would have my self-confidence, but no. At some point, I started to question my sexual preferences. No, I could not live with it.

I went to doctors; could not find a solution. A personal development specialist, who I met a short while ago, told me about root beliefs. This person helped me to find this belief in my subconscious codes.

Since my childhood, I had coded myself so much that forgiving myself, my mom, my dad, my relatives, friends, teachers, and everyone who made fun of me took quite a lot of my time.

Now, I do not have a problem and I am happy.

Love,

X.Y.Z.

NOTES FROM ERSİN PAMUKSÜZER REGARDING LIFE

A child of a Circassian mother and a father from Adana, I was born in 1956 in Adana. I was only six months old, when we came to Istanbul and settled in Kasimpasa, it was the start of my life story. As my father was a shopkeeper, I was introduced to trading and to the painful reality of doing business at a very early age. By the time I finished Pertevniyal High School, the fire to study abroad was burning so strongly inside me that, despite all sorts of difficulty, a friend of my dad (Uncle Nedim) reaching a hand out to me and giving me the money to make a start, opened the ways of Sweden to me. I'm glad I did it. Possibly, I had fallen into the world's most interestingly-balanced society. After studying Technical Physics and Applied Electronics, I studied for two years on a master's programme at Boğaziçi University (which I left before finishing my thesis) and then, saying to myself, "It is difficult for me to live here," I went back to Sweden and started working in Ericsson as a systems engineer. Until 2002, I did several jobs at Ericsson. When I left, I was the General Manager of Ericsson Turkey. In that time, I played a role in the establishment of Turkcell, Digitürk, Superonline and similar companies. I am thankful to all the people who brought color into my life during that journey. However, I would especially like to mention Mehmet Emin Karamehmet's and Murat Vargı's interesting touches, which made my life more joyful.

In 2002, when I retired from the professional world, I realised that I carried an interesting impulse; that I had the power to leave some things in life when they become ordinary and when I realise that I do not enjoy them anymore… Finally, in 2005 my entire previous life was terminated and I stepped into a brand new life. A master detox process that I experienced by luck in Thailand in 2002 caused me to investigate life in every corner of the world for two years, and in 2005 I established the first TheLifeCo in Bodrum, and stepped into the business of "Life Style". From that day onwards, lifestyle has been in my life as a "hobby-job". In addition, entrepreneurship: In the last five years, Startupbootcamp, Startershub and Başakşehir Living-Lab have been added to my life as new hobby-jobs. For me, hobby-job means being in the jobs that you find enjoyable and do not have daily responsibility for. Where you do not have a daily responsibility, creating a free agenda becomes very easy. The experiences from the first half of my business life have been good sources and inspirations. At the same time, in my new lifestyle journey, in every corner of the world, I tried to experience each discipline and to understand everything by trying it, from silent meditation to mindful chewing, from breathing courses to charcoal diet, and even to a 21-day water-fast.

The Art of Coping and Other Topics

Like myself starting to restructure my own reality in the September of 2002, when the time comes maybe you will, if you want to, also get into making such an effort, or avoid it if it feels difficult. This long chat is for the ones who chose to make the effort anyway… To avoiders, my suggestion is not to tire themselves for nothing by complaining… Empty complaints without effort only give tiredness. My father, living his life with the belief, "Let the horse die from barley," got vascular diseases and finally reached a sweet stroke, which arrived with a blood clot. He was only 69. I appreciated him for the fact that he never complained. God rest his soul.

So, going into some topics, what are the things that bring us to a troubled existence? The first step is forgetting that what we eat and drink are related to our body; our transition to a feeding based on our frailty. The second step is constantly being in the mode of flight and fight, in other words having a mental connection with the state of the world, which makes us live in chronic stress. We have reached the third step; here there is immobility and the body not flowing. And the last step is the environment that we live in… In the topics, what I am trying to say is: Our real problem is the mismatch between what happens and what needs to happen… This is the place where we will make an effort. I will mention the ways and methods of dealing with this shortly but, more importantly, I will tell you, "Never chase perfection! Always leave a margin of error in your pocket for yourselves. In this world, a search for a perfect existence will make a person a psychopath."

A Life Passed by Running Away and Fighting: Chronic Stress

Every day we come across the 1001 shades of life. Some give us joy and some make us annoyed, anxious or angry. Life goes on like this. A part of this journey happens on the water and the other part under the water, in our subconscious. For our body, the nuances are not important. All of them are gathered in two boxes: The boxes of threat and peace. The box of threat puts us in the mood of surviving. It means our body gets organised to keep us alive and, leaving everything else behind, it goes into a state of fight or flight. On the other hand, the box of peace puts the body into the basic activities of health, such as purifying and renewing when no threat is there.

The answer to the question of "What will we do to understand which box we are traveling to?" comes first of all from mindfulness. It means, when we get into the counting of "What is going on, which hormones are running wild in my body, what things are stretching us like the springs of the trampoline?", if "Mindfulness" is there, then its best friend "wise mind" is there too. The "wise mind" pushes us to observe the situation healthily. Instead of reaction (living like a leaf flying in the wind,) it carries us to the action (to form a thought-through idea.) The action is untroubled; it does not leave regret behind it. On the contrary, reaction locks us into many thoughts that tire us, with "oh damn"s, "what have I done"s, "what happens next"s. The journey to mindfulness is not easy.

Each person comes to life with their zen state and absolute mindfulness. Our minds, occupied by civilization, in a short time lose their ability to be mindful.

Much later, if God wishes, we start meditating, yoga, treatment and such actions. The subject is being able to live the moment and leave the pain of the future which has not arrived yet, or the never-ending settlings of what has already gone and finished, behind us. The future is worry and the garb of the past is depression. In addition, we have sets of behaviors on autopilot. When they are exaggerated, they destroy us. For example: While driving a car (first autopilot) and chewing gum (second autopilot) and at the same time speaking on the phone (third autopilot), getting annoyed by a word said to us; and at that moment if we crash into a truck maneuvering, we get destroyed. Each serious job should be lived only when we are busy with that subject, without our autopilot state, so that we do not live such emotional or physical destruction, and neither for a short while nor a long one.

The Environment and Us

The environment is a beauty of the world, a blessing, which feeds, airs, waters and colors our spirit. When we realise that, life begins; if we do not hear birds singing, it means we are not living, we are prisoners of mental games on a Ferris wheel. If we do not hear when a green-yellow lemon on its branch or a rosebud says to us, "See me!", it means we are disconnected from our environment or we have become blind from taking things so much for granted that we do not realise the beauty around us. What a pity! This disconnection causes us to lose the value of nature and the natural, and to build a life without them. Well, our beautiful Istanbul's state is obvious… More stone, more crowded and greyer… If we have reached this point, our world and environment lose their core and we spend our lives in the toxic atmosphere that we have created. Even if the beauties that we are not able to see live somewhere else, what we really destroy here is the nature inside us. I am not saying, "Let's save the world." There is no such thing. However, we can save our own environment; opening our channels, we can be good observers. In the environment that we observe, we can take out our healing items and make that happen. Speaking to and loving each other with these beauties in the world, we can come to experience them. At that point, it means we have reached and been living in the moment anyway. Beside that, in our existence, by embracing the philosophy of minimum destruction of nature, we can be the winner of that too. For example, we can make our consumption preferences accordingly. By consuming local products we can choose not to contribute to the hit that the world gets from transportation. Also, there are short-and-sweet, easy gains in this business. For example, putting an air ioniser in our bedroom will make us breathe quality air during sleep. A machine which makes our water alkaline and ionised will increase the quality of our air/water. We are addressing the basic problems as much as we can when we use something for protection against electromagnetic waves. The environment is the home of our descendants and ourselves; keeping it clean and perfect is a positive contribution to our future as much as to ourselves.

The Right Mixture of Food

The management of the digestion process is an art. "Which foods can we mix and when?"

You can mix slow carbohydrates; it generally means vegetables and especially green vegetables with other nutrients; however, it is suggested not to mix the other nutrient groups (fruits, animal products, fast carbohydrates) with each other, except for vegetables. In that way, we will be doing damage limitation by taking the function of digestion, which is one of the most tiring activities of the human metabolism, down to a reasonable level.

We Must Drink Water, Even Alkaline Water

The amount of water in our body, which is 90% when we are born, goes down to 65% by the time we die. In short, getting old is drying up. The important step in the continuity of life is drinking water. It is advised that during the day we drink as much water as matches 5% of our body weight. In addition, it is important that the water we drink is alkaline and ionised, etc., because nowadays making sure that the city water system does not get calcified is much more important than our health, water in plastic bottles is left under the sun, and plastic penetrating into the water is paid no mind, we have to take matters into our own hands. Nowadays, it is our responsibility to keep the water we need in an appropriate way and to consume it that way.

Ionised Air

Because environmental pollution has hit a peak and taken over our air as well as our water, there is a benefit in buying an air ioniser and guaranteeing breathing appropriate air for eight hours. This little investment would give us a pleasure like sleeping in a forest, beside a waterfall.

Interval Training

Flow and the movement of the body always face as necessities of a healthy life. The most proper way here is natural movement; however, in city life it can slip away from us very easily. Instead, subscriptions to sports centers or exercises that can be done at home take its place. The exercise method that I personally do and get benefit from is "interval training." In this method, the basic is to do a movement for thirty seconds fast and ninty seconds slowly and repeat it eight times. In that way, you are doing perfect exercise in sixteen minutes. For example, at home, jumping on a trampoline slowly for ninty seconds and jumping faster for thirty seconds and repeating it eight times. Similarly, we will be doing a very good work out if, on the beach, we walk ningty seconds in a slow rhythm and then move to double time for thirty seconds and repeat it eight times. Apart from that, exercises like squats and planks, which we do with our own body weight, are good weight training. Finally, if we can put a few stretching movements into our lives, then that will be realising a perfect exercise set.

Management of Agenda

We all have job lists to do. These gnaw at us non-stop in our subconscious, behind the curtains. Organising these in a priority order and keeping them beside an "okay if it does not happen box" is a life saver. At least the "okay if it does not happen box" in our list can seriously decrease the pressure on our lives and save us from being paralysed. One of the most important questions in the management of our agenda is the question: "What am I busy with at the moment?" This brings us to both our agenda and our mindfulness. One of the other important questions is: "If this does not happen, is that the end of the world?" If your answer is not "No," then we can say "I'll do the best I can, and not worry about the rest." Of course, for the management of these processes, definitely, there has to be an existing agenda.

Actor / Victim

We are all surrounded by a small number of actors and many victims. The actors take responsibility for their life flow and try to do the necessities of their lives actively, whereas the victims always live lives drawn by others and load the responsibility on their surroundings. Victims always have complaints and people that they accuse, whereas the actors stand on their own feet and do the best they can. The trap of acting is that, although the actors do the best they can, they have difficulty accepting not reaching the place they aim to, for reasons controlled by the outside world, whereas this is very normal and we should continue life without falling into this trap. Being a victim is a lifestyle full of unhappiness. Because in victims' lives everything is left to the outside world, not one responsibility will be on the person; there, the huffing and puffing about the world going wrong all the time would fill life. I invite the people I know to be actors and advise them to avoid being victims.

Drawing a Map of the Relationships in Your Life

Drawing the map of the relationships in my life is a method that I have been doing for a long time and I find it very useful. Putting the people, projects, feelings and thoughts that I am in a relationship with at that moment in some way into an order like a "mind map," analysing their positive and negative sides, also considering how each of them affects the others and optimising my life is a completely relaxing act. The result of these maps may be a decrease in the frequency of the relationship, just as it may be deciding not to buy that house after all.

While I am considering my relationships at work, I can take the decision that it is necessary for me to continue my tolerance towards a person. In that way, because we happen to look at the forgotten little details in the flow of time, our lives can be formed from a healthier decision chain.

Your Child or You Do Not Have To Do Anything

The only responsibility that nature gives us is "survival." Certainly, let's not forget that we are equipped with stimulations such as loving, being loved and developing empathy while doing this. When you first take your child in your arms watching their tiny nose, tiny hands and pure skin, do you think about them in the way of many daily responsibilities, such as that your child will have to work one day, do people favors, and be liked by everyone and be rich? No. So, why do we do it later? Because, our children and we are formatted that way. In short, if we put away that format, each person who can continue their lives according to their own possibilities should be able to live the life they want without harming anybody. There is nothing to be sad or ashamed about. However, while doing this, if we have demands beyond "survival," then the situation changes. If the necessary amount of what we want to have is not in our pocket, then we have to pay that cost in a way, and will have to enter into the system. Minimalists, the ones who are okay with less pay and less cost, have a fuller life.

Values / Mutual Values

All living beings live within the framework of their own values and those accepted by the society they belong to. It has always been this way. So, then what is the problem? The simplest answer is, in today's world we are being surrounded by unjustified values, meaning values not based on natural necessity, and this makes us alien towards life and our own core. This problem has wrapped around us millimetre by millimetre and is not an easy problem to solve. I personally, just like when changing lanes on the road, have warning lines saying, "Wake up idiot! Wake up idiot!" adjust myself by asking myself questions like, "Why should I do this and what is going on here?" and add freedom to my life. Mostly, these values are life-limiting and must be questioned. Of course, this does not mean that we will throw out and not respect the values up to a point at which we are alienated from society. As much as the environment can take, it will give us the necessary freedom anyway.

Health Starts Before Being Born

Parts of the qualities of life are the things transferred to us during the time we were in our mother's womb before birth and the ones we inherited from the time before pregnancy. Our existence and health start from then. Parallel to the dreams and self-devotion of the mothers sending their children to the best schools, they should also make the effort to bring them cleanly into the world. Today, in the newborn babies' systems, more than half of the poisons existing in the world are usually not seen at all. For the mothers to be able to gift a clean start to their children, they should keep the responsibility to have a clean pregnancy as a priority.

Societies are As Good As Their Populations

Lately, many people are uneasy about the way things are going in our country and in search of a place for themselves abroad; in societies they do not belong to. This can be understood as getting out of the environment being a treatment. During my childhood, they sent people with tuberculosis to places called "sanatoriums," which were surrounded by pine trees. There was such a place close to our district too.

The joyful, peaceful life that we search for is in fact in the place we belong to. Searching for the solution in other places will not bring permanent solutions. Staying in such protected environments like an aquarium for a long time damages people in different ways. (I can say this comfortably as a person who lived in Sweden for more than ten years.) If we want to create a world that we will live happily in, we must definitely direct our energy to contribute to the production of good people.

So, social entrepreneurship is one of the growing values of our world.

The Power of Words

When we take any word out of our dictionary, that situation disappears on a large scale too. On the other hand, however much we put any word into our lives, it becomes that much a part of us. Because in Native Americans' language there was not a word like "stammer" they did not get stammers. When stammering was identified in the Native Americans adopted by Americans, then the power of words showed itself. Think, when we get rid of making mistake from our dictionary, how free and creative a society we can become. A life which is beautiful, pleasant, full of love and tolerance would be very meaningful and full too. In short, we should be aware of the power of the words that we carry into our vocabulary.

Promises and Pains

Each view that we transfer to the outside world is a promise of our stance. While we are making promises, if we do not weigh the underlying responsibilities in a short while, we turn into people who make those in our surroundings disappointed. Or we get labelled as reckless, happy-go-lucky and irresponsible people. So, promises are sayings binding our existences and resources to varying degrees.

Promises should be short and sweet, so that we can stand behind them; so that we can be as straight as a die. And, not to be labelled as liars because of the incidents out of our control, we should make the point that promises depend on outside events.

My Life Prescription

First thing in the morning:

Mixed into a glass of water at room temperature the juice of a lemon or apple vinegar, and the current food supplements.

Sports:

Trampoline, Sonic Wave, Inversion Device, stretching yoga movements. Then sauna.

Instead of breakfast:

A mixed drink of the juice of cucumber, wheatgrass, ginger, spirulina, black seed oil, lemon, turmeric.

Until lunch:

Herbal tea, green tea, etc.

From lunch until dinner at 6 pm. Some snacks based on nutrition (pine-nut, almond, goji berry, walnut, etc.) and a lot of water and Oolong tea…

Late afternoon:

A light sport and stretching exercise.

Evening, 6 pm.:

A vegetable-based dish, then continue drinking herbal teas.

Before sleep:

I stop computer usage one hour before going to bed.
I listen to "deep sleep" from the Brain Wave 32 binaural programs app.
I take 15 mg. sublingual melatonin and sleep.

While traveling:

In my car and office, I keep herbal tea and high-nutrition snacks.

When I eat out:

I make my choice in the way of minimal damage.

Alcohol:

A glass, maximum two of wine. Sometimes, alternatively, a single whisky or cognac.

Coffee:

Maximum one shot of coffee a day (cocoa oil or coconut oil mixed in). The purpose is to prevent the sudden caffeine load by spreading the impact over a long time.

Eating for pleasure:

I eat everything if I feel like it. However, I keep the frequency of it to an acceptable level. (Max. twice a week)

On vacation:

Balanced and free. If exaggerated, when back I start water-fasting or vegetable juice fasting.

When I eat for pleasure I take a lot of digestion enzyme, HCI acid.

In my general world approach: unconditional positive regard, gratitude, transferring my own ideas by approving and accepting people, making an effort to be constantly mindful, the effort of using "wise mind."

My food supplement choices:

B3/Niacin, Pregnenolone, DHEA, enzyme, Bosmeric, Probiotic[20], B 12, Vitamin C, Magnesium, Calcium[21], Iodine[22], Turmeric, Omega-3... (Changing with other supplements from time to time, all of which are herbal and in food consistency, meaning the original state has not been changed.)

And of course, consumption of a lot of alkaline / ionised water.

So, that was my recipe.

What About Your Life Prescription?

What do you do when you get up in the morning?

What would be better to do?

All day, how do you snack?

How do you choose your lunches and dinners?

How much coffee[23], tea, alcohol, coke, fruit juice do you consume?

What is your exercise program like? Do you take the easy option when acquiring natural movement? I mean, do you take the elevator? Do you go to the grocery by car? What kind of body-working activities are there that you've involved in your life additionally? Do you walk? Do you do sports? Do you have a set up at home

20. Probably probiotics will gain more importance in the coming years. There are many unexplored functions of the flora of the intestines. When probiotics are given to pregnant women, the allergies in the child decrease via the flora of the intestine. When the intestinal microbes of people of average weight are given to obese people, sometimes the weight can decrease, etc.

21. There are works towards the fact that in a day, more than 1000 mg. of calcium supplement may increase coronary artery illness (heart vessel blockage.)

22. It is said that people who have thyroiditis (ex: Hashimoto illness) should not take an iodine supplement.

23. There are many studies about how moderate amount of coffee consumption might be beneficial. The newest of those is a very large study involving ten European countries and showing that coffee decreases the risk of death. http://annals.org/aim/article/2643435/coffee-drinking-mortality-10-european-countries-multinational-cohort-study. On the other hand, it is a fact that coffee generally accompanies unhealthy life habits and carries an addiction potential. Black organic filter coffee without cream might be a good companion to a healthy lifestyle.

where you can do exercise? Have you made stretching and moving your body every forty-five minutes during the day your routine?

What beautiful things do you see around you? How often do you speak to or touch them? Is your water clean? Ionised? Is your air clean? Ionised? Which chemicals are you surrounded by? What is in your shampoo? In your car scent? In your softener? How often are the moments that you are completely together with nature? How rare? How can you increase this?

Are you constantly obsessed with one thing or another? Getting angry and depressed? Are you blocked, and do you not know what to do? Do people make you tired? Are you distressed both at home and work? Do you need prescriptions to fix your head? If so, how about creating them yourself? How do you define your relationships: Toxic, tiring, more or less fixable/not fixable? How about ending the ones, which cannot be fixed? If you do not have to, it might be difficult to end the relations with mom, dad, sibling, etc. How about accepting the ones you cannot end as they are and living in peace with them? How about taking responsibility and opening a blank new page for the relationships that are possible to fix? The best type of therapy is achieved by making others feel good. You will escape from the tiredness of the world only when you accept it as it is. Despite making the differentiation between my job, his/her job, your job, the government's job, etc., just for yourself and approaching the others as an open buffet, can you still approach them in such a way as that they do not have to accept your ideas? Be an actor and take responsibility! Do not be a victim! Do not live an excuse-based lost life. Be realistic! The borders of acting end where your impact ends. Beyond is the cosmic world, which is outside you. Accepting everything as it is, you should create perfection with what exists!

People writing prescriptions for themselves are people writing their own life stories. I, at least every three months, look at my prescription again and renew it. And, I keenly suggest this to everybody.

Hormones and Beyond

Hormones are the chemicals produced by our body. They are the communication, warning and order systems behind the impeccable existence of the body. Hormones, as much as physically, touch every type of our existence mentally, emotionally and spiritually. Steroids and sex hormones are cholesterol-based hormones. Before getting into a war with cholesterol, it would be good to take that into account.

On the other hand, peptides are amino acid-based and they organise the uncontrollable vital functions such as sleep, blood sugar, and heartbeats. One of the secrets of keeping young is the production of healthy hormones.

The main thing is that we form what we eat, drink and think in a way such that they contribute to our hormonal structure. From time to time it is necessary to ensure the hormonal balance by using bioidentical hormones after the hormones that we lack, even temporarily, are identified. Because the synthetic hormones' ratio of contribution to the body is very low, they are not a solution. Especially, if we have gone through an illness, depression, or are facing a stressful period, the importance of our hormonal balance doubles.

The Balance of Being Individual and Belonging

The western world is a setup based on being an individual/hero. On the other hand, a human has needs like security, being liked, being loved and belonging. It is up to us to manage the balance between these. While the culture and the society suggest that we be individuals, to be happy and healthy they advise us, being social creatures, to belong to different environments. When we reconstitute the borders of individuality, belonging and integrating with the world will get easier anyway. However, this does not mean that we should belong to the unnecessary worlds that we do not approve of. Showing tolerance to the worlds that we do not belong to and accepting their existence is enough.

Alienating

If we are trying to develop ourselves faster than our environment, or if we have turned into new beings because of environmental change in our lives, the alienation will have started. I have lived both. When I came back, after living all those years in Sweden, I realised that I was alienated towards Turkish humor. Many patterns of thought were not suited to me. On the other hand, there is also the same thing at the spot I have arrived at while pushing the dimensions of developing myself; as well as being alienated and losing so many of my high school friends and, the language I use started to get different with my many later friends. Emphasis on alienation might cause you to be blamed, to feel apathy or lack of responsibility towards society, and to become distant from it. While you are trying to explain alkaline water, your friend might want to talk about the smooth taste that the newly launched rakı leaves on your throat. Alienation is a necessity of nature; being aware, not being bothered and accepting it, is necessary.

The Prescription of the Blue Zone

Nearly ten years ago, the regions called blue zones where people of more than 100 years old lived were determined in the world, and it was observed that those people had common properties.

Those common properties give us the simplest good-life recipe. The first common property is that they feed heavily on vegetables; the second is that they are active for their whole lifetime. The third common property is that they eat evening dinners early. And the final one is that they are sociable and in good relationships with people. If we also add the habits of positive thinking, a particular mobility, and having continuous mental activity to a recipe in which we abide by those four simple principles, then we will be managing to carry our recipe to excellence.

Digestion and Nutrients with Fibre

Digestion (the other one is gravity),which is one of the most intensive resource-needing events of life, is a topic that should be looked into. The secret of living well, having quality sleep, youth and many things, comes from eating easily-digested nutrients and keeping the time between meals long. Intermittent fasting gains meaning in that context. When we have a problem of digestion and we need to support it, HCI (hydrochloric acid) to regulate the gastric acid, digestion enzymes to ease the digestion and turmeric as an anti-inflammatory should be on our tables. According to my doctor friend's suggestion, especially when I think that I have been feeding badly, I use digestion-supporting products generously. High-fibre foods and food supplements such as psyllium are very important for the health of our intestines. These should also enter into our lives as easy gains.

Five Tastes in Nutrients

Things we eat reach our senses in five different ways. Sweet, salty, sour, bitter, and through their smells. Cooks can make us eat anything by hiding it behind a variety of sauces, spices, creams and oils. One of the reasons for chewing what we eat a lot is to reach the reality in the depths of tastes and find out the real face of our relationship with nutrients. Not doing any other job during eating is the second reason for reaching the real taste. If you also close your eyes, then your senses come together with that bite brlliantly, and the gourmet inside you comes out. In the journey to a healthy life, being a real gourmet is the definite solution. On the other hand, if we do not want to be cheated, we can consume our food in its pure state. Consuming avocado, carrot, and even meat if necessary, without sauce is an important step towards healthy eating.

The Management of Harm in Cooking

Before the journey of the food, which comes to our table starts in our system, it lives through some stories. The raw foods, which go through least, are the healthiest ones. The steamed foods are least damaged; along the road through boiled, shallow-fried, roasted, deep-fried and grilled, the damage increases gradually. Each process that happens to food changes the nutritional value and the structure of it and alienates it from our body. The more the toxic factors are, the higher the cost that the body pays. For that reason, while making our choices, we should always have raw nutrients on one side of our table. Being aware of each of our steps, we should decrease the amount and the frequency of eating. Decreasing the damage is in our hands with practical solutions, such as heading for rarely cooked nutrients and keeping away from the burnt or overcooked parts of foods.

Epigenetic

Until recently, the most important part of illnesses were based on our genetic structure. However, for a while now, the other side of this story has started to be based on epigenetics. If I put it simply, the most important thing other than our genetics is the environment we live in. For example, with your mom and dad, there were some illnesses, and you have inherited that genetic infrastructure. This does not mean that you carry the same risk of the same illnesses. If you live a clean life, the potential illnesses might not even come near you.

In studies done on identical twins, they kept one of the twins in the same lifestyle as their mom and dad and the other was kept with a more healthy one. As a result, it was observed that the one who was living a healthy life did not have the health problems that his twin had. The lesson we should learn from that is that our genetic structure does not need to be our fate; the actual definer is our lifestyle.

Uncompleted Jobs

In our ongoing lives, it is pretty important that we do not leave unfinished or half-finished jobs behind us. For example, you had an argument with someone and the problem was not solved, either between you two or inside yourself. This situation will stay inside you as a constantly burning fire. Maybe we haven't graduated from school, or although we got divorced from our partner we could not manage to separate mentally, or although we made the decision to move on to a quiet life we weren't able to leave the hustle. All the unfinished jobs keep burning bitterly inside us. We should learn to continue life by tying up the loose ends and paying the bills of all the unfinished jobs, which we try to leave behind.

Be Sensitive Towards Young Deaths

Every year, 1.7 million people die at an earlier age than the average lifespan. If we put aside accidents and hospital errors, nearly all of these losses, especially in our geographical area, are caused by lifestyle choices. The leading illnesses are heart disease and cancer. Here, what we squander should be examined thoroughly. In the average of our lifetime, at least thirty years and above are squandered. If the times we were dead while living are also added, we are talking about nearly fifty wasted years. However, with a little effort and a system, it is not difficult to keep our doors shut to the illnesses, which are not easy to catch in nature. As a person who has actively observed the illnesses related to vascular health, I am able to share this situation with you without any doubts.

Set Your Standards High, Accept the Result

The world we live in pushes us to reach some places or some things. What can be the problem with that? Of course, we will climb to highs… Target and run after something. However, we should not be troubled if we cannot manage to reach the high bars that we set, despite doing everything. Accepting the result, we should search for ways of getting better ones. If we have not done the necessary things for the journey, accepting the naturalness of the result, we may make the next attempt excellently. My management life has always passed aiming to dive fifty m. instead of forty m., being content with forty-five and having pleasure. In short, while setting targets, pushing our comfort zones will carry us to some levels; however, if we cannot manage to be at peace with what we have, we get blocked and stuck at where we are.

Put Your Priorities Ahead of the Jobs That Want to Suck You

While the world invites you to a variety of life experiences every day, you should try to live as yourself. A friend invites you to dinner, the boss gives a project, your child wants you to read a story, your spouse suggests going to the cinema, your dog wants to play. You, on the other hand, should answer all these invitations while trying to realise yourself in the frame of a plan or priority. Right at that point, you are supposed to show the ability to balance the process of realising yourself with the things expected from you. Otherwise, you turn into somebody who lives for other people and is overwhelmed by the unhappiness of neglecting yourself. We should never base our existence on selfishness, but we must not say "yes" to a system in which we ignore ourselves. Balancing unexaggerated personal priorities with the world's requests is a healthy stance.

You Are Not Your Career; it is Only Your Reflection in the Business World

I sometimes observe people talking for hours about their jobs as if their life is nothing more than their jobs. In one of my first jobs, when I met with the big boss, he/she advised me of two things. The first one was, "Be careful of the ones who insist on never making any mistakes; most probably they do nothing and just sit about," and the second one was, "We will not benefit from people who do not spare time for themselves and have nothing else to do in their lives apart from their work. If they do not have the ability to spare time for themselves, then how are they going to manage our jobs?" Since then, I especially cared about the balance of my work and my other existence in life. Every healthy existence should have an aspect other than work. As a hobby, socially, as love, etc.

All in One is Good

If we are a person made up of feelings and states such as being open-minded, open to the world, full of life, loving, happy, caring, with a positive approach, peaceful, comfortable, strong, honest, at peace and easy-going - how much more or less is not important - we should not have any doubts about being at the top levels in life regarding pleasure. For that reason, my suggestion is adopting each of these properties and, in a way, imagining them repeatedly and becoming them. Although in these days' terms it seems like a dream, if we focus our mind on these subjects, then they will find their proper places in our life stories.

All in One is Troublesome

There is no place to go for an "ego" which is full of psychological states such as anger, depression, confusion, desperation, carelessness, fearfulness, being wounded, bad, prejudiced or full of hate. To escape from such an "ego" one should pay every cost. One or two of them can be liveable with for a short time, but if we live with one or a few of them for a long time, then it means we are in trouble. It is necessary to escape from these destructive feelings and states fast, because they keep us from living as we deserve, and they fall over our existence like a dark shadow. Right there, in a mindful state, thinking that we have been in these feelings and states more than necessary, we need to question how to get away.

I Also Need Me / Stop the Flow and Stroke Your Spirit, Listen to Music, Stroke Your Body, Move

During the day, while we are sparing time for work, family, partners, friends, society, television, newspapers and social media, we must definitely remember ourselves too. We also need ourselves; let us not forget that. The quality time that you spare for yourselves means a time that is free from other things, which feeds you, adds beauty, makes you younger, opens your mind and keeps you spry. The benefits are too many to count.

I create breaks a minimum of three times a day, in the morning, during the day and in the evening, each of them from forty minutes to an hour, in which I take care of myself. I spend these breaks doing meditation, listening to music, watching self-development videos and reading books. I adopted the habit of saying hi to my body by moving, walking and doing a few stretching movements, even if only a little. These tranquil moments let the infrastructure of my body renew itself, as well as bringing balance to my hormonal structure. Of course, the bases of my future mental health are founded in those moments.

I became unable to go around without headphones to listen to music or the tones of the brainwave generator application, which puts me in meditation when I catch a break. The mindful breaks that you spare for yourself make a huge difference in productivity assessment. Let's not forget to take pleasure from being productive and doing a good job. It is a great richness to spare time for yourself during the day.

Ersin Pamuksüzer

ABOUT THE WRITERS

WHO IS ERSİN PAMUKSÜZER?

After studying Electronic and Technical Physics at Linkoping University in Sweden, he returned to Turkey and completed the post-graduate classes in Industrial Engineering at Boğaziçi University; he went back to Sweden without writing his thesis. In Uppsala University, he did post-graduate study in International Business Management.

He finished his adventure with Ericsson, which had started at the end of 1980, with the title of General Manager of Turkey and Israel in 2002. He was assigned to the executive board of Turkcell, in the foundation of which he played a role. This journey continued until 2006.

In 2002 he discovered many approaches to juicing-cleansing-detox and a change in lifestyle, then for two years, in various places in the world, he experienced them. At the end of these experiences, he founded TheLifeCo in 2005. In TheLifeCo, which provides services in Bodrum, Antalya and Phuket, programmes for both physical and mental purification are applied.

He led the Living-Lab project, carried out together with the Municipality of Başakşehir, in 2011. Living-Lab is a practicing, experiential space, where technology meets with people, schools and companies.

In 2013, after the Start-up Boot Camp Project, a platform in which entrepreneurs come together, he decided to set up a platform where he can share his experiences with entrepreneurs and get them together with different leaders and, in 2015, established Starters Hub together with MV Holding and Gedik Investment. Starters Hub has supported forty-two local and foreign entrepreneurs until today. Ersin Pamuksüzer continues to generate projects that contribute to Turkey's entrepreneur ecosystem.

In this book, Pamuksüzer, who is still continuing the purification journey since starting in 2002, shares with you his experiences about physical and mental purification, and his recipes and advice for living.

WHO IS SELDA TEREK?

She was born in Ankara on 31 July 1968. She graduated from Middle East Technical University in Business Administration.

Besides her professional work experience in the IT (Koç-Sistem), finance (Citibank N.A.), health (Ege Group) and education sectors, she also owned two personal enterprises called "Mahzen" and "Wishne Café." Between 2004 and 2008 she worked in the health sector, was assigned to be the coordinator in the establishment of two hospitals, and in the same period completed the "Hospital Management Certificate" programme of Anatolian Health Centre John Hopkins Hospital, and took part in the health study groups of TÜSİAD (Turkish Industrialists' and Businessmen's Association.)

She uses the corporate information carried from her professional life in the education sector and gives lessons especially to the women and young entrepreneurs of Turkey on the subject of company concept, and gives coaching to the owners of small and medium-sized companies about sales, marketing, business planning, preparing feasibility, promotion and using technology. She has always, at every opportunity, expressed the importance of young brains for a country to progress and develop, defended the necessity of youth always pursuing new and creative ideas, and at a private high school, for about three years, she gave lessons on the subjects of entrepreneurship and creativity. She transmitted her knowledge on the subjects of sales and marketing to our women entrepreneurs by having the role of instructor and coach in "10.000 Women" project of, carried out with the cooperation of Özyeğin University and Goldman Sachs. Also, in a similar project, she explained the use of technology to women entrepreneurs who use microcredit, with the cooperation of Özyeğin University and Turkcell, in different cities in Turkey. She still continues to give education and consultancy services to companies, gives mentorship for special projects, does literature editing and book translations.

Selda Terek is a novelist writer who writes realistic fiction. Apart from novels, she has works of short stories, biography, poetry, translation and painting. Until the Last Toxin is the writer's first personal development / self-help work.

Other books:

Lirik Prenses Tezer (Biographical novel) 2017
Mahrem Gölgeler (Novel) 2015
İnadına Yaşanan Zararına Aşklar (Novel) 2012
Duygu Koleksiyoncusu (Short stories) 2010
Aşk O Kadar Aşk (Amigdala) (Novel) 2008

Translations:

Dinlen - Rest (Alex Soojung-Kim Pang) 2017
Genç Milyarder- Young Billionaire (editor) 2017

E-mail: selda.terek@gmail.com
Twitter: seldaterek1@twitter.com
Fun page: http://www.facebook.com/Kitaplardan Seçilenler
Blog: seldaterek@wordpress.com

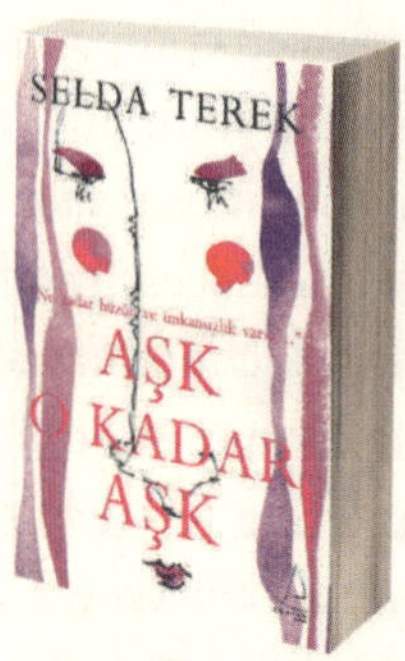

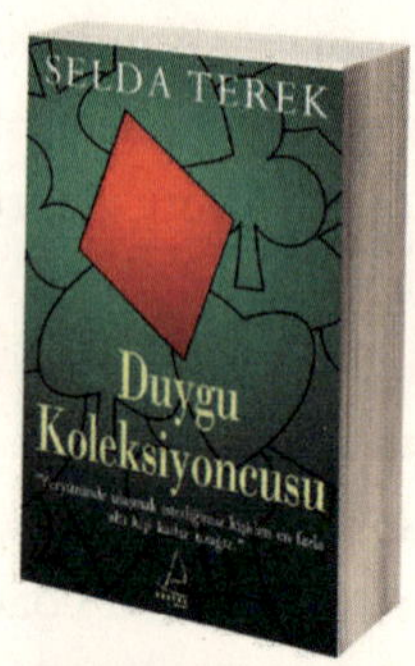

THANKS

Every life is a story with its actors, lyric fiction and adventures... Mine is too... Stories give us intermediate outputs, such as births, graduations, emotions, marriages, successes, failures, lessons, experiences and deaths... This book is one of those intermediate outputs, one which has started to be written tens of years before it was actually written.

And the stages, the places in which my story has happened... Even though I cannot list all the people who brought me to this stage in my life one by one, I would like to thank all the actors who have taken part in my story. Please accept this for yourselves, with no doubts. ☺

Also, I send my special thanks to my teammates, who made a critical contribution to this book, and at the same time played a role in the book coming into existence...

Critical Contributors:
To my mom, dad, granny, siblings,
To my husband, children,
To Nedim Amca,
To Fehmi Abi,
To Murat Abi,
To Mr. Mehmet Emin,
To the Japanese lady who directed me to a new lifestyle in my first detox...

My teammates:
Dr. Lodi, Güliz Altınbaşak, Beril Sinan Yılmaz, Gülten Dilek, all the teams of TheLifeCo, Startershub and Başakşehir Living Lab...
To Yelda Cumalıoğlu,
the group president of Destek Media,
for immediately adopting the project when I introduced it to them and making our job easy and to my dear writing friend
Selda Terek.

Ersin Pamuksüzer

SOURCES

Detox - Daniel Reid

The Dialectical Behavior Therapy Skills Workbook - Matthew McKay - Jeffrey C. Wood - Jeffrey Brantley

Duygusal Beyin - Bağırsak - Hüseyin Nazlıkul

You Can Heal Your Life - Louise L. Hay

Mutluluk Kürleri - Ümit Aktaş

Şifa Sende - Dr. Erhan Özer

The Power of Now - Eckhard Tolle

Yaşasın Hayat - Prof. Dr. Osman Müftüoğlu

Yol - Metin Hara

Web sources we recommend:

http://www.mindbodygreen.com/0-23399/6-secrets-for-warming-wintersmoothies-that-help-digestion.html

http://www.mindbodygreen.com/0-23354/a-smoothie-bowl-guaranteed-tomake-you-feel-good.html

http://www.jamieoliver.com/news-and-features/features/make-perfectporridge
http://www.buzzfeed.com/christinebyrne/cauliflower-not-carbs?utm_term=.ufKYO5XGxA#.xuOq6njOQG

http://www.forksoverknives.com/recipes/cauliflower-bechamel

http://www.huffingtonpost.com/2013/07/26/salad-dressingrecipes_n_1190214.html?ir=Healthy+Living http://www.mindbodygreen.com/0-9659/the-perfect-ayurvedic-smoothierecipe.html

http://www.mindbodygreen.com/0-9697/10-super-easy-smoothies-juicesthat-will-change-your-life.html

http://www.huffingtonpost.com/food-52/the-10-best-ways-to-eatr_b_3637030.html?ir=Healthy+Living

http://www.rawfoodrecipes.com/recipes/fruit-popsicles-with-coconut-milk.html

http://www.mindbodygreen.com/0-18438/coconut-pineapple-banana-cakewheat-dairy-free.html

http://www.rebootwithjoe.com/low-sugar-lemon-coconut-balls

http://kriscarr.com/recipe/easy-curry-lime-roastedcashews/?utm_source=011316&utm_medium=Facebook&utm_campaign=easycurrylimeroastedcashewsrecipe

http://www.mindbodygreen.com/0-13198/anti-inflammatory-coconutturmeric-cauliflower-vegan.html

http://kriscarr.com/recipe/raspberry-chia-seed-pudding

http://www.mindbodygreen.com/0-12923/cinnamon-oatmeal-with-cashewmilk-gluten-free.html

http://www.mindbodygreen.com/0-13046/vegetarian-kale-caesar-salad-withhomemade-garlic-croutons.html

http://www.mindbodygreen.com/0-13311/red-lentil-quinoa-cakes-with-basilcream.html

http://www.mindbodygreen.com/0-13120/red-velvet-beet-brownies.html

http://www.mindbodygreen.com/0-14642/quinoa-fritters-with-garlic-aioligluten-free.html

http://complete-health-and-happiness.com/it-was-hard-to-snack-healthyuntil-i-learned-these-22-delicious-metabolism-boosting-ideas

http://rawforbeauty.com/blog/the-healthiest-drink-ever-it-can-treatsarthritis-relieves-pain-inflammation-and-protects-your-heart.html

http://www.mindbodygreen.com/0-17857/5-cleansing-smoothies-for-alighter-breakfast.html

http://www.mindbodygreen.com/0-17504/20-minute-meal-red-quinoa-saladwith-black-beans-corn-avocado.html

http://www.mindbodygreen.com/0-17904/slainte-how-to-make-your-ownvegan-baileys.html

http://www.mindbodygreen.com/0-14058/perfect-on-the-go-meal-veganpeanut-butter-grape-wrap.html

http://foodmatters.tv/content/italian-quinoa-salad-with-basil-oil-recipe

http://kriscarr.com/recipe/classic-vegan-caesar-with-avocado-chickpeas

http://www.rebootwithjoe.com/baked-cauli-turmeric-poppers

http://www.mindbodygreen.com/0-18681/next-level-hummus-roasted-garliccauliflower.html

http://kriscarr.com/recipe/coconut-ginger-ice-cream

http://www.healthy-holistic-living.com/make-lavender-lemonaide-get-ridheadaches-anxiety.html?t=DM

http://www.youngandraw.com/vitamin-e-skin-booster-blueberry-almondmilk-recipe

http://www.mindbodygreen.com/0-18617/6-snacks-for-anyone-trying-to-eatclean.html

http://www.mindbodygreen.com/0-12188/dairy-free-chocolate-coconut-icecream.html

http://kriscarr.com/recipe/vegan-white-bean-waffles

http://kriscarr.com/recipe/raw-pomegranate-coconutmousse/?utm_source=011616&utm_medium=Facebook&utm_campaign=rawpomegranate&coconutmousserecipe

http://www.mindbodygreen.com/0-23307/cashew-milk-so-good-youll-forgetalmond-milk-even-exists.html

AFTERWORD

Although the only type in the homo branch of the primate team's great ape tribe that is now living, in its taxonomic name Homo Sapiens Sapiens, in other words human, has still not been able to figure out what and why this miracle is that we are a part of, we have already discovered a long time ago that nature's property of renewing and repairing itself occurs in our bodies too. Good news: As long as people create the conditions that will make them feel better, they know that nature is going to sort out the job… ☺

Selda Terek

We have said what we were going to say; now write your own life…

Ersin Pamuksüzer